Passage
to
More than India

A Journal

DICK BATSTONE

Passage to more than India!
Are thy wings plumed for such far flights?

Walt Whitman

Impressum

Acknowledgments: Compared with Gandhi and Tagore, Sri Aurobindo is little known in the West. For many in India Sri Aurobindo is a more significant figure, as the great patriot, pioneer yogi and philosopher of the evolution of consciousness and of the future of humanity. So I originally wanted to find an English or American publisher. In this I was unsuccessful as the book seemed not to be 'suitable' for their lists, being neither a travelogue nor a book about religion. Now, at last, it is being brought out in Auroville, the international community founded by the Mother in 1968 and which I have visited many times since its inauguration. Why was it not published here before? Because I wanted to reach a Western audience rather than 'preaching to the converted', but have now seen how truly international Auroville has become and that its diaspora reaches further and to a wider diversity of people than a Western publisher would. I am delighted my friends here wish to produce it.

If not otherwise noted, illustrations and plate pictures are either from the author's personal collection or in the public domain. Every attempt has been made by the authors to clarify the ownership of illustrations used in this book. Any oversights or omissions brought to the author's attention will be corrected in future editions. To send correspondence to the author of this book, send an email to prisma@auroville.org.in.

First Edition 2013
Second Edition 2022
Passage to More than India
Dick Batstone

ISBN 978-81-957301-2-4 (print)
ISBN 978-81-957301-3-1 (ebook)

BISAC Code:
TRV003040, TRAVEL / Asia / India & South Asia
BIO000000, BIOGRAPHY & AUTOBIOGRAPHY / General
BIO023000, BIOGRAPHY & AUTOBIOGRAPHY / Adventurers & Explorers
HIS062000, HISTORY / Asia / South / India

Thema Subject Category:
D, Biography, Literature and Literary studies
DNC, Memoirs
WTL, Travel writing

Cataloging-in-Publication Data for this title is available
from the Library of Congress.

Printed and bound in India by:
PRISMA, Aurelec/ Prayogshala,
Auroville 605101, Tamil Nadu, India

Digital Editions produced by:
DMI Systems Pvt Ltd, Vishnupuri,
Aligarh 202001, Uttar Pradesh, India

Published by PRISMA, an imprint of Digital Media Initiatives
www.prisma.haus, www.dmi.systems

Contents

Foreword

Sri Aurobindo, in reply to a would-be biographer, noted that "my life…has not been on the surface for men to see". The same could be said of Dick Batstone. For while Dick has been, among other things, a teacher, a bookseller and, indeed, a voyager to far-off lands, his real work has been a voyage within; a lifelong quest to discover himself, to discover his soul and the meaning of existence on earth.

In that quest, Dick's stay in the Sri Aurobindo Ashram in 1959-60, which is the subject of this book, was a turning-point. For it was here that he met the Mother who, along with the works of Sri Aurobindo, became his guiding star and doorway to greater knowledge.

Such accounts can be dry and of very limited interest. But Dick's journal sparkles with wit and with the minutely-observed portraits of the people he met on his voyage to India and in the by-lanes of Pondicherry. It is also a beautifully-observed portrait of the Ashram at a certain moment in time, when the Mother was still relatively accessible and hopes were high for the imminent transformation of her body and of life on earth under the pressure of a new consciousness; the Supramental.

More than anything else, however, this journal is the wonderful account of what happens when an individual's psychic being begins to open in the most propitious circumstances; how, time after time, Dick meets the right person at the right moment to allay his doubts and deepen his understanding of a yoga which has no readymade road-map (making the book a fine introduction to some of the key aspects of the yoga); and how the stars shine brighter and the birds sing more sweetly when one is in a state of grace.

These would not be Dick's words: he is far too modest to make such claims. Indeed, Dick is of a type which seems fast disappearing from the world – quiet, urbane, with the quizzical, understated humour of a man who has deep compassion for others and a lively sense of the beauty of the world: a man with whom one could spend a comfortable evening, the companionable silences broken only by simple remarks which reach deep into the soul.

But Dick is no recluse. In the 1970s he was one of the founder members of Auroville International U.K., in which capacity he gave talks about Auroville, organized events to raise funds and took an important stand at a critical moment in Auroville's history. He has also visited the community a number of times, latterly with M.E., his wife. For many years he was also the U.K. distributor for Sri Aurobindo's and the Mother's works and related books on the Integral Yoga.

Indeed, it can be said that his passage to more than India has never, and will never, cease...

Alan Herbert
Auroville
21st February, 2013

Author's Note

Compared with Gandhi and Tagore, Sri Aurobindo is little known in the West. For many in India Sri Aurobindo is a more significant figure, as the great patriot, pioneer yogi and philosopher of the evolution of consciousness and of the future of humanity.

So I originally wanted to find an English or American publisher. In this I was unsuccessful as the book seemed not to be 'suitable' for their lists, being neither a travelogue nor a book about religion.

Now, at last, it is being brought out in Auroville, the international community founded by the Mother in 1968 and which I have visited many times since its inauguration. Why was it not published here before? Because I wanted to reach a Western audience rather than 'preaching to the converted', but have now seen how truly international Auroville has become and that its diaspora reaches further and to a wider diversity of people than a Western publisher would. I am delighted my friends here wish to produce it.

I should like to thank:

Manoj Das Gupta, Chairman of the Trustees, for his permission to use the photograph of the Sri Aurobindo Ashram on the front cover; Kiran Kakad of the Ashram Archives for his help in finding the image; Professor Binu Mukherjee for smoothing our path in Pondicherry in every way; Tineke Smits and Saravanaraman for their research into Messageries Maritimes and finding the photograph of the ship, Laos; Franz Fassbender for his photograph of the author and for his expert advice concerning the design of the cover; S. Janarthanan for his help with scanning, spacing and formatting and Annemarie Bakker for her elegant initial layout of the text. Finally, immense gratitude to Tim Wrey and Alan Herbert for all their encouragement, support and hard work during the editing process. My wife M.E. is beyond thanking as she has been with me throughout.

Dick Batstone
Center Guest House, Auroville
February 2013

Introduction

During the 1950s I was working at the International University Booksellers in Gower Street, London.

I remember talking one morning to a customer about Indian spirituality. I asked if he had read The Gospel of Sri Ramakrishna. He replied that he had, and, after speaking of it with respect, he went on to say that the greatest contemporary Indian, in his view, was Sri Aurobindo. "He's the boy – the Plato of modern times."

I had never heard of him, but in the lunch hour I visited Luzac's oriental bookshop near the British Museum and bought a life of Sri Aurobindo by R. R. Diwakar. Certainly this was a portrait of a remarkable man – patriot, revolutionary, spiritual giant, pioneer of human evolution and a bridge figure between East and West. I was disappointed to find that he had died in 1950. However, his Ashram in Pondicherry continued, it seemed, under the guidance of a French woman known as 'The Mother', who had begun an international Centre of Education there. Remarkably, this appeared to be offering courses at a free university. On an impulse I wrote asking for more information about this. A reply came from the Mother's Secretary, Nolini Kanta Gupta, telling me that the free university had not yet started to function, but that I could contact Arabinda Basu, the Spalding Lecturer in Indian Philosophy and Religion at Durham University, who could tell me more about Sri Aurobindo. My ensuing meetings with Arabinda made me more and more interested in visiting Pondicherry.

Circumstances, however, seemed to conspire over the next few years to make this more and more unlikely. Arabinda, nevertheless, advised keeping the idea alive at the back of my mind, "And one day you will find yourself there!" he said.

The founder-manager of the bookshop was a remarkable Dutchman called Jan Bijl. He had been very good to me and had put me in charge of the buying of new books in English, and I did not want to let him down, especially as his blood pressure and heart were giving him trouble.

It must have been early in 1958 that he asked the head of the Foreign Department and me to come to his office. He began by telling us how, before the war, he and his wife had opened the shop, aiming to provide a service for London University comparable to that of Blackwell's for Oxford. They had lived with their children below the shop, working all hours, and it had been an adventure they had both enjoyed. Now it had become a nightmare. It was killing him. Publishers demanded payment monthly; Libraries paid quarterly. He needed capital to bridge the increasing gap, but he had been unable to raise the amount needed. The only solution he had been able to think of was to reduce the size of the business. It had become too large; the turnover of new books in the English and Foreign Departments had increased enormously. He was going to cut down the staff of sixteen to a size that was economic and manageable. We two members of staff nodded sympathetically, sorry for the newcomers he had recently employed, but Mr Bijl went on to say that as we were the most expensive he would begin by giving us both six months' notice, good references and as much of a handshake as he could afford.

In the lunch hour that day I visited Indian National Travels to explore the cost of a journey to Pondicherry.

Journal

26th January 1959

The train left London and went slowly to Dover, through patches of mist. SS Invicta left about lunchtime and crossed in a calm, with bright winter sunlight gleaming on the cliffs behind us, on the waves and on the white gliding gulls. Expensively muffled against the wind, an elderly American stood on the deck by himself. He said he was aiming for the Riviera. Down below, a Frenchman described his three years' service in Algeria. Most of the passengers on the second class deck were Indians. A Sikh, with wife and three children, asked where I was going. 'Bombay? That will be good, very good, all right.'

At Calais there was a train which was to go direct to Marseilles. 'Vite! Vite!' shouted the porters, as we struggled with our luggage. And then the train waited.

I sat next to the only Englishman in the carriage, a tall, slight, middle-aged man in a black overcoat and soft hat. He had beckoned me into the compartment where he was talking to and pulling the legs of half a dozen Indians.

'Now we are full up!' he shouted, 'unless a very pretty girl comes along, and then we'll sit her on the little flap by the window'.

The Indians laughed, and we settled down. The man introduced himself as Parker.

'Did you see the peripheral vesicles on that man's face, outside?' he said suddenly, glaring out of the window. 'Shocking! They drink too much wine, these Frenchies.'

He then asked where I was going. 'Bombay? Dormitory? The sods! I asked for Dormitory accommodation and they said no white people were allowed in it – too rugged. But it's perfectly all right, my dear chap, perfectly all right. I did it once before, and had a marvellous time, simply marvellous. I was able to teach them cards and chess, and had my own space on the deck, and I taught them English and French and looked after them and was king of my own castle there. I thoroughly enjoyed myself.'

All the time while Parker talked he kept breaking off to reassure Indians that they were in the right train, that it would start soon, and that it would go to Paris, but that we need not change – the carriage would be pulled round from Gare du Nord to Gare de Lyons without us having to shift ... He knew everything. His paternal attitude to the Indians was most impressive. 'They don't know French and I have to help them all I can,' he said. 'Why there's women and children, and they want milk and things, and don't know how to ask for anything. I'm in great demand as interpreter.' The train started. Parker stretched, and then said eagerly, 'Do you play chess?'

'Yes', I said.

'Good man!' he exclaimed, and slapped me on the knee. We went into the corridor and, sitting on some luggage, played two games. In spite of his confident manner he did not seem all that good, and I beat him. He became silent after muttering that his head ached. 'One of those chaps' had insisted on him drinking some whisky. He was not used to it and felt bad. By the time we had reached the outskirts of Paris he did indeed look wretched, and after taking a couple of Anadins he sat with his head in his hands for a while, and then tottered into the toilet.

While standing in the corridor I was spoken to by a healthy, well-built young Indian with an aristocratic face. He said that the Indian Travels man, Mr Patel, had told him that I was travelling Dormitory, and, as he was doing the same, he suggested we kept together and bagged a top and bottom bunk in the same section. 'I don't mind roughing it' he explained. 'I have been in a university training corps expedition for a fortnight in the foothills of the Himalayas, and that was really tough – forced marches of 20 miles, camping in our own tents, digging our own sanitary trenches, doing our own cooking ... I don't mind that sort of thing, but I don't like quarrelling, and these chaps are rowdy – did you see those Sikhs drinking and fighting at

Victoria? So we keep together. I like peace, and it's not half so bad if you're not on your own.'

I agreed, and we swapped information about ourselves as the train drew in towards the centre of Paris. He is a mechanical engineer, named Varma, a graduate of Delhi University, returning to his parents after two years of post-graduate work in Glasgow.

At the Gare de Lyons we left the train together for a twenty minute walk, down to the Place de la Bastille and back, while he told me of the great engineering schemes on hand in India – the irrigation projects and others, of which he was very proud. 'India has changed a great deal in the last ten years, but will change much more in the next ten. Up to now she has been consolidating. Now she can go wherever she wants.'

Back on the train we got settled for the night.

Some time in the small hours, when the train stopped at Dijon, huge Sikhs came and woke me, saying earnestly, 'Ask for water. We need water for our children. You can ask. Come.' I looked for Parker, but he had gone to another part of the train. On the platform there were no drinks for sale at that late hour. The guard said, 'The water is frozen. There is none.' At Lyons I was able to buy them some lemonade and Vichy water.

A young Indian aged about 17 came and sat beside me.

'How fast are we going?' he queried.

'About 60, I should think.'

'Don't you think 65?' he said.

'I don't know.'

'Do you know Reg Parks?' he asked.

'No.'

'He is the most famous body-builder. I have written to him.' He showed me a physical culture magazine, full of Charles Atlas and other strong men.

'I myself am weight-lifter' he went on. 'I lift 285 pounds and do many bends. When I begin I weigh 8 stone. Now I am 11 stone. A man needs a power in his body.' I agreed. 'I shall join weight-lifting club in Bombay' he went on, and he showed me from his wallet the cut-out photograph of a negro strong man. 'He earned £300 in one year, just for showing his body – £300. He is in the army now.'

After a few hours sleep I woke to find it 7.30 and the train stationary, at Marseilles.

We crowded, stiff and uncertain, on the platform, and collected our baggage. Outside the station the hills of Marseilles were rising through the morning mists like so many Monts St Michel crowned with spires and towers. The shipping company's bus took us to the quay-side, and after having our passports checked we staggered with our luggage up the gangway onto the deck of the waiting ship, the Laos. She was a fine looking boat, with lofty passenger accommodation and graceful lines, the hull splaying out in the bows to give a wide deck. She towered above the docks, her grey and white paintwork dazzling in the clear morning light.

A man at a little table checked us on board, and then 4th class passengers were directed across the forward deck, past the hold, to the fo'c'sle. Entering the left of the two doors, there, we turned right, down a steep iron staircase. At the bottom was a deck where there were lavatories, washbasins and cold showers. Down another bent iron stair we came to the Dormitory level, which ran the width of the boat, being about twelve feet of space all round the opening into the forward hold. This space was filled with groups of two-storied double bunks. Each group centred on two iron pillars from which metal frames hinged outwards on either side, supported by chains. A strong canvas was laced inside each frame to make a shelf. There was also a third tier on top, which served as a luggage rack. These double-banked double bunks were stacked two deep all the way round. At a rough guess there seemed room for about 100 people.

After the stevedores had finished loading, covers were fitted over the hold at our level, making an open floor in the centre of the Dormitory, over which a vast dusty tarpaulin was dragged. Then the deck-covers were fitted overhead and it became dark except for a scatter of electric lights and the sunshine from a few port-holes.

Slowly the place filled with Indians, Arabs, Chinese, Malays, Africans, Sikhs and Japanese. They settled down with much noise, getting their cases up on the luggage racks and undoing their parcels.

Many of the Indians had all their belongings in cardboard boxes, and some Sikhs brought huge bundles done up in striped carpet, laced round with cord.

Varma and I tossed for bunks and he got the lower one. Then we queued for an issue of blankets and a small square pillow each, and made up our beds and got our belongings organised. After that we went up on deck to watch the ship cast off and head out to sea.

Around midday everyone crowded up for lunch in the fo'c'sle, at the 4th class canteen. Behind a high metal-topped counter stood a massive Chinese cook and his helpers at their vats and pans. The trays which we pushed forward were stamped into six various sized hollows into which the servers ladled or slapped boiled rice, a lump of curried meat, a spoonful of dahl, a hunk of bread and an apple. Last of all, to keep us happy, we got our glasses filled with rough, sour red wine. We then trooped round to rusty metal tables, that had once been painted grey, and settled down on iron benches to eat. Varma and I sat together. He ate very fast, and soon we had had enough. The metal trays from which we ate had been shiny with grease, and the glasses cloudy with dirt, but the food itself was not too bad.

This evening, lying in my bunk, I have watched Arabs unroll their prayer-mats on the floor over the hold, and kneel to Mecca and then stand in dignified silence, praying. From the shadowy background came high-pitched voices and laughter, the sound of a Japanese boy playing a guitar, and of a gramophone record of an Indian singer, while under it all were the throb of the ship's engines and the swish of the sea passing along the hull outside.

Parker, who looks rather like a smaller model of Sir Malcolm Sargent, came and stood by my bunk and asked how things were. He said he'd been told by an officer to tell me that, as the only white man down there, I was responsible for preventing panic and keeping order if the ship started to go down... Then a French journalist, a tall young fellow with a big mouth and friendly eyes, came and asked questions – what did we think of the conditions? I said it was all right, I'd expected it to be rough. But he said, 'Yes, of course, you can accept it for yourself, but is it good enough for these others?'

Later a Swedish journalist arrived and took flash pictures of us in our racks of bunks, like a war-time air-raid shelter. 'It is disgraceful' he said. 'I would never have believed it possible nowadays.' It was all vaguely exciting and flattering to be seen as such objects of compassion.

Actually the people around seemed quite content and settling down philosophically enough.

*　*　*

31st January

Dear Anthony and Mary,

Now I can tell you what Dormitory accommodation is like. No wonder it is cheap. It is a cross between a bad youth hostel and a prisoner of war camp. However, the company is good. There is a splendid Englishman called Parker in the 3rd class who penetrates below stairs to see how I'm getting on. He has been an army sergeant for about 20 years, and spends his time looking after people – he interprets for the Indians, gives them medical advice and aspirin, shouts at the French crew and stands up for the bullied, and laughs at them all! Today he discovered that we in the Dormitory had not been issued with life-jackets according to regulations, so he chased up a ship's officer and had the life-saving equipment locker opened and, with a sailor and me to help him, had a distribution made – enjoying himself greatly at showing bewildered old patriarchs and indifferent mums how to fasten the things on, if need be.

Yesterday he took me on a thorough and brazen tour of inspection of all classes of the ship. He said it was important to accustom the stewards to the sight of one in the 2nd class early on in the voyage, and he made a point of buying cigarettes in the 1st class lounge and tipping the man there, to establish a contact. He also sat himself with a superb gesture at the grand piano and struck defiant and Beethovian chords from it. He found some ship's stationery there, too, which he needed.

In the Dormitory itself I have another friend, Varma, an Indian engineer, and we are gradually consolidating a group of like-minded

8

travellers around us. Actually the people all about are quite OK –
harmless and friendly, though sorely tried by the conditions – yet the
conditions might be much better if it were not for the people! I don't
know which is the root of the trouble. They interact. For instance the
French say it is useless to try to make the place clean, because it is
made filthy again at once. The Indians on the other hand complain of
the dirt and say it is useless to try and keep the place clean because
the French make so little effort. What happens in practice is that
once a day a sailor pushes his broom round the premises, and, as
soon as he has gone by the inhabitants are spitting and throwing
down orange peel and pea-nut shells from their bunks, so it is soon
just as bad. They need a Gandhi to teach them both to stand up for
their rights and be irreproachable themselves.

Meals are pretty swinish. We crowd into the fo'c's'le and collect
our food from a counter and then sit at long tables on metal benches,
which collapse now and then. Some people have to stand. Also
present are some most ferocious looking French colonial soldiers,
black Spahis. One was removed roaring the other day, after rather
too much wine. Rumour had it he was put in irons. At the evening
meals the noise becomes tremendous. The wine we get warms us
up; quarrelling starts, and occasionally people have to be restrained
from using the knives and forks on each other; everyone shouts a
bit louder to make himself heard and throughout there are Indians
gargling and cleaning their teeth into the gulleys down the sides of
the 'saloon'.

Teatime, too, is picturesque. We queue up on deck for a hot sweet
brew ladled out of a galvanised bowl by an impassive Frenchman.
This is the most prison-like scene – the jabbering crowd, pushing
out their dirty glasses and getting the stuff poured over their hands
as well.

I must stop. Hope all goes merrily on the farm.

Love, Dick

*   *   *

9

1st February

Yesterday Parker brow-beat the steward into letting me eat in the 3rd class saloon for a change. Parker said something must be done for the morale of the Dormitory passengers, as there was no entertainment provided. He proposed a variety show. Now he is scouting for talent. He asks everyone if they can sing, conjure, play an instrument, dance or even tell a story.

I asked him what he was doing himself, and he said the compère and producer was exempt. I said I could play the violin, but fortunately had not got one. Incredibly, alas, he has found an Indian whose young son has been learning it in England, and has his instrument with him.

Now Parker is drafting a programme, full of circus-like turns and bogus artistes. It is to be typed for tomorrow. He is busy as the devil.

*　*　*

2nd February

The great entertainment has taken place. People squatted on the tarpaulin in the dimly lit Dormitory and waited, according to Parker's instructions, many of them not knowing at all what it was all about. The celebrated violinist Peristalsis opened with a Gavotte by Purcell, without music and without much applause. A Swede from the 3rd class sang his National Anthem and there followed two love-songs by a Pakistani, and a magnificent dance by an Arab, who did it solely for the love of the English, he said, not for anyone else; then a Sikh began to sing. At that point there was nearly disaster; an Arab in the background somewhere began to make mocking cat-like howls. Other Sikhs, jealous of the honour of the Punjab, moved in on him. There was the beginning of a scuffle and a knife was drawn. Parker and I rushed to maintain the rule of law, and after much passionate argument, there was disarmament and withdrawal to previous positions.

Parker quickly produced the next item – a conjuring trick by a serious-looking Austrian from 3rd class. He made a broom-stick

10

stand up and dance, and the audience was mildly amused. Finally a Hindu sang a long and rather miserable devotional song.

Parker seemed satisfied, afterwards, that something had been done for the troops, and said there would be another show in a few days, and we were to practise.

*　*　*

3rd February

Drama! Parker has again been busy. He decided today that the Dormitory crowd must not put up with the squalor of 4th class meals any more. 'These Frenchies could at least wash up the crocks with soap,' he thought. What should we do? A hunger strike was the best gambit, he said, because the 4th class steward would not want the captain to hear of any trouble down in his part of the ship, and would be likely to give in.

So at lunch time, Parker was moving among the masses, organising, explaining and being indignant. He picked interpreters to explain to the different nations what was going on, and with Varma and me and a young LSE student to help, told them, 'No food – until they wash up properly.'

When the bell went for us to go into the fo'c'sle a crowd surged over as usual to the counter, but Parker was there to fend them off, directing them to stand back and not touch a single fork. They did so, unwillingly, still not clear what was happening, except that it seemed they were not going to get lunch.

Then Parker turned to me and said, 'Go and find the steward and tell him there is great discontent over the grease on the trays and eating equipment. Tell him to bring soap at once and get hot water, and say I am holding them back down here, but he must hurry if there is to be no bloodshed. Right?'

I found the steward, a large red-faced man in a white jacket, and delivered my message. He turned even redder, and said he would come. And come he did, with packets of soap-powder, and he himself washed up, there and then, before our eyes. Justice was seen to be done.

11

The Indians were delighted, and so was Parker. Only the Chinese cook and his gang looked disgusted.

FROM SUEZ TO ADEN

The sea passes beneath a dull evening sun.
An Indian asks, 'You write poetry now it is sunset time?'
The sea passes, white as watered milk.
But what is there to say? What muse hovers here
Over the Red Sea? Only the sun is red,
Sinking below the horizon, visibly sinking...
Five black gulls fly past low over the water.
Before the muse can speak
That sun has gone.

*   *   *

5th February

The heat is pleasant, though in the Dormitory, now, the roar and rattle of the ventilation system is another deterrent to living there.

Last night Parker and I slept on deck. Varma would not come. Before sleeping Parker reminisced about Dunkirk, and I listened to his slightly cockney voice recreating a scene rather different from my previous idea of it '...and they were in such a panic some of 'em to save their skins that they piled into boats that were full already and sank them. I had to tell one hulking big carcase from the Guards that if he climbed into my boat I'd shoot him. Meant it. Otherwise my men would have never got back. Thank God it was calm...'

He talked, too, about how he would have liked to have been a doctor or an actor. During the war he had once understudied for the part of Napoleon in a play at the Windmill – marvellous stuff. He felt he'd understood Boney. Now, he supposed, when he left the army, he'd take up chicken farming...

We woke early to the sound of the crew hosing down the deck. Parker whispered to me to lie low, and when a matelot came within reach he came alive suddenly and grabbed him by the ankle and nearly had him down.

* * *

7th February

Dear Anthony and Mary,

Since my last letter, the voyage has been enlivened by a visit to Aden. Parker and I went ashore together, which was quite an education for me. He seems to know the whole world like you do your village – having walked, hitched, bussed or sailed in small boats over everywhere. He was convinced that Aden was the place where one could buy a camera cheapest on the face of the globe, and so began by asking in every shop by the harbour. Then we took a taxi to Crater, nearby, and plunged into a most colourful scene. After a while he was sitting doing a wonderful act in a little back room behind a shop, with me beside him and two Arabs passing us Zeiss field glasses and cameras and Coca-Cola. He made out he was a businessman who was only interested in buying something cheap so that he could make a profit – that if he found what he wanted he might come back from his ship with orders for perhaps twenty more, and he would be passing this way again in a few weeks' time, but they must be cheap... To cut a long story, the price of the Zeiss binoculars fell from £15 to £7 ('Specially for you, Sir', in a whisper) and the camera from about £5 to £2.10. He bought the camera but left the binoculars.

After that, we wandered through bazaars and back streets, testing the prices of cigarettes, resisting children who ran and caught hold of our hands, and looking at the stalls and little shops. P. appeared quite ruthless. 'Shut up' was his mildest remark, and I really squirmed when he came upon a hunchbacked black cripple squatting on the pavement, and patted his hump and explained to me how the condition arose from a fibrous development of the shoulder blades, just as if the man was an exhibit in a showcase. He also delighted in pointing out a case of elephantiasis, and he said everyone here had the scab as a matter of honour. The beggars got nothing out of him,

13

and nothing from me, as I'd left my money on the boat. Usually P. is most friendly with everyone, but in a very paternal, benevolent way – and then curses them all to me in private. I don't think he likes me to think him soft enough to feel any of the nobler emotions.

Cairo was fun. A brilliant French journalist called René Delacluse, Yusuf Kolenski (an American Buddhist), John (a young Dutch student) and I left the ship at Port Said and got a taxi to Cairo, rode camels to the pyramids, blinked at the sphinx, gazed at a mosque, viewed the bazaar, saw Tutankhamun's treasure and got a taxi again to Suez where we were picked up by the ship as she went by. No time to describe all that. Nor the hunger-strike that Parker and I organised in the Dormitory dining-room, nor the petition sent to General de Gaulle and seventeen other eminent authorities about 3rd and 4th class travel for Indians on French ships, nor the four entertainments put on by P. to raise morale. What a man!

This morning, soon after dawn, our ship tied up at a substantial western-looking quay in the Bay of Bombay. As we came in towards the land the sun was rising over mountainous and misty islands, and dozens of small lateen-sailed fishing boats were gliding towards us out of the east, over a calm white sea.

The Dormitory passengers were crazy with excitement. They got up at about 4.30 a.m., with much shouting and noise. All quite unnecessary, as there was time to pack after breakfast, because we couldn't get off the boat until about 9 o'clock anyway

I said farewell to Varma and to Parker, whom I last saw waving to me from the 1st class deck, as I went into the Customs shed. He had told me he was on his way to Australia, in connection with army tests on atomic weapons, in some desert.

Outside the Customs office I was mobbed by a crowd of shouting, gesticulating porters and drivers, all wonderfully eager for one's money. I capitulated to a clean looking man who was offering a taxi, and after much bargaining, and with a very thin boy who attached himself to me as a luggage carrier, I was brought to a hotel quite near where the boat arrived. I'm on the 3rd floor back. It is cheap, but I'm not happy about staying, as it is repellently dirty and there's a chain of ants running down one wall into a crack in the floor, and I don't like the food.

From my window I can look down into an alley-way, which runs between the hotel and some five-storey flats opposite. Just now I saw four lion-coloured cats down there. On various window-sills and balcony parapets of the flats sat large sleek springy crows, while a kite flew keenly up and down. Then an unseen hand from above threw out some offal or guts which fell smack on the stones below, and at once everything went into action. It was fascinating.

The street-life around here is amazing – dozens of shoe-cleaners in every road, people ready to cut your hair or shave you, sellers of fruit, nuts, fountain pens, shirts, ties, socks, gold rings, paperbacks, newspapers, handkerchiefs, and more, all spread out on mats on the pavements, or, sometimes, on the inside of an open umbrella. And there are the beggars – some of them horribly incapacitated, pulling themselves after you, muttering and holding up their hands.

This afternoon I went to an interesting exhibition of modern paintings by a man called Satish Gujral, with titles like 'Down and Out', 'Wail', and 'Christ in the Wilderness'.

It was getting dark when I came away and the pavements were crowded with people lying down, swathed from head to foot in white cotton, like corpses. I am told there are over a million refugees from West Pakistan living in Bombay, and only a very small fraction of them can be housed. It is fortunate that it is warm and dry.

A little man came up to me and told me that he had not had a clean shirt for three weeks, and that he was 40 miles from home – 'And if you will look you will see there are real tears in my eyes because I speak from my heart'. He wanted 4 rupees, 12 annas or something. I gave him 2 annas, which broke both our hearts, and we left each other weeping.

That's enough for today.

With love, Dick.

PS. I have moved to a haven of sanitation – the Red Shield Salvation Army Club, where I have a room to myself, apart from a very black crow who sits in the window and pecks at the curtain from time to time.

* * *

16th and 17th February

The Janata Express was to leave Bombay at 1.30 pm on Monday and was due to arrive at Madras at around 8 pm the next day.

A friendly Methodist minister whom I had met had offered to take me and my luggage to the station in his car. He is a huge burly north countryman, bursting with energy and very genial. We had an early lunch before starting, and he ate fast and appreciatively, making whimsical sad remarks about his figure and his diet and how good his cook was. He advised against drinking tap-water at the stations, and against eating from stalls or from salesmen whose food was uncovered and open to infection from flies or dust. 'But you can always get tea or coffee, and fruit that you can peel, so you'll be all right. And if,' he added, 'you do get dysentery, don't get alarmed about it. Most white people get an attack of it sooner or later after coming out here, but it need not be serious. Just see a doctor and do what he says.'

Soon we were driving fast through the town centre to the Victoria Station. This is an enormous and imperially complacent building like several of the hotels in Russell Square piled together. There is something very magnificent about its ebullient ugliness, which makes one proud to belong to a people who could make such a mark on so alien a land.

Mr Philips, the minister, quickly had things organised, with a porter to carry my luggage on his head, and some chocolate for me to eat, and then, telling me to come and see him when I came back, he was gone into the crowd.

The porter settled me in an oblong 2nd class compartment. It had a rexine-covered seat round three sides of it and a long seat down the middle. Altogether about sixteen people could sit down and there were shelves over the seats on which one could lie full length. These were already occupied by Indians, who had unrolled sleeping-bags

16

and bedding and one of whom was busy with a primus stove. I had hoped to be in time for one of these shelves myself, but had to be content with an end seat by one of the windows. These windows had no glass but were fitted with shutters which could be pulled down. At the end of the compartment, by the doors, there was a space for standing and for luggage, and opening from it, a lavatory and small washing room.

I arranged my luggage under the seat and relaxed. A notice, pasted on the cream planking of the walls, said 'Travellers are warned not to accept food from strangers or fellow-passengers; it may be drugged.' Another read 'Passengers are asked not to allow beggars to board the train; they may be bandits.' I began to look at my fellow passengers more carefully. More of them began to arrive, piling in huge bundles tied up with rope, suit-cases, bags of food (how much of it drugged?), metal tiffin-carriers, musical instruments, trunks... Soon it was impossible to move even one's feet. The train started late, after much shouting, last minute sorties for more food, arguments with porters, tearful farewells and heaving about of bedding and bags. I was the only European, but a young couple with a baby, next to me were talking in English. I read and looked out of the window and time passed.

In the late afternoon the countryside began to become more hilly, and the line climbed steadily until the train was travelling along the side of a steep ridge of mountains, overlooking a fine panorama of scrub-filled valleys and rocky peaks, and back over the plains we had crossed. We went into tunnels through the rock at intervals, emerging to find the view now on one side, now on the other. Then came army encampments and Poona, where we stopped. Here at once we were assailed by vendors of food of every kind – chewla and chivda and sweets and nuts, fruit and tea and coffee, with each salesman shouting and jostling and pushing up his tray to the windows or trying to enter the compartment. Then, too, there were men with hats and fans and toys and cigarettes and cardamom and areca-nut and pan... And so it was to be at every station, even at night.

In time the English-speaking couple with the baby began to prepare a meal, and the young man, who it turned out was a jazz saxophonist, asked if I'd join them. I refused resolutely, but then his wife urged me to change my mind, and the food looked very tempting: (hard-boiled eggs, chapattis and fruit), so, throwing caution out of the window, I accepted, greedily. They were really very friendly people, and we talked intermittently throughout the journey. They had lived in France for a while, and were more western than eastern in their tastes and outlook.

At intervals during the night the train would stop and the mournful cries of the tea-sellers would break in on one: 'Char, charloe, char' and then again the rattle of rails. I remember one voice of particular dignity and charm, as if from a man of much patience and experience, who had a real sympathy with passing travellers – so sweet a voice that I had a strong desire to see the man's face, but the effort needed was too great and I fell asleep again.

Next day the country was brown and flat and monotonous. Wastes of sandy uncultivated land, stuck with tall palmyra palm trees. 'The palm tree is a queer plant' said the musician. 'You start from the bottom and it is just bare trunk, and you say 'Not yet,' and you go on and it is still 'not yet', and then suddenly at the top, 'Ah yes, that is what it was all for!' He handed me the baby to hold and composed himself for sleep.

Getting out stiffly at one stop I had some tea and fruit, washed under a tap, and, after a deadly Charminar cigarette, began to feel a bit more awake. Old men in the compartment were winding on endless crumpled turbans. The lavatory and washplace were already dry of water. Once again people were eating. A man on one of the shelves was sitting cross-legged in meditation.

Reading, eating, looking out of the window, talking occasionally or dozing, we passed the day quite easily. Towards evening the countryside began to grow much more lush and prosperous. There were a few lakes and canals, and many wells, with oxen harnessed to water-raising screws and windlasses. There were more villages of palm-thatched mud-walled huts, surrounded by animals and naked children. We could see herds of slow-footed fawn-coloured cows, many with huge humps; groups of black water-buffalo wallowed in ponds, some with just their ponderous horns, their eyes and their nostrils showing. And then there were glimpses of women in bright sarees, carrying water pots on their heads or hips, and others washing piles of clothes by the edges of rivers, and spreading them to bleach on the grass.

The bright green paddy fields were a new sight too: their even level growth and vivid freshness of colour, lying in neat patchwork among water and dykes. Then, around 6.15 the sun set suddenly, a fiery orange plunge over the horizon, with a moment of dark red, behind scattered palms.

Eventually, just before 8 o'clock, the giant engine drew us into Madras station. Deciding not to go on to Pondicherry that night, but to get some sleep in a bed, I got down, blank and awkward, from the carriage and waved goodbye to the musician and his wife.

At once I was beset by fierce, desperate, piratical-looking porters, dressed in red shirts, shorts and turbans. However, with the help of a friendly Indian I got my more bulky baggage stowed in the station left-luggage office and was soon in search of somewhere to sleep.

The station rest-room was full; even on the floor men were lying asleep, wrapped in their sheet-like garments, so I went outside and a cycle-rickshaw man said he would take me to a hotel.

We left the station yard and were soon bumping and swerving through streets in a fast hubbub of traffic, surrounded by moving lights and the sounds of creaking bullock-carts, the trotting of pony-carts and the tinkling of bells on harness and from the necks of oxen. Around us were dim mysterious buildings, towers, palm trees and a warm breeze carrying strange smells of cooking, tobacco, sweat, cattle. Horns blared as cars tried to make their way through the hurrying crowds, drivers shouted, the rickshaw cyclist grunted and rose on his pedals, braking and straining as he swung us round pedestrians and porters with fantastic burdens on their heads.

This was 'the East' at last. Bombay had been, superficially at least, like any large city of the west, but now one was being swept along like a piece of flotsam on a flow of humanity and beasts unlike anything one had ever experienced before. Anxieties about where

I was being taken, the fair price for the journey and of a place for the night slipped from me. I relaxed and began to enjoy it, senses marvellously awake.

A turbaned man in white showed me a room opening onto lawns and flower-beds. It did not seem expensive. And then a meal brought to the room – and bed! In spite of greedy mosquitoes, sleep, deep and unstirring, came swiftly.

*　*　*

18th February

Woke this morning at 6.30, all disconnected. No idea where or who I was. Soon I remembered that today I would see Pondicherry, my goal that for years had seemed so remote – the place where Sri Aurobindo had lived and where his companion, the Mother, still lives. The day's beginning was filled with stillness.

After breakfast I went for a short walk. Just opposite the hotel, to which I had been brought in the dark, was the station for Pondicherry, waiting to offer its services. Nearby stood rows of taxis and rickshaws. It looked a curious part of the town – areas of waste ground, cut by roads and railway tracks, with a few scattered houses standing in their patches of garden, and some small shops and hotels opposite the station. Yet there seemed to be the skyline of a town all around. Nearby was a large church, of early nineteenth century Gothic style, set in a field of brown grass and surrounded by an enclosure with impressive padlocked iron gates. Having collected my bag from yesterday's station, I went back to the hotel.

The hall porter was so insistent that I should not carry my own luggage that I let him have his way. If one is a European it is, apparently, unseemly to carry heavy cases, and worse, it can be seen as an attempt to do the would-be carrier out of his tip. (In fact I had that in mind, of course.) But the wish to help may have been as genuinely disinterested as that from the man at the stationery stall who offered to post my letters just before the train started, and refused to accept anything for his kindness.

20

Leaving at 10 o'clock, we joggled slowly off through the suburbs of Madras, past white and yellow flat-roofed buildings, dusty common-land dotted with cattle, and here and there a modern-looking factory or work-shop.

There was one old man on the opposite seat, with a dark strong-jawed face and short bristling white hair. He watched me very intently, so I got out a book and began to read. It was an Indian paper-covered edition of Sorokin's Reconstruction of Humanity. After a while I looked up and the old man was still eyeing me sternly. He put out his hand and indicated that I should give him the book. Adjusting his glasses he slowly leafed through it, and then settled down to reading.

I got up and looked out of the doorway. The countryside was becoming even more prosperous and fertile-looking, with much water and paddy, also some maize and sugar-cane, and plantations of banana and of tall coconut palms. Groups of children stood and waved to the train as it went by.

The old man was a slow reader, but at last, when I had sat down again, he gave the book back with a slight smile, still saying nothing. Then he shut his eyes.

At about 4 o'clock we came to Villupuram, a junction where we had to change trains. Sitting opposite me in the new train were two young Indian women, very small and slender, with beautiful dark faces and black hair in looped plaits. One wore a saree of vivid orange silk with a golden weave in the border. The other was in scarlet and black. In their ears were golden pendants, and one had a jewel pinned to the outside of her left nostril. On their tiny feet were delicate sandals of soft red leather, tooled with gold. They sat together very graceful and demure, saying nothing, their faces radiant beneath a plum-like bloom. A heavy scent wafted across to me from the white flowers in their hair. Surely Sita must have looked like this, I was thinking. Suddenly one of them gave a resounding belch, and then so did her companion. I felt embarrassed, but they continued to gaze in front of them, with large liquid expressionless brown eyes, until, after a few stations, they got out.

It was odd that a train that appeared to keep moving at 25 miles an hour, at least, should take 8 hours to do 100 miles, but it managed it. It was about 6 o'clock when we drew into a station where the board said 'Pondicherry' and I got down.

Beyond the low line of station buildings was a sandy yard, where a few beggars stood and sat. Here too a group of rickshaw men waited, and once more there was the usual drama of shouting and fighting to get hold of my bags. They undercut each other in their offers to take me to the Guest House of the Sri Aurobindo Ashram, until I thought I had a fair price. I climbed into a lofty rickshaw and the man set off, running between the shafts at a surprising speed. His back soon began to glisten with sweat.

The sun was setting and the solidly built white and yellow garden walls and villas that we passed were lit with a golden glow. I felt a sudden exhilaration – the swift pace of the runner, the gentle radiance of the evening light, the sense of arrival. No-one was about in the streets. There was a stillness, and I had a sense of coming to a holy place.

The rickshaw man stopped at a doorway in a high wall, opening into a little court, and I got down. Handing him the money in a daze, I turned to go in. But he was shouting and coming after me. What was the trouble? Three rupees he wanted, and I had given him three annas. No, I argued, I had never mentioned rupees. We raised our voices, and then a tall slender young Indian in a white shirt and grey trousers came out and asked who I was and what was wrong. I told him my name, and he said they had been expecting me. 'Go in' he went on. 'I will settle with this fellow', and he turned sternly on the rickshaw man.

Inside all was silent. A tall date-palm rose in the centre of the court. Bushes of bougainvillaea bloomed around the door-way, and pots of large plants with variegated green and yellow leaves stood around the walls.

A small pale-complexioned Indian girl, dressed in a mauve muslin saree came forward, smiling, and said 'Welcome. We thought you would arrive earlier. My name is Bapsie. The man you just met is Behram. We look after the guest-house here. Let me show you your room.' She went to one of the tall doors that opened from the court, and going inside turned on the light. I followed her into a lofty square room where there was a huge double bed, a low dressing-table and a few chairs.

'It is good to be here ... after so long', I mumbled, still feeling dazed, and looking at her thick brown hair which fell down to her waist behind her back.

'We hope you will be very happy', she smiled. 'Does the Mother know you are coming?'

'Yes', I said.

'Then you will be all right.' She paused, and then, 'You would like some supper? It will be ready for you in a few minutes.'

Behram came in. 'These fellows always try to cheat a newcomer. We have tried to make them agree to a fixed charge from the station to here, but they try to make as much out of it as they can. But he's gone. I gave him one rupee. Even that is four times more than it should be, but he said your bags were very heavy'. They showed me the bathroom and then left me.

Supper was a huge meal, course after course: soup, hors d'oeuvre, fish, meat, sweet, dessert and tea. I overate. I sat alone at a big table, in a room with pale green distempered walls, from which looked down large framed photographs of Sri Aurobindo and the Mother. In one corner stood a fine carving of a goddess, done from some dark wood.

Now and then Bapsie and Behram came in to see if everything was all right.

After the meal I went back to my room, and sat and listened to the silence; the very walls seemed to emanate a feeling of peace. An old man had put up a mosquito net over the bed, and very soon I was undressed and asleep under it.

*   *   *

Today I was woken by bright sunlight from the windows and by two sparrows flying in through a space over the door to attend to a nest which they have behind one of the inside window-shutters.

There seem to be no other guests, and I had breakfast alone. Then Behram directed me to the Ashram main building. It is quite a long walk: down Rue Suffren to a large square of sandy waste-land, which is being laid out as a park, then down another street on the opposite side, past the Post Office and a small temple, and then one comes to it, on a corner, surrounded by a high, pale grey wall. The entrance has the Mother's circular symbol over it, and inside there are palms and ferns and a small rock-garden, with a path, ahead, under a pergola, leading up to an old grey and white two storied building.

In front of this building was a row of chairs, where a large man in a white dhoti was sitting. He asked who I was and said I had better come with him and see Madhav in the office. He would give me the necessary information for my stay, and would show me the latest Ashram publications. He took me across a courtyard surrounded by pots of flowers. In the centre was a large tree, leaning over a massive raised rectangular tomb, covered with blossom, which I recognised from photos I had seen as being that of Sri Aurobindo.

At the office Madhav, a busy energetic-looking man, was writing at a desk. He asked how long I intended to stay, and explained the various charges for the places where one could live. The New Guest House, where I am, is the most expensive. Then comes Golconde, the modern and very beautiful hostel about which I had heard, and finally there is a place called Parc à Charbon, which is the cheapest. I think I shall go there, as then I can stay longer with what money I have.

Madhav also gave me two volumes of Sri Aurobindo's letters, called 'On Yoga I' and 'On Yoga II', which I could take away, he said, and I could tell him later if I wanted to buy them.

The man at the gate, whose name is Charupada, said I should come to the Playground in the evening at 6.45 to see the evening programme there. It was very hot by this time so I went back to the New Guest House, keeping as much in the shade as possible, and sat in my room and read the books I'd been given, and some Ashram magazines from a bookcase near the dining room.

In the afternoon, while I was having tea at a small table in the courtyard, a middle-aged Indian, clothed as if for tennis, came in and began talking. He was an Ashramite, and said he had known other visitors from England and had had some good talks with them. But, he said, they stopped at the intellect always, and did not go beyond it to the experience which only yoga could give. The practice of yoga was an act of faith, or, if you liked, a scientific experiment to test an hypothesis. This hypothesis could only be verified by personal experience, but I would find plenty of people here to tell me it 'worked'. The questioning mind, he went on, could be a great barrier to yoga, but Sri Aurobindo, he thought, had made yoga more acceptable to the western mind than had any other writer he knew of. He told me he had lived in the West himself and had kept a boarding-house in Glasgow.

After this man had gone, I set off to find the Playground, which I managed to do after some false turnings, by about 6.40. It was already dark by then. Many people were standing in the street by a closed door in a high wall. It was apparently not yet time to go in. There were people of all ages there, men, women, boys and girls, the older ones in white dhotis and sarees and some of the younger in white shirts and shorts. The girls wore tight-fitting muslin caps. There was little conversation but an atmosphere of concentration as they waited. Then a light came on, illuminating the Mother's symbol above the door which was then unlocked from inside and we entered.

This 'Playground' is a long rectangle of sandy earth enclosed by low buildings of various heights round three sides and by the street wall on the fourth. There is a gym on the right, class-rooms, a children's dormitory, and several small rooms and doorways which I have not investigated yet. The focus of the place is a room in the centre of one side, where there are large photographs of Sri Aurobindo and the Mother, with incense sticks burning before them.

Near the door to this room a young athletic-looking Indian stood by a microphone. In front of him a number of groups of men and women, in shorts, had fallen in and were standing at ease. Soon he called them to attention and marched them round the Playground. On a space of wall, on the right of the little room with the photographs, there was a large golden symbol of the Mother, set in the centre of a map of the Indian sub-continent. This symbol was illumined by fluorescent lighting from above, and, as each group passed it, the leader flung out his right arm in salute and there was an 'Eyes Left'.

After this march-past, the groups formed into four columns and began to do marching and gymnastic exercises to their instructor's word of command. The non-participants sat down cross-legged on the sand opposite and watched.

A white-haired old man sitting next to me explained that, whereas in other Ashrams the body was disparaged and thought of as a hindrance to the spirit, here it was trained and developed. Sri Aurobindo had taught that the body must be made a fitting temple for the Divine. Hence, the P.E.

Among those taking part were some quite elderly men. My neighbour told me that there had been one sadhak of 89 who had regularly exercised. 'But,' he added sadly, 'he died'.

After half an hour the marching stopped and the groups re-formed. They stood to attention and then suddenly the lights were switched off, and for two minutes we stood in silence. This was intense and seemed to reach up to the stars above and away to the sea that could be faintly heard in the distance. Then the tube over the map and Mother's symbol flickered alight, the groups saluted and broke up, and everyone began moving about.

After this, some men started to bring out straw mats and unroll them on the sand. Two boys carried out an arm-chair and set it under the wall-symbol as if the Mother were to come and sit in it there.

More people came into the Playground and soon the whole area was covered with cross-legged figures sitting on the mats and on the sand. Again the lights were turned out and again there was a serene silence. Then the music began; it was a tape-recording, played over an amplifier, of a strange searching melody on an organ. It was neither distinctively eastern nor western, but very simple and, in the setting, created a definite mood of purposeful tranquillity. It stopped and there was a deep stillness. An occasional breeze fanned among us and rustled the leaves of a tall neem tree standing in one corner of the Playground. The lighthouse by the shore flashed its beams on the buildings at intervals, and gradually the mind grew quiet, and aspiration began to rise in one. A light flickered and one was dazzled by the return to visibility of the map and symbol. Slowly people began to stand up and walk off. Men came and rolled up the mats. Solitary individuals continued sitting here and there, deep in meditation.

I left and went back to the New Guest House, through streets full of starlight and moonlight.

*　　*　　*

20th February

Today they woke me at about 5.30 am, so I could go to Balcony Darshan at 6.15. Behram explained that they had let me sleep late the day before, after travelling, but that most people, Ashramites and visitors, went every morning 'to Balcony', as now, since her retirement into seclusion, it was the only opportunity they had of seeing the Mother.

I set off as it was getting light, walking through straight empty streets to the Ashram. The roads in Pondicherry all seem to be straight and at right angles to each other, as in a Roman town. I had been told to go past the Ashram buildings to the street beyond, where I would see a crowd of people, waiting. Following a hurrying Indian, who I guessed was also going there, I came to a broad sandy turning where several hundred people were standing. Men and women of all ages, and some boys and girls, they were looking up intently to a roofed balcony that projected from the first floor of one of the Ashram houses.

I went in among them and stood on the pavement on the opposite side of the road to the balcony, but was too late to be really central. Near me was a young Indian with a rather Grecian face and short curly hair; his head was thrown back, his eyes closed, and a slight

27

smile on his lips gave his face a radiance that seemed almost ecstatic. Another man, old, with white hair and beard maning him like a lion, gazed with a fierce penetrating stare at the balcony.

After a few minutes there was a movement up there, and the Mother had come forward and put both hands on the balcony rail, and was looking down at us. Slowly she seemed to read the sea of faces below, her head and eyes turning, with a pause here and there, to encompass the whole street. Then, unsmiling, she looked ahead of her and her gaze seemed to rise above the houses opposite to some station in the sky, and her body to stiffen slightly. In some curious way her face began to change until it seemed to become set like a mask, or figurehead, or, again, like the Sphinx, its eyes lifted and set upon some distant horizon beyond human sight.

There seemed to descend a palpable silence; one sensed an invocation of spiritual power and a presence of grace. And from the street came an offering, a laying open of the individual's being to the invisible light that would purify and transform, an aspiration to surrender all to the Divine, a dedication of the effort that would ensue during the coming day.

And then, after what must have been about ten minutes of clock-time, there was a lessening, a release of pressure, and looking up, one saw the Mother's eyes moving back to earth, and her face softening into gentler lines. She looked down at the people below the balcony, at the upturned heads and the hands raised in pranam, and she smiled, and it was a melting intensely human smile of love, so that her whole face was alive and suffused with it. Slowly she seemed to inch back, still smiling and radiant, until she was in the doorway of the room, and then she had stepped back into it, and had gone.

People began to disperse from both ends of the street until only a few groups were left, talking, and a few individuals still looking up to the balcony, or standing motionless where they had been, with closed eyes.

The sun had by now fully risen, and a new day had begun.

*　*　*

28

Yesterday, after morning Darshan, as I was leaving the Balcony street, I was spoken to by a tall active-looking Englishman in grey flannels, aged about 45, I should guess. After asking where I was from and how long I intended staying, he suggested I came along to his flat after breakfast for a talk. He pointed out where he lived, and later in the morning I went to see him.

We sat together in a large lofty room on the first floor which overlooked the sea. He introduced himself as Norman Dowsett, and explained how he and his wife Lena, and their 18 year old son Norman Junior, had been living at the Ashram since the end of the war. Their daughter had also been with them until recently, but had decided she wanted to return to England, where she was now training as a nurse. Norman asked me why I had come and, after I had told him, described how he himself had arrived here.

It seems he was in the RAF during the war, and had been stationed at Cuttak, higher up the coast on the Bay of Bengal, where he flew coastal patrols and sorties against the Japanese as far east as Rangoon. One time when he and some fellow RAF men were on leave in Madras they saw a notice in a paper advertising a hotel in Pondicherry, which boasted a French cuisine. They went there, and very good it was. At that phase of his life he had become interested in the writings of Vivekananda, and one day he went to the town library in search of a book by him. This library however seemed only to have got abreast of the latest novel by Voltaire, and he was going away disappointed, when one of the staff suggested he should try the Ashram library, which he said, was a good one, and the only place in Pondy where he thought the book might be found.

At that time Norman did not even know what an Ashram was, but he went along, and was lent the book and allowed to read it on the spot, though not to take it away. So he went for several days and read, and talked a little with the people he met there. And then, one day, one of the library attendants gave him 'The Life Divine' by Sri Aurobindo, saying that if Vivekananda appealed to him, so would this.

Norman said he would never forget the effect this first contact with Sri Aurobindo had had on him. He had been shown into a small bare whitewashed room with a chair and a table in it and had sat down to read, and it was as if this book had been the goal to which all his past reading and thinking had been leading him. He could not recollect what he read, perhaps only a few pages, but here was the voice and spirit of one whom he had in some way known all his life. He had lost track of time and sat there knowing a great stillness and peace and that he had found what he had been looking for.

As he came day after day to read, his curiosity about Sri Aurobindo grew. Could he see him? He was told that Sri Aurobindo never left his room and could only be seen a few times a year on Darshan days, and even then did not speak. He could however, if he liked, meet the Mother, the French lady who was Sri Aurobindo's 'companion in yoga', and who looked after the practical day to day running of the community. It was arranged that he should meet her. At the agreed time he had come, having in mind some picture of the Mother as the epitome of all the saintly women he had read about since childhood – some demure figure in black, perhaps, with a white headdress, like a mother-superior... He had had a shock. This person he met was bedecked like some eastern queen, in silk robes, with a crown of pure gold on her head, set with a flaming ruby. She wore golden anklets and rings flashing with jewels. Moreover her face was heavily made up. He was so disappointed that he said none of the things he had intended, but had tried to chat in French, which was a piece of conceit since she could speak perfect English and he had not used French conversationally for over twenty years. And the time had passed with commonplaces, the Mother asking politely about his earlier life and he telling her of the war, and so on.

When he had got back to his hotel he had flung himself on his bed, deeply unhappy and in disgust with the whole business, and then he had happened to pick up a book he had recently bought, a record of conversations with the Mother, and had read 'The whole mental world in which you live is limited ... do not judge the Divine by outward appearances nor by the preconceived ideas of your limited intelligence ...' This so opened his eyes that he lay and wept, full of anguish.

The next day he had got up early and gone to the bazaar and bought a bunch of the most expensive roses, and taken them to the Ashram, and asked to see the Mother. She met him and, before he could speak, said, with the greatest compassion, 'I know. It is all right'.

And he told me he knew then that his being had come back to its home.

• • •

I asked Norman how he suggested I could make the best use of my two months' stay here. He said I should avoid the sightseeing tours which were laid on for visitors, on which one was shown the activities of the various departments of the Ashram organisation – farms, bakery, laundry, printing-press, foundry, and so on. These things were not important for a deeper understanding of the place, he insisted. I should try, rather, to be quiet in myself and become open to the Mother's force, which was all that was needed for inner growth if one had aspiration and sincerity. Although this force could be contacted wherever one was, it was particularly concentrated in and around Pondicherry, and if I stayed for long I would know what he meant, as did all those who had lived in it as followers of Sri Aurobindo's yoga.

He also suggested I read books by Sri Aurobindo himself, avoiding commentaries and secondary stuff. He said that for ten years after coming here he had read nothing except the writings of Sri Aurobindo or the Mother. He said they have 'a mantric quality' about them, that is that the very sound and rhythm of the words have the effect of raising the consciousness.

Before I left, Lena came in and gave us both 'soup' to drink. This is the vegetable-water produced by the kitchens while making the community's vegetable curry. Lena, apparently, serves it outside the dining hall every morning for elevenses to anyone who wants it, and is known as 'the Soup Lady'. It is quite harmless, though tepid and not very inspiring. Lena said it was full of vitamins. She also told me off for not wearing a hat against the mid-day sun.

Norman said I could come and visit him on any morning when he was not taking a class in the school.

MEDITATION

Marching is over and the Gym has emptied.
The lights go out, all but the moon and stars.
Music begins, persistent melody
Searching and yearning, threaded focus of sound,
While on the sand hundreds sit,
White-draped, anonymous at this hour,
Silent, silent as the sand
The overture ceases.
Now only the susurrus
Of waves on the distant beach,
The high flash of the light-house lamp
And the night-wind touching our faces.

* * *

22nd February

Today I visited the Ashram Library. It is a splendid building, once the home of the Deputy Governor of Pondicherry, standing among glistening palm trees of various kinds. It is looked after by Medhananda, a tall grey-haired German, who was sitting in the entrance hall at his desk.

He says there are over 40,000 books, and that all have come to the library as gifts or bequests. Many people who have come here to live as sadhaks have presented their own libraries as offerings to the Mother. The result, naturally, is considerable duplication, but also it mirrors in an interesting way the reading habits of an intelligentsia that finally finds itself at Pondicherry. Apart from the many cases of books in Indian languages, about which I could not form an opinion, there were large sections of English and French literature, philosophy and sociology, and some shelves of excellent books on oriental and occidental art.

Upstairs there is a long gallery, where the sea wind can enter between white pillars, and where there are small tables and wicker armchairs, and a remarkable array of periodicals from all over the world. I was able to find Punch, The New Statesman, The London Magazine, Encounter and The Listener from England, and America and France were equally well represented by The Atlantic Monthly, Harper's, Time, L'Oeil, Cahiers du Sud and other well-known titles.

In the entrance hall there are complete sets of the writings of Sri Aurobindo and the Mother. Selecting the 'Synthesis of Yoga' which Norman had recommended, I began reading in a cool and quiet place overlooking a garden.

• • •

I later visited Norman again and he went on with the story of how he came to be here.

After that first visit, which he'd told me about, he came again whenever his leave allowed him. He attended a Darshan and saw Sri Aurobindo for the first time, and he wrote to the Mother on occasions for advice – whether, for example, he ought to accept the offer of a commission. (Sri Aurobindo said he should.) He became conscious several times of a new providence in his life, and even before the war ended, he knew he wanted to come one day and live at the Ashram.

Describing his early visits here, he said how it often seemed impossible to come – all sorts of circumstances intervened to prevent him, as if testing his resolve. Once the train was stopped by flooding, and he had to get out and wade; another time he had suddenly developed a fever, with a very high temperature. A colonel in his compartment had given him aspirin and then got out at Madras to arrange for an ambulance to take him to hospital because he looked so ill. He had realised what was in the air and had evaded him, and, in a state of great weakness had got to Pondicherry, where suddenly the fever left him, and he was perfectly all right. He said this experience of difficulty in coming was a common one for many

33

people, and that he was very happy for my sake that I had succeeded in reaching the Ashram.

Before leaving India for service elsewhere Norman had asked the Mother if he might come and live here one day. The Mother had said yes, as soon as the war was over, he could come. He had been surprised, as he thought he was in too impure a state to come right away. But no, Mother said it would be all right to come as soon as demobilisation took place. 'But how, Mother?' he remembered asking. 'You will fly out first, and your wife and children will follow by ship,' she had said. He forgot this at the time, and only realised afterwards that that was exactly how it happened when the time came.

Meanwhile the war continued; he had various assignments, including the flying of Churchill to Yalta, and then at last peace was concluded. He now had a series of obstacles to encounter, two of which seemed, on the face of it, decisive against his going to Pondicherry. For one thing, he had developed an ulcer. A Harley Street specialist told him that if he went to the tropics he could say definitely that he would be dead within six months. This was confirmed by a second opinion. Secondly, he had no money at all for the journey to India. There were temptations, too. The RAF offered him a position which would have soon led to Air Vice-Marshal rank, doing very interesting work. Also his pre-war employer was offering him a partnership in the running of a huge chain of hotels and would have probably made him his heir if he had accepted. His parents thought the whole idea of going to India was madness. Lena, however, was willing to try it. She had had letters from Norman while in India describing the Ashram as a 'paradise on earth', full of love and sweetness, and she too had begun to feel the influence of the Mother.

Then the miracle happened. It was decided by the RAF that officers should be allowed to wear uniform for two weeks after demobilisation with full use of privileges – including free travel – so as to give them an easier transition into civilian life.

As soon as Norman was demobbed he got tickets for Lena and the children to go to India by boat, quickly settled his affairs, and, after a final argument with the authorities as to whether travel to an Ashram was or was not a return to civilian life, he was flown to India, and once more met Mother.

'Do you believe what the Doctors have told you?' she asked.

'No, Mother, not if you say I shall be all right,' he had replied. And that was fifteen years ago. He certainly looks fit enough now.

Lena gave me some tomatoes and small cucumbers to take away with me.

Back at the Guest House this evening I smoked the last of my cigarettes, savouring the occasion with attention, as I do not intend to buy any more while I'm here.

The Ashramites are expected to keep four basic rules: chastity, abstention from intoxicants, from smoking, at least inside Ashram buildings, and from eating meat (unless for special health reasons). There is also, rather strangely, a ban on talking politics, or at least it is 'discouraged'. I suppose this was necessary because in the early days many of Sri Aurobindo's followers were ex-revolutionaries, and so the discussion of political topics led very easily to strong feelings and fierce arguments.

Although it's not obligatory for visitors to keep these rules, it seems reasonable to try to during my stay.

*　*　*

23rd February

I have now moved to Parc à Charbon, where it is cheaper. This Ashram property is right at the southern end of the sea-front. One of its boundaries is actually a continuation of the sea wall, from which one can climb down onto a strip of sandy beach where small pale crabs scuttle with surprising swiftness into vertical bolt-holes as one approaches. There are two main buildings, one each side of a wide sandy path which leads from the entrance to a small exposed garden beyond them, where there is a miniature lotus pool and a flower bed laid out in the form of the Mother's symbol.

The building on the left of the path is a large barn-like affair with a ridge roof, divided up inside by partitions, about seven feet high,

35

into many small cells which open above into a common lofty roof-space. One can hear every movement made by the people living around one. On the opposite side of the path is a large low building used as a dormitory for visitors who cannot afford the guest-houses. It is now nearly empty, but it fills up, apparently, on Darshan days. It is bare inside except for a number of string-beds.

In my cell there is just room for a narrow wooden board-bed with a net over it, a small table and one chair. Its window looks out on a passage. The floor is concrete, and some ants are coming up through a hole by the door-frame.

*　　*　　*

24th February

I am in two minds. Should I stay here altogether, or should I go back? To have seen the greatness of Sri Aurobindo's life and thought, to have sensed in them the qualities and power that drew the disciples to Christ, to have come to a community where the members are filled with the purpose of perfecting human existence on earth, where they are centred on a person who is living in union with the Divine ... How can I leave?

February 21st was the Mother's birthday. There was a special 'Darshan' – literally a 'sight' or 'vision'. Norman explained that to have the Darshan of a person who has realised a high state of consciousness is to pass in front of him or her, and receive something of their spiritual power during the silent eye-contact that occurs.

Aware of a feeling of peace and serenity, I joined a long queue of people waiting to see the Mother. We moved slowly upstairs and through the dim but splendid rooms where she lives. I felt a tremendous expectancy. Then someone called out, like a footman at a ball, 'Mr David Baxter from London', getting the name wrong. I was in front of the Mother, who moved, holding out her hand to me, smiling almost, it seemed, diffidently, a humble old lady. Suddenly I was utterly confused. I neither spoke nor bowed, nor took her hand, nor made pranam as the others before me had done, but stood, the image of awkwardness, hardly seeing her, then passed on.

36

Why was I so disturbed? I felt insincere. I have come here, attracted by the ideas but not to the extent of making a serious sacrifice. The Mother must see this, and so what place have I before her or at her Ashram? The same thing holds me back from asking to meet her, though she does grant interviews to visitors from abroad.

I am extraordinarily divided; the wish to give myself and stay is offset by the inability to abandon family, friends and country. I do not really seem to want what I want to want. Indeed, my motive for coming here – was it one of genuine search, or did I come as a break, to escape from some personal relationships I could not sort out?

Yesterday I experienced a great feeling of relief when the man in charge of the sleeping quarters down here at Parc à Charbon said, 'Oh, you are a visitor. I thought you were one of us'. Yes, I am only a visitor. Let me enjoy my stay, and see what time leads to.

*　*　*

25th February

They do not serve food in Parc à Charbon, so one goes to the main Ashram Dining Hall. This is on the north side of the big square, near the Governor's Palace. It was probably once the home of some French official, and is a remarkable building in the form of a Greek temple. It lies some distance back from the street, in a garden rich with hibiscus and oleander and deep herbaceous borders, its pillars and pediment rising beyond a round flower-bed that centres on a fountain.

Arriving at meal-times one leaves one's sandals on the steps or in the portico and joins the queue of waiting sadhaks inside. One collects a tray and is given a bowl of curried vegetables, some rice or wholemeal bread, a bowl of curds and two small bananas, or maybe a bowl of milk, and, finally, a tin of sugar. One is then free to sit where one likes in any of a complex of beautiful lofty rooms which open from each other through massive archways. Or one can take one's tray outside to one of the arcaded terraces, under the projecting eaves, and enjoy a view of the garden.

37

At the left of the entrance to the Dining Hall there is a blackboard on which is written up a quotation from some work of Sri Aurobindo's. It is changed every day. Whoever does the writing has a very clear and beautiful hand. There is another board elsewhere on which is written some saying of the Mother's.

Inside there are no tables or chairs, but rows of raffia mats to sit on and small lightly-made black wooden stands, about nine inches high, on which to put one's tray. These low stands are copies of a type seen by the Mother when she was in Japan, so I am told. The absence of large furniture makes the place seem spacious, and many people can sit down on those neat rows of mats without it feeling crowded.

Against one wall is a row of large chattis, earthenware water-pots with taps, from which one fills one's metal cup.

On the walls are portrait photographs of Sri Aurobindo and the Mother, taken at different times during their lives. There are also a number of large oil paintings by Ashram artists: pictures of lotus blossom, birds perching among flowers, peacocks, and a mysterious landscape in which an immense crowd of people stream away across rough country towards distant mountains. Also framed and hung are various facsimiles of Sri Aurobindo's and the Mother's handwriting, and printed exhortations such as:

'Let us work as we pray, for indeed work is the body's best prayer to the Divine', and 'All work done for the Divine, from poetry and art and music to carpentry or baking or sweeping a room, should be made perfect even in its smallest external detail as well as in the spirit in which it is done; for only then is it an altogether fit offering.'

People, on the whole, eat quickly and silently. Mealtimes are not looked on as social occasions, except perhaps by the children and young people. The older sadhak collects his food, sits down cross-legged, offers it to the service of the Divine in his heart, and eats it, remembering and thanking Mother, and then briskly takes his utensils to the washing-up department outside, distributes his tray to one man, his bowl and cup to another, his spoon to a third, and then goes himself to the washing place. There he rinses his mouth, spits and gargles, cleans his hands and returns to his room or his work.

Meals are usually served in more than one shift, so that there is not too much congestion. Not all the Ashramites eat here, since, by special arrangement, some families and individuals collect their food from the kitchens and eat in their own dwellings. Nevertheless perhaps around 200 people come at a time.

When all have gone, an energetic bald man appears and rapidly collects and stacks the tray-stands, rolls up the matting and sweeps the floor, which is of beautiful hand-painted tiles. He works with a concentration and economy of effort that would delight a Time and Motion expert.

*   *   *

26th February

It seems harder to find the place and the opportunity for stillness – for sitting and trying to go inwards – than it usually is. There is certainly an atmosphere of peace, and people I speak to say, 'Don't concentrate on the surface, the activities of the Ashram and all that, but try to feel the deeper spiritual current that is here.' Also Norman speaks of 'the very strong atmosphere of this place. The Mother will not allow new-born or very young children to live here. It is too strong for them.' But I seem so far not to have made use of this milieu, as, for instance, I have made use of the Gym for exercises. However I've only been here a week.

The more I think of questions like marriage and family life, the Mother, a new job and so on, the more I discover that thinking, after a point is reached, is futile. Norman was talking today of becoming silent inwardly, and waiting, listening, attending, still as a rock, until more light came on a problem. Now is certainly a time for learning to do this. As it is I can find reasons for so many contrary attitudes to situations, but I don't hear any categorical imperative. Answers must come from a higher or deeper level of consciousness to have real authority.

But there are other reasons, too, for trying to 'Be still.' Sri Aurobindo, in his letters, constantly stresses the importance of 'quiet in the mind'. It is the first thing needed in his yoga. 'I mean,' he writes,

39

'a mind free from disturbance and trouble, steady, light and glad so as to open to the Force that will change the nature. The important thing is to get rid of the habit of the invasion of troubling thoughts, wrong feelings, confusion of ideas, unhappy movements. These disturb the nature and cloud it and make it difficult for the Force to work; when the mind is quiet and at peace, the Force can work more easily.' He recommends a standing back and dissociation by one's true being from all the surface movements of one's consciousness. And if one can't do this? Then he says aspire, 'call very quietly and steadily,' and cultivate a strong 'pressure of understanding and will in the mind'.

*   *   *

1st March

Fever. It must have been the sun. By 9.30 a.m. it is really hot, and walking back from the Ashram is quite a feat. It takes about twenty minutes, and the last lap is in the open, out of the shadow of the houses. What with sickness and headaches I've not stepped out for three days.

One can't sit on one's chair without being bitten all over by mosquitoes, so I've been lying and crouching under the net, on the bed. But this bed is so hard that one can't stay in any one position for long without getting stiff. However I've slept a lot, and passed the time in a sort of dream-filled hectic daze, unable to read, watching the grey house-lizards crawling upside down on the roof overhead, and in the power of all sorts of circling thoughts and negative emotions. No-one has been near me, which is perhaps a good thing.

With much determination I tried for a while to preserve a piece of cheese – a last relic of food brought from England. The ants found it the first night, but I cleaned it and wrapped it in a plastic bag. They ate through this, however, and got at it again. Before going to sleep for the next night I balanced the wrapped cheese on a pot of marmalade on the table, and ringed it about with a thick circle of DDT. In the morning however it had vanished completely. A rat?

*   *   *

40

Woke feeling well. People banging about and being unselfconsciously noisy from 4.45 onwards. They do not seem to have the consideration for others that even a child has in the West. As for their morning throat-clearing noises ...

Breakfast in the dining hall. Bread, hot cocoa and banana. Afterwards, while putting on my shoes outside, Ananta, the American, passes. We say good morning and he adds, 'Care to have coffee with me at El Greco's?' This is a very unexpected gambit in an Ashram, so I agree at once.

'It's a little habit of mine I shall never give up,' says Ananta, and leads off towards the bazaar. He is an immensely sturdy, bull-necked fellow, ex-U.S. navy, about 30, with freckled bronze face and short fair hair that goes back in crinkled waves, flecked with grey at the temples.

'I got these white shorts in the States during my last visit, and are they comfortable ... Gee, are they comfortable. I need another pair, but how can I describe them by letter?'

We reach 'El Greco's', and sit in a little alcove near the front, looking out on the street, where an old man is preparing pan, carefully wrapping up grated vegetables and spices in little packets of pale green banana leaf.

'Don't you get restless here?' I query, watching Ananta's masterful way with the waiters and the abrupt ferocity of his movements.

'Sure. Yes I get restless. But ... if you look inward it goes. If you can look inward and experiences begin, then it is so rich and interesting – the restlessness becomes pitiable, trivial. Oh yes, that's the trouble with my people. We are terribly restless, full of vital, and I've as much of it, more probably, as most of them.'

Coffee is brought and two plates of food. 'Try this. Come on. Eat this. It's rice-cake. Ever tried South Indian food? You may like it ... Yes, you see this change in people as you go West. I went back last time through Russia and Europe, and there you notice the growing alertness and activity of the peoples. But when you get to the States, it's madness, a frenzied, feverish activity – rushing around, ceaseless carrying on and excitement. And what for?'

'What was Russia like?'

'Oh, mind you I only passed through, was there a week – but I'd come from the Ashram, and that maybe had sharpened my perceptions a bit. Anyway, I liked the Russians. Sure, I'm no communist, and nothing like one, but the people I met were decent human beings. Now that's something people won't believe back home. This incessant propaganda in the papers makes them believe every Russian's a devil, always and all the time. These papers like 'Time' and 'Life' – fine papers on everything except Russia – and Nasser – but they're letting up on 'Dictator Nasser' a bit now, because he's opposing communism. But it's crazy. You know 5,000 U.S. tourists came back from Russia and said the Russians were human beings like ourselves and that they didn't want war. And these tourists were sober old men and ladies, retired people, some of them, as well as youngsters, and they didn't go as an organisation or in parties, but separately, just as they do in India. But they've caused no end of trouble back home.'

We talk more, about Dulles (who was crazy), Red China (which should be recognised), Senator Fulbright (of whom he approved), and then the boy brings plates of vegetables and fried crisp-like wafers on to which we edge the veg. He eats his but mine we send back. He gives me a piece of his to try. 'Not bad. You might like it more than the rice-cake if there's not too much onion...'

As we come away he falls upon an Indian at the cash-desk, saying, 'After nine years I come here after being away for a year and you haven't my iddli!' Everyone smiles at his vehement mock anger.

Outside, where the sun is beginning to get up its strength, Ananta tells me never to give to beggars, as, once the word gets around that one has, life becomes intolerable because of the crowds. I mention the saying of Jesus that if you give to one of them you are giving to Him. He replies, 'There is the opposite tag that the poor are always with you'.

We talk about the Ashram on the way back to the main building, and he says how he'd never intended to stay. For the first year he was still 'on the way to Ceylon'.

Referring to the article in Life Magazine about himself, with pictures of him in orange robes and of him planting rice in a paddy field with six servants, he tells me what trouble, endless trouble it had caused. 'My family said I had let down my country, my town, my religion, and betrayed them, the family. And that picture of me and the native servants; you know what people said? They said that's what I was doing it for – sexual relations with the natives – would you believe it? As if anyone would want sexual relations with a collection of old crocks like my workers! If that's what I was after I should have stayed in Athens. Do you know Athens? It's a beautiful place. I like Athens'.

*　*　*

3rd March

Norman has arranged for me to live in a visitors' hostel which is nearer than Parc à Charbon to the Ashram Centre, where, too, there is a splendid little roof-top restaurant nearby, which I can go to for meals instead of the Dining Hall. I had mentioned to Norman the sad effect of the food on my digestion, and he had at once thought of this place, where special North Indian food is served for the benefit of visitors from that part. The place is run by two sadhaks called Ganapatram and Mungatram, who have both been here many years.

Ganapatram says I am to tell him at once if I don't like the food, and he will try other dishes until he finds what suits me.

It seems rather a failing in 'equality' to quibble about food, but, as Norman says, it is much better to be physically fit if one is to make the best of one's time here. Ganapatram agrees and says it is worse for a European coming to stay than for a North Indian, as nearly everything is different from what one is used to.

My new room measures about 8 by 12 feet, with a bed, table, chair and a spare bed against one wall to use as a couch. There is

43

no window, only a ventilator high up above eye-level, but there is a large electric fan in the middle of the ceiling, which is a great luxury.

* * *

4th March

Philippe, the tall bony Frenchman with the deep voice, shouted to me across the dry water-course, 'Where is the Ashram restaurant?' So I jumped down the bank and crossed over to him.

'Aha, the crossing of the Red Sea!' he cried, and we went on together, past the mud-huts and tethered cows towards Ganapatram's restaurant.

I had had the feeling earlier that Philippe had avoided me; whenever we had met he had made no effort at conversation, and I had not made the effort either, since his ironic mind had made me react out of harmony with the spirit of the place. This evening he was different. He said he was really leaving next day. He had put off going several times, but it was too expensive to stay, and he could not find one man in the Ashram who was able to explain with any enthusiasm why he was there and what he was doing.

'Now, I am not joking,' he went on, 'I have spent recently three weeks at Ramana Maharshi's place, you know, reading and meditating there, and, besides the Maharshi's very weighty little books, I read there Sri Aurobindo's 'Life Divine' which was in their library, and I made notes on it, and really thought it might be the way for me. But now I come here I think not. Now you tell me, do you think the Supramental race will be born here in Pondicherry?'

We arrived at Ganapatram's before I could answer, and Ganapatram himself stood there to greet us at the entrance. 'Now what is your name?' shouted Philippe. 'I have it somewhere here,' and he began looking through a bag of books and papers.

'That's right' said Ganapatram. 'I will tell you when you've found it,' and he chuckled.

Philippe did not find it, but called for whisky and cigars. This delighted the old sadhak, who of course allowed no smoking or drinking in his place.

44

Going upstairs, we sat down at a small table on the roof, and Philippe went on. 'Why did you come here, tell me?' I tried to do so.

He then said that he had tried reading more of Sri Aurobindo's books but found them full of mistakes – and why did he always try to reconcile opposing points of view? His voice became deeper and fiercer as he went on, 'How can he reconcile the view that all this world is unreal, nothing, with the view that it is real, the Divine? Why reconcile, reconcile ... you cannot reconcile fire and ice, truth and error, light and dark, reality and illusion. We must have WAR. War is necessary'. He gazed earnestly through his spectacles in the most amiable way.

He bought me pineapple juice and had coffee himself. 'Now look at this book 'The Ideal of Human Unity'. I shall quote it in my book on Kingship, because it is so completely wrong. He has no idea of the magic or ritual of kingship as the representation of the gods here on earth. He speaks of democratic governments alone being stable, as they are founded on the broad will of the people. You know how in France the democratic governments before De Gaulle were the laughing stock of the world because they lasted such a short time'. He laughed, and went on, 'and Krushchev is not stable. There is another little Krushchev waiting to push him out ...'

Ganapatram brought me my supper. Philippe was dashed. 'I thought you had come here with me out of brotherly love,' he said, 'and now I see it was for love of your supper. I am a disillusioned man. All these Ashram people call me brother, but they don't mean it. If you asked a brother for one rupee, the answer would be 'Sorry, brother!'

'You're unfair. They don't have money of their own anyway ...'

When we left he kept talking about Advaita Vedanta, and its incompatibility with Sri Aurobindo's philosophy. I think now that the answer to his point is that these doctrines of monism, dualism and so on, are not, according to Sri Aurobindo, doctrines about the world in itself, but about different experiences of the world – so that it is possible for them to be valid without contradicting each other.

As we walked on in the dark towards the Playground, a little boy ran up to Philippe who gave him a chapatti which he had pinched from my tray. Another little boy arrived and he told the first one to share it with him.

'The wonderful thing about the Indian philosophy' said Philippe, 'is that it tells one to test every word by experience. We stand on the threshold of the temple together, and we cannot understand each other, but we talk and then each must go inside to do his own sadhana'.

*   *   *

5th March

Met a man from Tibet. He said that the Chinese are only in control of border territories in the east; that the central administration is still in Tibetan hands, but that the Chinese army will not leave until guerrilla warfare stops.

He was a small cheerful-looking man whom I would have taken for an Indian. He said he had been to Sweden and also Switzerland where he had stayed when one of the Dalai Lama's relations was recovering from a brain operation. He told me he was very curious to visit Africa and see the wildlife there. He asked me about the social structure of South London.

He said from his inmost heart he was wanting to stay in Pondicherry always, but that he had certain commitments he had to fulfil before giving up his job, which was that of Government Publicity Officer.

It had taken him 12 days to get here, via Sikkim.

*   *   *

6th March

Dear A. and M.,

For a while letters and news came back. Then, after a crumpled postcard from Madras, there was nothing. The Orient had swallowed him up. Among the teeming and anonymous millions it was as if he had never been ... Actually silence must not be interpreted as indifference or forgetfulness. I have often wished you were with me to share some of the sights and experiences of the last weeks, and imagined your responses at times. I wonder how you are, both of you and the young ones. A letter, if posted air-mail, takes four days to reach Pondicherry, by the way.

I am writing this in a small white-washed room on the first floor of an old Tamil cottage, in a street on the edge of the Indian part of Pondy, not far from the Bazaar. Outside there are some babies crying, some street vendors shouting, crows cawing and hand-bells ringing. The streets, planned by the French, are on a grid plan; the main ones are tarmacked and the others have a surface of rammed broken stones. The pavements seem to be the responsibility of the houses they serve, thus they vary in height and solidity according to individual prosperity and civic consciousness. The houses vary too, from mud-walled huts thatched with palm leaves, to quite solid little two-storey villas in their own compounds, where coconut palms and bananas are growing.

Everywhere there are children, sometimes quite naked. There are also large hump-backed white, fawn and piebald cows, and grey water-buffaloes with long horns sweeping back along their sides. Many small black swine, of a very primitive sly appearance, like miniature wild boars with bristles down their spines, trot eagerly or sadly through the gulleys and rootle among the refuse. Sometimes they stand rather self-consciously with crows on their backs. Fortunately there are not many cars. People, if they don't walk, get about chiefly by bicycle or coolie rickshaw.

The streets are very dusty ... and the smell ... apart from the cattle the humans contribute quite distinctively to that, as there is no indoor sanitation in many of the houses. Children come to the doors and piddle straight into the street, and in the early morning – don't go out! As for the cows, I saw in a paper the other day that someone had worked out that in Madras there were over 3,000 head of cattle in the North West sector alone. They pick up quite a lot of greenery and edible rubbish free, I suppose, and the municipal authorities have to do the mucking out. There are also goats and donkeys, chickens, jungle-fowl and, of course, dogs and cats in reasonable supply, and quite a few chipmunks – small rat-like squirrels, with three pale stripes down their backs and tails almost

as long as their bodies. They chatter very fiercely from the trees and
sometimes run along the telephone wires squeaking. Overhead there
are hundreds of black crows, which keep up a constant comment
and complaint, a few kites and eagles, and some green parakeets,
pigeons and house-sparrows. The total effect is not as bad as you
might think. The people are very leisurely and dignified, and there
is an apparent acceptance of their lot, even among the beggars and
very poor, though some of it may have the apathy of malnutrition
behind it, I suppose.

At the start of the day and in the early evenings it is cool enough
to go up on the flat roof of the cottage where I am staying and look
down on the streets and houses all around. Opposite, there lives an
elderly fuel merchant, with a very hairy chest. In the mornings he gets
bundles of young casuarina trees delivered to him by bullock cart,
then, during the day, he sits in the road stripping off the twigs and
cutting up the trunks into short lengths which he ties up in bundles
and stacks on the pavement. Of course half the road is blocked up at
his point on it. His wife sits outside the door of their house with half
a dozen pots, cooking. It smells quite good.

The French part of the town is next to the sea, behind a very fine
broad promenade, and is built up with much more solid bungalows
and houses in the French colonial style, which I admire immensely.
These buildings, although massive, are beautifully proportioned,
often with classical pillars, pilasters and panels, and for coolness
have lots of arcades and balconies and lattices; the windows have
little glass and the doorways have few doors. The walls are colour-
washed with much taste and variety – grey and white, cream and
white, cocoa-colour and white, or sometimes in three or four colours.

Most of the Ashram property is in this part of the town, scattered
about. There are the school buildings, the International Centre for
Education, the Library, several clinics, a theatre, the 'Playground'
and gym, lecture rooms and laboratories, and a number of houses
and flats inhabited by Ashram members. These, with their children,
number a little over 1,200 now, I think, so it is a pretty big community.
Then there is the central group of Ashram buildings, where Sri
Aurobindo himself once lived, and in one of the courtyards of which

he is now buried. The Mother, who since his death has continued the running of the place, also lives in this part, mostly in seclusion.

When I first arrived I stayed for a few days in the Ashram's New Guest House – a kind of caravanserai of most romantic character – a shaded court with palms and bougainvillaea, and rooms opening off it, a charming and beautiful hostess, an electric fan in one's room, and four or five course meals! But for economy I moved into another lodging on the edge of the sea, where I had a little cubicle in a large shed, divided up into many such. There I struggled for a week or so with sunstroke, ants, mosquitoes and myself. The elderly man in charge lay for much of the time on his bed, while quiet-voiced young men read to him or cooked food in a corner of the room. I felt rather bitter about him until I found he was ill with elephantiasis in both legs, which were horribly swollen and quite black, and must have given him a lot of trouble. The wash-place, there, was a concrete shed, its walls stained with green slime. It contained a cold tap and some really enormous lizards. One morning I was standing there cleaning my teeth and spitting into a gulley in the floor when the old man hobbled up. He smiled benevolently and said, 'Is this your first experience of living in a spiritual atmosphere?' (Spitting and spluttering noises from me.) 'You will get used to it', he added, as he moved off.

For food I went to the Ashram Dining Hall. This was an old French mansion built like a classical temple and standing in a lovely little garden. It was self-service and we sat on the floor. It was good – except for the food which did not agree with me. Apparently once the menu was looked after by the Mother herself and was perfect – really well thought out. But the disciples grumbled. The Gujaratis said it was biased in favour of the Bengalis, the Bengalis said it was only edible by Tamils and so on. This came to the ears of Sri Aurobindo, who in disgust said, 'Right, in future you can do it yourselves', or, according to another version, inaugurated a diet that everyone would dislike equally, so no-one could say there was favouritism!

Anyway now I eat at a little roof-top restaurant run by a placid fellow called Ganapatram. He is about 50 I should say, and is in charge of the Ashram workshops where poor people are taught cottage industries – furniture making, basketry, papier-maché work and the manufacture of incense and scent. He has curly black ringlets down his back and a slow huge smile like a crocodile. He is concerned about finding me the right diet, and really is most kind. At lunch and supper I have a round metal tray on which are four or five little bowls containing such things as curried cauliflower, boiled beans and peas, curds, dahl, curried potato, a ball of dried curds in syrup, cucumber and tomato and so on. To eat with these goes a pile of hot chapattis, which are a bit like bannock, and very good. At breakfast he produces 'iddli' which are rice-cakes, eaten with a kind of white chutney, followed by lemon tea. When Ganapatram is not around there is his friend Mungatram who looks rather like him, and is also very helpful. From time to time other guests come in too. There is a cheerful little man from Lhasa in Tibet who comes occasionally, and is interesting to talk with. He suggests I visit him in Tibet, but I don't think I shall.

Food and lodging cost 9 shillings a day, i.e. £3.3.0 a week. Laundry charges are a penny an item!

So far I've said nothing about the essence of the Ashram – what it is doing and why. Let me try.

Sri Aurobindo, as maybe you remember, began his rise to fame in India as the leader of Indian nationalism in Bengal. He really got the 'Free India' line going in Edwardian times, before Gandhi. Then he took to yoga, frankly to increase his own energy and capacity for work as a political leader. In 1908 he was shut up by the British, and had various profound experiences of a spiritual nature while in prison, which quite changed his purpose. He left politics, arrived in French Pondicherry and became absorbed in the practice of yoga. At first he said his was the 'yoga of humanity' because all the emphasis in previous Indian yogas had been on saving the individual and had left the rest of the world where it was, in wretchedness, whereas he was not concerned with his own salvation but with 'changing human nature'. He proposed a synthesis of the best elements in the three main traditional yogas of India, and explored and expounded this synthesis in a modern, un-obscure, experimental way, making it acceptable to the scientific mind. He found that the Bhagavad Gita had attempted a similar synthesis in the past, which had been lost sight of. So he commented on the Gita, in a series of essays, showing how the yoga of Knowledge, the yoga of Love or Devotion and the yoga of Action could all be combined to lead the individual soul towards the realisation of its true nature, and also that this was compatible with work and enterprise in this world.

By now he had become convinced that Indian political freedom was assured, in due time, but he was concerned about how it would be used. He saw that otherworldliness had been a cause of India's social stagnation and economic apathy, and began building a new cultural philosophy. His aim was still probably 'for humanity'. Later this changed, and he stated that his yoga was 'for the sake of the Divine', when his own experience deepened. But he always maintained his opposition to the escape into Nirvana or bliss in the beyond – though he recognised the validity of the experience these words represent. His point was that one should certainly find Nirvana or Moksha or the Kingdom of Heaven, but not stay there or even get other people to stay there. Rather, bring back that consciousness into the world to transform it. And here he went further than the Gita, saying that not only the mind and heart and will, but also the material body of man must be transformed.

Ethics based on love and right thinking are fine, but are always fighting so precariously and inconclusively that people, as you know, can doubt whether humanity has really progressed at all over the last 2,000 years except technologically and in the accumulation of knowledge. So Sri Aurobindo maintained that the root of the trouble lay in the inconscient part of man, and particularly in the body itself, which he saw as the last stronghold of the old selfish impulses and obscurities. These are still latently there even in the saints, ready to attempt a come-back whenever the chance offers. If the Kingdom was ever to be realised on earth, Sri Aurobindo insisted, man would have to change integrally, so there was no longer this conflict between 'higher' and 'lower' within him, but rather the whole being – right down to the cells of the body – would consciously collaborate with the divine will.

Transformation is, then, one of the emphases in Sri Aurobindo's philosophy.

Another is the evolutionary element: he saw evolution as the unfolding of what has been involved – the divine power, consciousness and delight have plunged into the density of matter, and the history of the world has been the gradual emergence of these qualities back into the light, as it were. So, life and mind were latent in primordial substance – consciousness sleeping in inconscience – but they have evolved through the descent of the transcendent uninvolved forces and the ascent of the aspiring, immanent, involved forces. Each stage transforms and uplifts what has gone before; life does not abandon matter but lifts it to the stage of organic matter, and mind builds on and transforms that. And why should mind be the end of the series? Why should man be the final species?

Sri Aurobindo asserted that there is another step possible – to Supermind. This is not just mind in an exaggerated form, but something unthinkable to anyone below its level – just as unintelligible to us mental beings as human behaviour is to dogs. (Sri Aurobindo's Superman, by the way, has nothing to do with Nietzsche's exuberant egotist of the same name.)

The Supermind would have, finally, the power to deal with the inconscience of the body.

Sri Aurobindo became convinced that this new development of consciousness was now, for the first time, a practical possibility, and he worked 'under a supreme inner guidance', to pioneer the descent of Supermind, in himself, in the Mother, and in a group of dedicated people in the Ashram. Already, according to the Mother, some fundamental change has taken place in the nature of mankind – in its possibilities of consciousness and its future development.

This bringing down of Supermind would be something new, Sri Aurobindo said, because previously even the greatest have only, at best, come into contact with it in trance or contemplation, and it has never up to now entered into the earth's evolution and been embodied in waking everyday life.

When the new principle eventually becomes established, it is said, people will be born with the Supramental capacity, just as men, now, are born anywhere in the world with the mental capacity. They won't have to practise a strenuous individual yoga to get there.

Meanwhile, as things are, we live as transitional beings, full of imperfections, ugliness, suffering and frustration. But this is not to say that the world is irremediably evil or should be written off in favour of a better after-life. Rather, press on to the next, more perfect stage on earth, when illness, misery and even death will disappear or be modified through the power of the divine manifestation.

The people here are trying to do that.

With love to you,

Dick.

*　　*　　*

14th March

As soon as D. is peaceful and in the right receptive attitude, he thinks, 'This is perhaps the place where I should be. What else can ever really satisfy me?'

When he says this a syndrome of thoughts is set in motion which destroys all peace. The vital and mental minds produce picture after picture of the root elements of his attachment to his previous life: parents, family, P., old Mr Clarke, friends, and England itself. This goes on until in misery D. recalls that he is only a visitor at this place anyway, and no-one has asked him to stay, or even expected it of him, so he should just relax and enjoy his time here. Peace and receptivity then return. And the cycle begins again.

*　　*　　*

22nd March

'I was interested to see your poems in 'Mother India', said a bald patrician-looking Indian in white shirt and shorts, who met me outside the Playground last night. 'My name is Mehdi Imam. Norman tells me you are an Oxford man'.

He spoke in a fantastically Oxford way himself, and soon told me why. 'I was at Oxford myself. I was educated entirely in your country. You know the Dragon School? Yes, well I was sent there when I was six, and then went on to Harrow and Oriel. My tutors there were Ross and Tod – yes Tod of 'Greek Inscriptions', so you see I have a great feeling for England, and Europe too. I have been right through Europe nine times; stayed in Spain; visited Greece. Have you been to Greece? No? You should go. The Parthenon – so beautiful you never want to leave it – the blue of the sky, the whiteness of the marble ... and Greece itself – still breathes of the classics – its rounded bare hills and temples and olive trees – so beautiful. I visited Delphi – spent a day there – remarkable. And of course after I left England my father, who was a judge in the Supreme Court, a very brilliant man, saw to it that I should follow in his footsteps in Bombay. But after years and years there, people would ask 'Do you miss England?' and I would say 'But of course I do, after spending a third of my life there'. And now it's all different – all that part of my life is falling away. But all that education is coming out now. Wonderful. It is all being given out here. I teach B.A. English and help produce Shakespeare. Madame Pitoeff has had experience of dramatics and I tell her how the lines should sound. Together we are putting 'Macbeth' on tape. And 'Hamlet' too. You must come and hear them. I have just recorded 'To be or not to be'. And the children are wonderful here – wonderful'.

'Yes' he went on, 'I had to come here. A time came when my work just ceased to interest me any more; although I was earning thousands of rupees a month in the courts it didn't mean anything any more. I said to the Mother, 'Is it coming to this?' and she smiled and nodded – and I had to come here. But I said to her, 'Let me be absolutely frank and honest with you, you can do nothing for me unless I do it myself', and she smiled again and agreed. It's a strange thing one can do nothing, really, yet without one's co-operation the Divine will do nothing either. Although He is omnipotent He will not lift one up the mountain, but if you will open to Him He will help you climb it yourself. And that's much more fun, much more exciting. It's very interesting, very interesting'.

He paused, looking into the distance. Then a new thought came to him, and he continued, 'But when you come here you must not rely on your mind. It can't help you here. Intellectual queries and perplexities actually block the Divine light from entering your head. It's a pity you are not clairvoyant. It makes things much more convincing if you can actually see these things – I have seen them – the Grace coming down, the Lumen Christi descending like a golden column onto one's head ...' He broke off and raised his hands as if to guide down the descending force, and, looking up, smiled and chuckled, and muttered 'Oh now that's naughty, that's naughty' as if the Divine Playmate were teasing him with actual clairvoyance as he talked. 'Yes, it's real all right' he went on, 'and similarly if one's mind is full of doubts and perplexities it is as if there were fumes or clouds of fog – yes, like London fog – rising from one's head, and the light cannot enter, it is screened off'.

'How do you quieten the mind? The best way is to read noble and inspiring literature. Fill your mind with lofty and beautiful thoughts, and dedicate whatever you do to the Divine. When you pick up your pen, do it for the Divine, and so with everything you do. Another thing: don't criticise. When I came here first I was full of criticism. I found the people dull and stupid. Where was the Supermind? And I thought there was no love here. But then I found it was all a reflection of myself, my own condition, and so I radiated love and then everything was lovely, everyone was beautiful and so wonderful to me – because love returns back to one from other people if one radiates it out. Now I don't criticise, and if I hear a clever remark against myself I don't make a retort but turn a beam of love to whoever made it, and forget it. And love is power, there's no doubt about that. Jesus was no weakling, but had tremendous power too. He had love and power, not just love. I realised that when I had a vision of His face last Christmas. It was in the Playground on Christmas Day, and the Mother was there and I saw her face change to the face of Christ – it was wonderful. Afterwards I went to a friend and told him about it, and he said, 'Why you are the second person who has come and told me that he saw Christ instead of Mother today'. But the love and the power were wonderful. And, if one opens to this, the work is done in one, behind the scenes. One must aspire, and quieten the mind, and then everything is done for you – it is wonderful'.

COMPLAINT FROM INDIA

In this country the songsters at dawn are crows
And cockerels. As if the heat had dried up music
Into a croak and a little trumpet.
These black crows, cawing and muttering,
Wrangling over the justice of everything, -
Over the right ration of refuse, and the existence of eagles,
Lowering their heads like geese, at the slightest trespass,
Indignant to hoarseness and open-beaked astonishment
Over trivialities best left without comment,
STAND TOO MUCH IN THE PUBLIC EYE
Here in India. Someone should tell them
To be more reticent, and not bounce around so much
Like spring-heeled jackdaws.
And let them forget they are in the Ramayana.
I don't mind the cockerels.

*   *   *

30th March

Yesterday, Easter Day, the Mother gave a special blessing to Ashramites, in commemoration of 29th March 1914, when she first came to Pondicherry and saw Sri Aurobindo.

She sat in one of the Ashram courtyards, embowered in flowers, a small, humble old lady, with a most human smile, but with eyes of unfathomable spirit, radiating, searching for a sign of response: life-giving eyes. For forty-five minutes Ashramites and visitors filed past her, silently, each being handed a printed copy of the message for the day: a quotation from Sri Aurobindo concerning the nature of the appearance of Supermind.

In the evening I went to a small neo-Gothic chapel dedicated to St John. It might have been in England except that there were potted palms each side of the altar, and among the flowers decorating the lectern were pink lotuses. On one wall was a marble plaque to Anna, dear wife of a Major Felton, who recorded his grief and loss in 1865. 'Blessed are the pure in heart for they shall see God'.

The congregation was all Tamil and the minister was a sturdy Bengali. Some of the girls were most beautifully dressed in silks and muslins, with braided blossom in their black hair, which hung in heavy shining plaits and loops.

The minister preached about Jesus and women; how they loved him and were last at the cross and first at the tomb, and how when they came in the morning Jesus was not there, but 'gone hence'. He exhorted us that this church should not be like the empty sepulchre nor like the whited sepulchre, nor like the synagogues in Galilee and Capernaum which Jesus left – 'passing from them'.

He told a story of how Gandhi in South Africa, when a young man, used to attend a church there regularly. The white congregation told the minister, who'd been there 40 years, 'Either you tell this black man to leave, or else we leave'. The minister told Gandhi, who said, 'Pray to your Jesus about it and let me know what He says next Sunday'. Next Sunday the minister came and said to Gandhi, 'I had a vision last night, when Jesus said you should be told to leave because you are a Hindu'. 'Oh' said Gandhi, 'I had a vision too, when Jesus said to me he had been trying to enter this church for forty years, but had not been allowed in'. Gandhi never went to a Christian church again.

*　*　*

31st March

Dear A. & M.,

Many thanks for your letter. Let's begin with your question, 'What is an Ashram?' A glossary I have here says, 'Ashram – Hermitage. It is usually used as a centre for penance, sadhana, education or social service'. 'Hermitage', with its associations of solitude and a cell by a spring, is a bit misleading, when one is applying it to a community of over 1,000 people, and this ashram here in Pondicherry is not a centre for penance, education or social service – though there may be incidental traces of these things in it. It is a centre for sadhana, and sadhana, says the glossary, is 'spiritual discipline for attaining self-realization'. Again, one may quibble with this definition, as Sri

57

Aurobindo's yoga is not confined to self-realization. But you get the idea, I hope.

Another book I have here says, 'An Ashram means the house or houses of a Teacher or Master of spiritual philosophy in which he receives and lodges those who come to him for teaching and practice.' I believe that in the past they were often in forests, and varied in size from that of a sage with a few followers to the equivalent of a university.

At present there are many ashrams, all over India. Tagore and Gandhi, for example had their own, and there is another famous one near here, founded by Sri Ramana Maharshi, which is visited, I think, by Larry, the hero in Maugham's 'Razor's Edge'.

People who practise sadhana are called 'sadhaks', by the way.

The Sri Aurobindo Ashram, it seems, is different from the accepted pattern of what such a place should be. The traditional Hindu thinks of an ashram in terms of poverty, asceticism and otherworldliness, where the body is tolerated as a necessary snag, but here the emphasis is on the Kingdom of Heaven on Earth, and life more abundantly – physical, emotional and mental, wherever it's consistent with the primary aims of sadhana. Thus although sadhaks have a minimum of private possessions, they don't cultivate unnecessary hardship, and the Ashram as a whole owns a good deal of property and equipment.

The people here, however, do live very simply. A man apologised to me recently for having a bookcase in his room; it was, he said, necessary for him, for his work as a teacher.

One sadhak told me how shocked he was when he first came here, to find men and women doing the same physical exercises, and wearing shorts, too. Asking where the Mother was, he was told she was playing tennis. He found no ochre robes, no chanting of Sanskrit, no ashes on the face. But also, he noticed, there was no dirt and no dysentery. Gradually he came round to the view that an ashram could aim at a spirituality that was incarnational, and expressed the Divine in terms of this world.

Beauty, too, is given an importance that you wouldn't find in an ashram that looked upon all visual distinctions as illusory. For instance, there is a great appreciation of plants here. The Ashram courtyard is like a Japanese garden – really very beautiful, with flowering trees, slender palms, cacti, shrubs, climbing bougainvillaea and all sorts of Indian and European flowers – most of them in pots – roses, dahlias, morning-glory, verbena, canna and many more whose names I don't know. They are in pots because the soil is so poor and sandy that any moisture drains away or evaporates very quickly. As soon as a plant is past its prime it is taken away to the nurseries and a pot of something else is put in its place. The effect is wonderfully refreshing, especially when contrasted with the bare, dusty ground seen elsewhere, all burnt up by the heat.

Today I saw my first snake-charmer. He was sitting by a road playing on a bell-bottomed pipe to a huge dark cobra in a basket. The snake seemed critical, and not very charmed.

Love, Dick

*　　*　　*

1st April

At supper yesterday evening I talked with an Indian mill-manager. He told me all big Indian business firms employ an income tax expert, whose job it is to produce a special set of account books for the Income Tax Inspectors. This 'expert' is the highest paid man on the staff. The Government knows this double accounting system goes on, but can do nothing about it. The Government would take half the profit – if it could – from the mill where this fellow works. Under French rule there was no income tax at all, and 'fortunes were made'.

This manager also said he could not understand the Message handed out by the Mother on the recent Darshan day. I tried to explain, but he said he guaranteed that at least 60 per cent of the people who had been given the Message would not have been able to make anything of it. The Message, printed on a card of Ashram hand made paper had said:

'It is not perhaps very useful to forecast by the mind what will be the precise results of the descent of a Supramental consciousness

59

into a world in which up to now the mental intelligence has been the highest evolutionary product and leading power. For the Supermind is a consciousness which will work in a very different way from the mind and the lines laid down for it by the latter are not likely to be respected by the greater energy in its self-organisation and operation here'.

Sri Aurobindo

*　*　*

4th April

Restaurant talk:
'The absolute limit to asceticism is reached by the Nagas. I saw a procession of them once.'
'Like living skeletons?'
'No. All types – tall men, short men, fat, thin, lank, broad.'
'Men and women?'
'Men and women, and stark naked.'
'Nothing on at all? Loin cloths?'
'Mother-naked. And they walked like kings, as if they owned the world, heads up, erect. It was a sight. It was something. People began to ask themselves 'What are these clothes, these possessions……?'
'And did they carry nothing? No weapons at all?'
'Yes. Some carried an iron bar, as weapon. That was all. And they walked past – without seeing anything, in trance, all the time in a higher state of consciousness. They didn't know where they were, or what they were doing.'
'But how did they find their way?'
'Their guru was leading them, and they followed. It is believed that anything they touch with their feet will be blessed with good fortune. I saw a man holding out a big bundle of notes and one of the Nagas kicked it right out of his hand down the road. Of course he never saw it. And another man held out a very valuable gold pot, and it was kicked far away...'
'And is it true that one cannot ever go to their camps and come back again?'

60

'Yes. They very rarely come down from the Himalayas, and if one searches for them, and even if one looks just like a Naga oneself – takes off all one's clothes – they stop you when you are a long way away. The guru knows by occult power if you are coming....'

'How do new recruits join, then?'

'Only exceptional people, who have the inner aspiration and the call, can join. They hear the call and give up everything and are led to a Naga guru, from wherever they are. But it's quite something to see them, I can tell you. I was impressed.

• • •

'I'm not usually impressed with holy men. I go up to them and look at them and say 'Number One Fake', and they are usually men like I am, and don't answer my questions. But two or three times I was impressed'.

* * *

10th April

Earlier this week a tall aristocratic young man appeared at Ganapatram's restaurant for lunch. He was dressed in white, and wore dark glasses, I remember, and spoke with quiet authority to the party of visitors he was showing around. We got into conversation, and he asked where I was from, why I had come, how long I intended to stay and so on. At the end of the meal he invited me to join his group and visit the Lake, a property in the country north of Pondicherry, which is being developed for the Ashram. I went with them, and we had some more talk. He is an industrialist from Calcutta, I think, very much interested in the Ashram, and devoted to the Mother.

Today, when I went to pay my account with G. for the week, he said, 'How long will you be staying, Mr Dick?' I told him I could afford to stay one more week and then must leave.

Lowering his voice, and looking at me in a kindly and serious way, G. explained that a visitor, who wished to remain anonymous, had asked him to tell me that henceforward he would pay for my board and lodging. It was his wish that I should not have to cut short my stay for economic reasons, but remain as long as I felt the visit was of importance to me. G. added that although this benefactor had wished to be an unknown one, he thought I could guess who it was, and he could assure me that this man was rich and I should not hesitate to take advantage of his offer.

He said he was happy that this had happened, and that the Divine must wish me to stay on longer.

*   *   *

17th April

I have seen the Mother. At 9.30 I called on Norman, who had arranged the interview. He took me to a building where flowers are distributed to people who want them for puja. We chose three flowers to give to the Mother, and then went to the main Ashram compound. There Nolini, the Ashram Secretary, met us and led me up green-carpeted stairs to the Mother's flat. At the door a strongly built elderly man, naked to the waist and with a fine beard, ushered me into the room and then left with Nolini.

On the right of the door through which I had come sat the Mother on a small high-backed chair. Behind her head was a green woven figure of her emblem; at her feet a deerskin. On her right, half facing her, was a small arm-chair, to which she signalled me. I gave her the flowers, which she put down on a little table on her left, and I thanked her for seeing me.

When I had sat down I lost all energy to speak for a minute or so, and remained, silent, waiting for peace and order to return to my mind. When I looked up she smiled at me and we laughed.

'Should I stay here, at this Ashram, Mother?' I asked, conscious of the effort of putting the question, and of supreme suspense as to the answer.

She looked into my eyes and then said, in a high, slow, gentle voice, 'Yes, if you want to stay here ... You must feel within yourself a definite call to the Supramental life. Do you really want to stay here?'

I went on, 'Part of me gets into a panic at the thought – but part of me makes me have to ask you if I should stay – if it is best for me or not. I promised my people in England to come back, but since I have been here I have been uncertain what I should do.'

'You say you have promised you would return; that is a serious thing, then. You have to be very sure of the Divine call if you are to break that promise without harm to yourself. If you stay you must be able to feel that you can do your family more real good from a distance than if you go back to them.' She paused, and then went on, 'You see the question may not be "Pondicherry or London?" It may be that you should come here and then return, or alternate between the two, or even not come again in this life. The question need not be so clear cut. I have followed you at Darshan and at Balcony in the mornings and I have felt that it may be right for you to go back and face your old life until it becomes ridiculous for you – until the people you live with become like strangers to you. Then there will be no question about where you should be. Have you been happy while you have been here?'

'Yes, except when I have been thinking about whether to stay.' We laughed, and she said, 'Except for the problem!'

'Yes, I don't seem able to get below the surface-mind to find answers to questions from within, for myself.'

'That is because you put the questions in the wrong way – you expect an answer either yes or no. But it doesn't come like that. Have you done any work here?'

'No, not yet.'

'I think you should stay for another month or two – will your parents be all right for that time? – and do some work, putting the problem out of your mind. Then you will be able to judge better for yourself how it suits you here. You will get more into the spirit of the place, and see how it works in practice – doing your work as an offering to the Divine, and testing how the various parts of your being react. Then, when you see more clearly, or have a greater resolution, let me know, and we will have another talk about it.'

She discussed the money side of staying and what sort of work I should try. She suggested I should teach in the Ashram school, but seeing the consternation in my face asked if I would like to help, instead, with proof-reading in the Publications Department, and I said I would. She then went out of the room to find the bearded man and ask him to find Nolini, who would arrange for me to begin work.

While she was gone I looked round for a moment. Against the far wall was the big double throne, covered with a tiger-skin, which is to be seen in Cartier-Bresson's photograph of Sri Aurobindo and the Mother giving Darshan. The room contained many carvings, bronzes, ivories – objects of Japanese, Indian and European art.

The Mother came back and said, 'Have you seen Sri Aurobindo's room?' and led me to the door into a parallel apartment, equally large but rather dark, as the window-shutters let in little direct light and because of the colour of the floor and furniture. Everything gave an impression of solidity and massive proportion. There were book-cases, a writing-desk, a sofa and two or three tiger skins. The bust by Elsa Fraenkel, which I had seen before in London, stood between the windows.

'Is that like him?' I asked.

'No', said the Mother, 'it is not a physical likeness, but it shows very well a certain quality of his mind – his vision of intellectual truth, which is why I like it and keep it here.'

She told me how Sri Aurobindo lived in this room for 24 years without going out of it. Then Nolini came, and she told him to take me to Prithwisingh, to start work proof-reading.

'Voilà' she said.

Before I left she gave me two flowers: a pink and white hibiscus, and a rose. 'Has anyone told you the names we give to the different flowers here?   This one is Divine Grace, and this is Psychic Love. Voilà.'

• • •

In appearance the Mother looked old and frail, her head perpetually sunk forward, as if from much intent gazing into people's faces. She had some dark cosmetic round her eyes. These, her eyes, and her smile were not old at all. Nor was her mind. She gave the impression of absolute accuracy of judgement based on direct insight, and of a concern not to impress for irrelevant reasons, or say things in any way other than the best for the person concerned. Combined with endless patience and kindness she had a brisk practical sense, and a lightness of touch.

She wore a white dress with a pale golden-coloured scarf tied tightly over her grey and black hair.

*   *   *

18th April

Yesterday's account of the interview with the Mother was not accurate. I see the fallibility of eye- and ear-witnesses where such meetings are concerned, for almost immediately the ego begins reshaping the pattern, bringing some things forward into prominence and relegating others to the background. The mind and heart are so intent on a comfortable memory, so biased in their selection of foci that a detached version must be rare and difficult – even after two days, let alone fifty or sixty years, as with the Gospels.

I have, for instance, omitted Mother's question as to what there was to be said on the positive side for staying at Pondicherry, and, again, what led me here in the first place. I did not mention herself, but told her about the effect Sri Aurobindo's writings had had on me, and about the experience that had come while staying in Durham with Arabinda Basu, a follower of Sri Aurobindo. I tried to tell her briefly how this had resulted in a deep change in the way I was aware of the world – how people, houses, trees, all objects, had lost their separateness and become a shadowy film behind which was an indefinable, overwhelming, silent Reality. I said how Sri Aurobindo had written about a similar change, which had had a lasting effect on his consciousness, but that with me it had faded until, by the end of a fortnight or so, it had become only a memory. All the same, I felt it had been the most important event in my life – a kind of revelation.

The Mother nodded as I tried to describe what had happened, and said it was a true experience, and asked if anything like it had recurred while I was here. I told her it had not.

*   *   *

A black day. Toothache. Horrible band starts playing in street at 5 a.m. in preparation for a wedding celebration. Thunder-storm. Swelling in left nostril. Funeral in afternoon. Procession goes down the street with gaily decorated coffin carried head-high. Weeping women.

No resolution of inner conflict. It is still 'To stay or not to stay' in spite of my instructions to forget the issue. What work is more worth doing than sadhana for mankind – for the Divine, and where better to do it than here, where the atmosphere and environment are prepared for it? Yet there is seemingly an insurmountable block in the way. Do I accept this and wait for growth and grace, or do I fight it? Today was certainly unsuccessful – the only bright beam was 'Blessings', in the morning, when Mother gave each of us a flower and to me the most wonderful smile and 'eye contact'. Her eyes are indescribably rich, penetrating without censure or assertion, loving without sentimentality, deep .... alive.

FRENCH MARIGOLD

Poor plucked flower-head
Cut off from Earth,
What is your gold crown worth
So soon devalued and dead?

Emblem of Consciousness,
For your short hour,
Earth-born sun-aspiring flower -
Such transience is not valueless.

And when your petals
Come to me from the Mother
I would wish no other

Blessing – not even in lasting metals.

*   *   *

Wake to the band again at 5 o'clock. Go to Balcony. Afterwards Niranjan, a young man who works at the Library, tries unsuccessfully to borrow a bike for me, so we can go back with Ananta to have breakfast on his island. Eventually Ananta persuades him to give up the one he has borrowed for himself.

Ananta and I buy bread in the town, collect some food from the Dining Hall and go south, out of Pondi, until we come to a dusty lane off to the left. We go down this, between cactus hedges, until we reach a palm plantation by an inlet of sea, across which is the island.

Ananta shouts over the water until a Tamil boy punts off to fetch us in a little boat, decked over with corrugated iron.

We soon arrive at the island – a low-lying plot of land bordered by well-trimmed hedges. We leave the boat and go along a sandy path between tall green paddy, then turn left past a white temple about the size of a gazebo, capped with a dome and a golden ball and spike, with gilded peacocks – symbols of victory – over the entrance. Further on is a large pool of pink flowering lotus, and, next to it, another containing white ones.

At the end of the path is a small but massive cube of concrete, washed in Indian red, standing on white blocks. This is Ananta's house – two rooms: sitting room opening eastwards and overlooking a third pool of pink lotus, and bedroom behind it. It has a prefabricated ridge-roof, with a layer of palm over it for coolness. At the back is a separate very solid sanitary unit. Sloping away to the side is a hedge-enclosed lawn, in the middle of which are two fish pools. One has a small white wall at its end, on which Picasso-style fish swim frescoed under a golden sun. Sturdy young palm trees grow down one side of the lawn, and many pots of flowers stand spaced around.

Five Tamils are busy catching all the fish in the nearer pond and tipping them into the other. Ananta says he will enlarge one pond and fill in the second.

We sit at a small table under a leaning tree, and a boy brings a photograph of the Mother and puts it on the table. Nearby is set a pink lotus flower, with a thick stick of incense stuck through its centre. The pale blue smoke drifts in the light air-currents over the lawn.

We eat omelettes, toast and peach jam and drink coffee. We speak very little. Once Ananta says, 'You know it seems to me that the Mother is getting strawnger and strawnger every day. I don't know as much about these things as Norman does, but I have never known anything like these last few weeks; and yesterday she was amazing. Did you see how young she looked?'

When we finish eating he shows me the little temple. It is like a shrine inside, with photographs of Sri Aurobindo and the Mother. Everything massive, bright and clean.

He also shows me a strange squat white column, up which golden hooded cobras coil. This, he says, represents the Mother as Power – the Serpent Power.

*　*　*

21st April

This morning Norman was saying that it was the Mother's wish that the Ashram should be a place where all those who sincerely wanted to find God could devote themselves without distraction to the search, and develop their inner potentialities to the full, without material anxieties. Once she was convinced that someone was a genuine seeker, whatever his or her religion or philosophy, then she was prepared to feed, clothe and house that person, free, for the rest of their life.

I asked about the economics of such a community. His answer was that many disciples living all over the world sent gifts, some gave a proportion of their income, and others left legacies to the Mother when they died. Then again people who became full members gave the Mother all they had when they joined. In many ways, too, the Ashram had become self-supporting: there were the farms, the bakery, the departments for laundry, building, clothing and footwear and so on, and there were other departments which earned a profit

68

from selling to the public, such as the hand-made paper factory, the soft drinks bottling plant, Cottage Industries and other ventures.

He said, however, that profitability was not the criterion of the success of a department. The idea was always that the work should be done for the Divine, and be a means of sadhana, a part of the process of spiritualizing the individual consciousness in its relation to outward activity and to other people. A man might spend many years doing some work for which he had no aptitude, but from the inner point of view this might be seen to be necessary for him as a means of developing a weak side of his nature. Thus there were, in the Ashram, well-qualified intellectuals who were doing simple manual work, such as washing limes.

The Mother had warned visitors that there was probably nothing done better here, in the way of institutional work, than could be found elsewhere, but that the attitude behind the work was different. Slowly a group of human beings was becoming self-aware and prepared for development.

The twelve hundred or so people cared for had never been short of food or any real necessity, however. If there was a special need, then the Mother prayed for the necessary provision. She had always stressed that the money was from God, and must be used for the service of God. I mentioned the way George Muller had run his orphanages in Bristol on a similar day by day trust in the love and providence of God.

Norman said, too, that although the Ashramites did not use money – he himself had not touched any for years – the Mother did not disparage it in any ascetic way. She maintained that the money-power was only one more of the various forces in the world that must be captured and used for the Divine Life. In practice, as in a Kibbutz, most Ashramites just did not need money.

Once a month each sadhak wrote out a list of his requirements, and these were met, as far as was economically possible at the time, on the first day of the new month. This occasion was called 'Prosperity Darshan'. The Mother would be present, and each person would receive soap, a new shirt or saree, or a pair of sandals, according to his or her need. Many would be content just to receive the Mother's blessing.

I like very much this idea that people should be chosen for jobs not because they can do them well, but because they can't.

*   *   *

23rd April

Today I had a look at some more of Pondicherry. Instead of turning right when I came out of the hostel and making for the Ashram buildings in the clean deserted roads by the sea-front, I turned left towards the centre of the town.

There is a different atmosphere, almost at once. It is the world of the merchant and the worker. At first I passed by single-storey Tamil houses, with wooden pillars between which could be seen ante-rooms and interior courtyards. Then I came to small shops, open-fronted, a few steps up from the street: shops selling tobacco, pan, betel-nut, cardamom and peppers, bananas, grains of all sorts and sweets. And then further on there were bakers, furniture-makers, weavers, grocers and intriguing hardware shops which were displaying brass ornaments for the horns of oxen, bronze figures of Krishna, incense burners, strange-looking lamps, knives and all sorts of mass-produced cooking utensils.

After about ten minutes I reached the market, very congested, with fruit and vegetables piled up on the ground and salesmen squatting behind them. In the clothiers' section I was momentarily fooled by a plaster figure draped in a golden saree, smiling at me over the bales. There was also a fish market – a grim place where dogs and flies bustled among heaps of small fish and shrimps lying exposed on the scale-glistening earth, and the sun drew up stink enough to discourage a yogi.

In another street I came upon silversmiths, sitting cross-legged on their work-seats, hammering bangles and ear-rings and fine filigree jewelry.

Everywhere among the crowds were emaciated beggars, naked except for loin-cloths, each holding a staff in one hand and a

70

begging-bowl in the other, some like mediaeval portrayals of Death himself, moving slowly, with staring eyes, some with crippled and deformed limbs or missing extremities, all uttering their cries, patiently, insistently, filling me with a sense of their hopelessness, their timeless endurance. And even more importunate were the children. They followed me for streets, clutching at my hands and staring up with large impertinent and imploring eyes, refusing to take no for an answer, holding up even younger children and babies for my charity, and leaving an unforgettable image of humanity helpless among swarming flies, under the implacable bright glare of the sun.

I also saw a fakir, a man naked except for a lunghi, but his dark skin plastered with grey mud, and his hair caked and thick with it, so it stood out round his head, and, most terrible, his cheeks pierced through and through by skewers of wood and with long splinters hanging from his ears and mouth. Silently he held up his bowl to the shopkeepers, and the talking died away wherever he halted.

Beyond the shopping area there were again quiet streets where middle-class Tamils lived and beyond, still further, I came to districts of mud-built huts, roofed with palm-leaves, where bare babies played with cats and dogs on the baked ground, and to small gardens where palm trees rose, with large pots hanging among the nuts, in which sap was collecting to be made into palm wine.

At the far side of the town was another drainage ditch, and then unbroken groves of dark, silent coconut trees.

*　*　*

24th April

There are no beggars around the Ashram buildings since the Ashramites have no money.

It seems to be a common criticism, though, that the Ashram does little to help alleviate the general misery. I suppose people contrast it with Gandhian settlements or with Christian missions. The Ashramites whom I have talked to about this have two points to make in reply. Firstly, they say, philanthropy is not their purpose or their province. One does not reproach a research laboratory or

71

an engineering shop for not taking up the rehabilitation of beggars, and they may serve the community none the less in their own ways. Similarly, the Ashram – itself largely dependent on voluntary donations – has its own work to do; and if and when it succeeds in its long-term aim of pioneering the emergence of Supermind it will have served humanity in the most constructive and radical way possible – cutting at the very roots of poverty and human misery, since everyone would feel the benefit even if only a few people became fully transformed. Nothing really new would be achieved, on the other hand, if they raised the standard of living of the whole of South India to the level of that in Europe.

The second point the Ashramite may make is that, although social service is not its primary aim, even so the Ashram has done an enormous amount for the people of Pondicherry and the countryside around. The Mother not only started the Honesty Stores in the town, where food-grains, for example, are sold at an 'honest' price, without hoarding or profiteering, but also the farms, factories and constructional services belonging to the Ashram employ an outside labour-force of many hundreds. In fact Sri Aurobindo once said that when he first came to Pondicherry it was a town in decadence and decline, whereas now it is thriving and expanding.

Sri Aurobindo writes, in a letter, 'Carrying on anything of this magnitude without any settled income could not have been done if there had not been the working of a divine Force. Works of charity are not part of our work, there are other people who can see to that. We have to spend all on the work we have taken in hand ...'

*   *   *

26th April

Each morning, now, I go to work – proof-reading – in Prithwisingh's room. This is in a building opening off the main Ashram courtyard, near the Samadhi. Passing a notice-board for group athletics activities and timetables, one enters a lobby where incoming letters are displayed. At the end of this is a large rather dark room in which Prithwisingh sits, at a massive table-desk, his back to the door.

His locks of white hair curl down to his shoulders, and he has a drooping golden moustache. He wears strong spectacles, for he is very nearly blind. In spite of this, though, he seems to sense in some way who it is that has come into the room, saying very sweetly 'Good morning, Mr Dick' and talking for a while before passing me anything that has come in for correction. He has given me an H.M.S.O. guide to the symbols used in proof-annotation, and some clear advice on how to set about it. Before his own sight began to fail, about ten years ago, he did the work himself, and proof-read all the works of Sri Aurobindo published in English during the nineteen-forties.

Today he told me how he compiled the Index to 'The Life Divine', which is indeed almost a book in itself. Every day, he said, he would read a paragraph two or three times until the central thought became clear to him. Then he would summarise it, wherever possible in Sri Aurobindo's own words, and link it to the key thought or concept appropriate to the Index. At the end of the day he would send his précis of paragraphs to Sri Aurobindo himself, who would return it to him next morning with his approval or emendations. In this way he must have read the whole of the massive 'Life Divine' three or four times, and in a way few other people have done.

Sri Aurobindo's pencil-written revisions, he told me, he keeps as a treasured memorial of that time. 'You may find it difficult to imagine how in those days we valued every scrap of writing that came to us from his hands – and in this way I had a constant contact with him for over twelve months. It was a very happy time.'

By then Vallabhdas had arrived. He is a visitor from Gujarat, a small elderly man, a barrister, who has been working with me. He never talks, but does what is necessary with a reverent attention to the matter in hand.

As we settled down, a girl began reading aloud to Prithwisingh the morning's book-orders that have come through the post, for he is also in charge of the book-selling department, handling all the publications in English, French, German, Chinese and the Indian languages that come from the Ashram press. The room we work in has tall book-cases down two sides, in which copies of every available title are displayed.

If somebody comes to ask for a book Prithwisingh will get up from his swivel arm-chair and go slowly to the cases, open the glass doors and with hardly a fumble pull out the right volume, at the same time telling his enquirer the price. I think he is helped in doing this by the wide variety of format in the publications, and by putting away all the stock-replacements himself so that he knows the feel and contents of each shelf. If he asks me to bring him something he will give an exact description of where it is and what it looks like. Sometimes if I have been unable to find a book he has come triumphantly to my help.

Around 11 o'clock I went to the Dining Hall garden, where Lena was ladling out 'soup' to a queue of sadhaks. After I had had mine I was spoken to by an Indian who, after introducing himself as Ravindra Khanna, asked me to have tea and read some English poetry with him, as he wanted very much to read with a person from England who could explain the particular national allusions and imagery which were difficult for an Indian to understand. I said I would be glad to come and do what I could.

*　*　*

27th April

Surprise. Ravindra, the man who invited me to tea and asked so humbly for help with the English poets, has been a lecturer on the subject and has a gold medal for English Literature from Lahore University; he was able to appreciate what we read much more deeply than I. However, we had a most pleasant talk. He said how much he had come to love England through her literature, and how one day perhaps, when the yoga had progressed, he would come to visit the places he had read about. He said he was surprised how the Englishmen he had talked with had seemed to know very little about their own poetry, which he considered the greatest in the world.

74

He lives with his wife and young son in a large ground-floor flat with a garden at the back, in which he said he often sees a mongoose. When it looks at him, he told me, its eyes are like a human's.

*　　*　　*

Read long stretches of 'On Yoga II'. There is no doubt about it, Sri Aurobindo's yoga does not have much in it to encourage romantic lovers! Nor seekers who are after Supermind or immortality for themselves. It is a heroic yoga for God-lovers only.

It seems that the prospect of not marrying has a powerful deterrent effect on one's vital nature. But if one is to give oneself wholly to the Divine one must do so unconditionally, and if necessary forego anything and everything, otherwise surrender is just a word. This must be seen quite dispassionately and without illusions, and then only can the vital be persuaded to co-operate. Otherwise, if unconvinced of the value of one's intentions, it will remain a latent saboteur.

This yoga calls itself a yoga of acceptance and 'of this world', but in the matter of human physical love it is rigorously negative.

In 'The Listener' recently there was an article on the western conception of romantic love, in which the author argued that only now, after hundreds of years, was the physical and sexual side of marriage becoming freed from the collocation of world and the devil. He claimed that even the Romantics of the 19th century were still obsessed with the evil of sex, but that now more people than ever before could enjoy the mutual satisfaction of true romantic love, freed from guilt. From this point of view Sri Aurobindo seems a return to the old gnostic disgust with matter and generation.

On the other hand men like D.H. Lawrence and Alan Watts, modern psychologists and wise sacramentalists, are not trying to pioneer the descent of Supermind and a new 'leap' in evolution that will overcome all the ills that flesh is heir to. It is only in this context that chastity is emphasised, for the release of the energy tied up in the vital processes, and for the freeing of the mind from

75

desire, egocentric motivation and restlessness. It is a specialist job, for the few who feel called to it. Even among the followers of Sri Aurobindo there are many who live family lives outside the Ashram. Each person, one is told, must find for himself how he stands with regard to marriage; the self-discipline of the sadhaks, then, does not imply any general rule for mankind, but a particular vocation.

The other day Norman recounted how a team of Russian gymnasts had visited the Ashram in 1956 and had coached the athletes here. They had been impressed by the community, but had asked Nolini, the Secretary, why, since children were obviously so loved and cared for, the Ashramites did not live a normal family life and produce children of their own. Nolini had asked in return why they did not drink or smoke, and had explained that similarly a self-imposed restraint was necessary for Sri Aurobindo's yoga, in order to develop a new capacity – for the transformation of body, life and mind. He said the human race was unlikely to die out because they were not adding to the population.

The differences between the old asceticism and that of Sri Aurobindo is perhaps that the old was for the sake of the soul in other worlds, whereas his is for the soul expressing itself in this world.

* * *

30th April

Today, after balcony, I went with a few others to the sea-front and watched the sun finish rising over the Bay of Bengal. Then about ten of us went swimming before breakfast. The sea was wonderfully warm, and very calm.

I walked back across the Place Dupleix, the arid weed-covered park at the centre of the French part of Pondicherry, by the sea-front. It is being laid out as a public garden, gradually. In the middle of it is a strange and massive monument built in the French neo-classical manner of the early nineteenth century. It consists of a phoenix-surmounted dome, supported on four arches, with pilasters and pediments. Its plaster facing and stucco is washed a striking

76

orange-pink. The inscriptions at its base commemorate the history of the town, from ancient times until its rebirth into glory under the influence of Dupleix and Suffren. Inside there is an insignificant fountain playing into a bowl, over the bronze bodies of some naked French nymphs.

Tree-lined paths and drives radiate out from this incongruous sight to the sides and corners of the square. All round stand the chief buildings of the former French administration: the Governor's Palace, the houses of senior officials, the Chamber of Commerce, a Bank, the Hospital and Medical School, the Post Office and, on the seaward side, the Customs office and the light-house. In one corner of the Place are the crumbled remains of Fort Dupleix, taken by Clive and afterwards dismantled according to treaty. However, between the park and the beach, on a pedestal of short granite columns, taken from some ancient temple, stands the bronze figure of Dupleix himself, swaggering his sword hilt and looking defiantly at the sea.

Crossing the wide concrete drainage canal that separates the French from the Indian part of the town, I made my way to Ganapatram's, ready for breakfast.

*   *   *

4th May

Just getting better after a nasty cold. At the Ashram clinic they give one warm salt water to gargle with. Today I continued the treatment by going swimming again. A heavy breaking sea, full of little shrimps or water-fleas...

'The problem' has wonderfully subsided. Two weeks ago I wrote the Mother a letter in which I told her I had been unable to follow her instructions, to put it out of my mind, and asked for her help.

I said that I saw now that the issue was not 'London or Pondicherry', nor 'marriage or not marriage', nor 'this work or that', but 'Do I want to find and realize the Divine more than anything else?' It seemed that if I could be open and offer my being to God then all problems would wither away and be solved incidentally –

77

that heroic decisions and dramatic gestures were unnecessary. I saw, as I wrote, that the real problems were lack of aspiration, peace, detachment, and the absence of genuine love either for God or man. The answer to these could only be by effort on my part, the divine grace and time. It does not matter where I am.

• • •

Mehdi Imam's dream: "I saw a room full of people. 'What are these people doing?' I asked.

'They are working very hard making their own problems.'

Then I was shown a room full of people solving problems. 'How are they solving their problems?' I asked.

They stand back from them – and ask 'What have I to learn from this? Why has this problem come to me?'

So don't think about problems. You never chose to be born – it was decided for you. You never chose the most important things in your life – so don't worry. Stand back and enjoy being here."

He also said, with a far-away look, that he saw a sea voyage and a marriage or engagement. Stand back!

*   *   *

18th May

At 3 o'clock I called on Ravindra Khanna for tea. He was sitting on his bed, reading, and looked up with that frowning smile of his. 'I've been waiting for you. I have something for you to taste'. He went over to the window and produced two large yellowish-orange fruit. 'Mangoes. I was given them this morning, and I said to myself, the Divine intends these for Dick who's coming today.'

'You must have some too.'

'Yes, we'll eat them – though I've had literally thousands in my time.'

We talked of fruit, English and Indian, and about fruit-juices, and how Indians made tea. Then I changed the subject to the Ashram, and asked what was meant by the Inconscient. I had heard that the Mother was now engaged in an attack on this plane of man's being. But what precisely was it?

78

He pointed to his heart and said 'If a man hears bad news his heart will speed up. With me now I feel such things in the solar plexus. But this', and he pinched a fold of the flesh of his thigh, 'this part of me is really insensitive. It never responds to mental or emotional shock; it is dead, inconscient – the inert physical. If you bring the light down into your body and the centres open, they will all open down to the navel and below to the sex centre, but then there is a dark barrier – you can feel it like a hostile consciousness opposing the light. Now it is only the Supermind that can change that. The overmind can change one down to the vital consciousness, but the Supermind alone can change the body itself. It is only one step, but it is a vast one. That is why when someone asked in 1950 if there was far to go before Supermind descended and began the change, Sri Aurobindo replied 'Only one station – but there is no railway yet'.

'You see the Inconscient is not only an individual thing. It is circumambient, and conquering it in oneself is not enough. One must defeat the force itself on its universal plane, and then everywhere it will be easier for man to aspire and progress with unheard of ease and speed. It will be as sudden a change as when an object leaves the earth's atmosphere and then flies with unhindered momentum through space.'

We were sitting cross-legged on some mats on the floor. Ravindra began pumping away at the primus, preparatory to tea-making, and while the kettle warmed, he talked of Sri Aurobindo's death. He said how, in 1950, the world situation was very bad – Korea and the threat of a third world war – and that he and the Mother were very concerned that it should get no worse, and that also at that time the hostile forces were attacking his body so that he should have to concentrate on it more and more, and his energies be used up on that, and how, finally, as a strategy for more effective action, he had left the body.

His body, he said, lay in state for 115 hours, and was radiant with a golden light – so far had he gone towards the transformation of his own physical nature. It is forbidden in Pondy to allow a body to remain unburied for more than 48 hours, because of the climate. So Mother asked the chief medical officer to come and give a report on the body after two days. He examined it and said that every tissue of the body was still alive. After four days Mother said the Supramental light was withdrawing, and a faint blue scar was visible near one collar-bone...

I asked Ravindra if it was still easy for a newcomer to go through the stages through which the Ashram as a whole had already passed. He replied that it depended on a man's motives for coming to yoga. He had come himself because he had realised the transience and mortality of life and its ineffectuality – although, strangely enough, he had suffered no personal tragedy or betrayal as had others he'd known. Always he had been surrounded by love, from parents, wife, family and friends – so much so that now not a day passed without his praying for them and their souls' welfare.

Some people, he went on, approached the Divine through work; he himself, though he did offer his work to God, too, found the greatest happiness in meditation. He had meditated before coming here, until he had felt the descent of love into himself. Everyone appeared to him to be lovable; he had a great outflowing of love for the people he met – everyone, beggars, animals ... plants and flowers even. And this was not himself loving, but the loving of God acting through him. It became so intense that he only lived to open even more fully to the transformation. It became a marvel to him that there was so much love to be found in the world – for it was returned to him from every side. He was imprisoned by the British for political reasons, and put among habitual criminals of the hardened type – people with 12 or 15 convictions, but they too could recognize this love and return it. And then there had come to him that knowledge of the eternal nature of his soul, the central certainty that it was immortal, that he was immune from all accident or evil. He said he saw that nothing in the world mattered or could touch the soul, but said he could see this might shock a westerner.

When he came out of prison he was to marry a girl. He met her and agreed to marry on condition that they should lead a spiritual life. People had tried to dissuade the girl, and said 'Look at him, he is a sadhu!' 'And at that time', said Ravindra, 'I had long hair and a black beard. But she insisted and said she loved me and would look after me, whatever I was. Then for two years she supported me while I went to college and took my degree in English. She was a lecturer in Sanskrit. And then our child was born, and she cared for us both.

'Then came the pathetic part. I felt I must come away and lead a spiritual life, and that I must come to Pondicherry. I remember pacing up and down, looking at my wife and child and feeling a pain gripping my solar plexus as I thought 'How can I leave them?' and then I turned to God and there was the yogic calm which said 'Leave everything. It will be all right. God will take care of them', and then I would look at them again and think, 'How can I do it?' So I wrote to Mother and said 'May I come?' and then waited in agony for the reply. Mother said 'Wait a while', and it was like a reprieve!

'And then, you see how it worked out: my wife herself went to the Ashram, to a Darshan, and saw Sri Aurobindo and was overwhelmed by him, and wanted nothing so much as to stay there, and she and my son came here first, and still Mother said to me 'Wait a little longer'. So when, after two years of lecturing at a college, I eventually came, in 1949, it was as easy as anything, and I had no regrets or pain at all at leaving.'

Ravindra then asked, as we ate the mangoes and drank tea, how things were with me. I told him how I seemed to have scared myself, and now had no aspiration or energy since I had seen where they might lead me! He said, 'I know how you feel. When I waited for the replies from Mother, to say if I was to come here, I was like a condemned man standing on the scaffold and wondering 'What next?'

He went on to say that sincerity and aspiration were enough; there was no need for anxiety. If I stayed I would be given the necessary strength. If I went I should have no self-condemnation or the feeling that I'd missed an opportunity. Just let all thoughts rise into consciousness and offer them to the Divine, saying 'This is what I am like: you can see what is best. Please change whatever is necessary.'

He paused, and the room was very still. Then he went on, advising me against living in big cities, if possible, since in them one wasted much energy in repulsing bad suggestions and influences.

'But there is no going back in yoga', he said, 'no going back. The soul will grow and put pressure on you and your surroundings: you cannot stop it. And there is nothing in the world like the satisfactions of yoga. Norman and all the true sadhaks here will tell you that. There is nothing so real as the peace, and the love and the certainty that come with spiritual experience. It will be all right, the Mother will guide you, and by the time you are ready to come here your ties will be no stronger than gossamer threads ...'

* * *

20th May

Went to work with Prithwisingh in the morning. He was describing a dream or vision in which Sri Aurobindo had come and silently embraced him: 'a very sweet experience.' Vallabhdas was solemn and concentrated on the work. We stopped at 11.10 and I went to see Purani.

Purani is a large, very vigorous man, now in his sixties but still humming with energy. He was one of the earliest disciples of Sri Aurobindo, and had known him before he went into seclusion. He now has a room opening on a small courtyard near the Meditation Hall, in the main Ashram complex. He said he would take me to see an English lady, married to an Indian who had brought her to live here in the Ashram.

On our way, we met Eric Bass, a tall American visitor, who was carrying a parcel very carefully. He asked us up to his room in the Golconde Guest House (cool and beautiful) and told us he had been to see the Mother, and that she had told him about a previous incarnation of his when he had been an artist in thirteenth century Japan. He was childlike in his simple delight at having been told this.

He said, too, that he had meditated in the Mother's presence, and that she had told him afterwards that he had been drawing a picture all the time as he had sat there. Mother had lent him three paintings by herself, to talk about in his art lecture in the afternoon. It seems

82

that she had known many of the great artists working in Paris at the turn of the century, and had herself exhibited work in the Salon.

Purani and I left, and finally succeeded in tracking down the English lady, Mrs Pinto, who asked us both to tea on Monday.

While we were waiting to see her, a girl had brought us glasses of fruit juice, and Purani had discussed Eric's earlier lecture. He said Eric was a genuine artist, with understanding, though he himself could not admire modern art as wholeheartedly as Eric apparently did. Too much of it remained ugly – whatever the artist's manifesto.

After lunch, fell into a heavy inconscient sleep, then had a shower and went to find Eric and his lecture. In a street near the school buildings, I met Ravindra, and suggested he should come to the lecture, too. He asked me to tea. We decided to have the lecture first and then the tea.

Eric confessed it was only the second talk on art that he had given in his life, but his sincerity and simplicity carried him through. He talked of the elements, the principles of painting: the balance of tensions within a frame: vertical, horizontal and so on, by line, tone and colour. These rules, he said, were essential to great art of all periods, but each great period had to achieve its own style, and make its own discoveries, although the rules were eternal.

Modern artists such as Picasso, Klee or Matisse did not do what they did because they could not draw naturalistically, but only after long apprenticeships to older styles ... Art was like meditation – it must start in sympathetic surroundings and one should learn the rules from a master. It could be a high path to the Divine. He described how he himself had sacrificed success in music, athletics and as a playboy, for the sake of art – how he'd 'built his raft' through work, and had had a calloused bottom through sitting for nine hours a day at his drawing. Now his craft, like Noah's ark, had carried him to the Ashram and to the Mother. One must, he insisted, have a knowledge of technique before the Divine could use one to pass on what one has learned. Sri Aurobindo would have remained unknown if he had not been able to write English – would have been no more to the mind of the world than if he had lived in a cave in the Himalayas ...

Painting, Eric said, was a mystery that sprang from the psychological relation between the artist and three-dimensional reality – to be expressed on a two-dimensional canvas for three-dimensional viewers. The elements necessary for a work of art were, firstly, the potentially beautiful subject; secondly, the spiritual sight and intuition of the artist; thirdly, his knowledge and mastery of the methods and principles of art; and, fourthly, the grace of the Divine.

Afterwards at tea Ravindra said he had been impressed by Eric; he had not been, like some other Americans he had met, hard, restless or hollow.

We discussed D.H. Lawrence. Ravindra liked him for his refusal to deny the beauty and colour of the world, and for his affirmation of the goodness and richness of life and love. But, he said, Lawrence had been ignorant of the way to find the true richness of love, which was not any more the old way of human love – but could only come through the Supramental change, or else by sacrificing human sex-love, as Eric had forgone music and athletics, for the sake of a greater divine love. He said how he had experienced both kinds of love himself, and that when the sex-power was diverted, to rise up the body, the ecstasy of communion with the Divine was far greater and more intense than in union with a woman. He laid much stress on the up and down character of Lawrencian love – the moments of intense love and sympathy and understanding, alternating with periods of black depression and bitterness and disgust.

Ravindra also described how he had brought the light down into himself and made it shine on his sex-centre, until the sex-power had been driven down into his thighs and then his legs and finally out at his feet. Later his wife had embraced him and he had felt no reaction at all in his sex-centre. He had been like an impotent man, and then he felt the sex-force coming up his legs until he felt response in his knees, and then it slowly crept up to where it had been.

• • •

Ravindra is bushy black-haired, swarthy, with a beaky nose. His smile reveals fine white teeth. His eyes are often screwed up or half shut, but they open wide in moments of mutual understanding. He is quite solidly built, but at times, he says, he suffers from asthma.

*　　*　　*

21st May

This morning Norman talked about surrender. He said many westerners who visited the Ashram admired the organisation, were interested in the philosophy, and indeed were looking for something and wanted spiritual progress for themselves – but of all these how few were prepared to surrender themselves to the Mother. Their minds were so active, and they were so identified with their minds, that the prospect of giving up their independence not only scared them, but seemed wrong. Surrender, he said, was the great stumbling-block for Europeans and Americans.

'Surrender to the Mother' he describes as a trusting and a self-giving, 'that the work may be done in one'. It is a dependence on her grace and a belief that she will guide and help one according to one's need and aspiration. If people are open to her and accept her, the Mother can act upon them, and, through the force that she mediates, can transform them at every level of their being.

All this does not mean that a person who surrenders to Mother loses his individuality, nor that he becomes passive and does nothing. Instead, such a person comes to express his own true uniqueness, and, beginning to act from the divine centre in himself, becomes an instrument for the manifestation of God in the world, actively and according to his own particular potential. Nor is he a puppet. In fact he is freer than he ever was before when subject to external stimuli and his desire-nature. It is the old paradox of the service that is perfect freedom.

I mentioned that it was easy to be glib with the word 'surrender' but that in practice there were parts of one's nature which did not want it, or could not practise it for more than a short stretch.

85

Norman agreed that this was of course true to begin with, hence the need for effort at first, but later the Force took up the sadhana. If one could surrender to the Divine straight away one would already be an enlightened person, in a state of union. What was important was to make the central, general resolve, and then implement it in detail as one could.

He also told me of his early struggles to remember the Mother at all times. He had found it very helpful to associate an object with her, as a kind of memory-jogger. Thus if he made the effort to think of Mother when he entered a certain room or when passing a particular building or tree, then, after a while, the association became automatic, so that these things brought him back to recollection whenever he came to them.

When he speaks of Mother his eyes kindle with love, and he becomes very gentle and full of bhakti.

*   *   *

22nd May

'Surrendering to the Mother' might certainly daunt a typical westerner. The words evoke associations quite different from, say, 'doing the Father's will', which might not sound quite so bad.

I myself find phrases surfacing in me such as 'Mother fixation', 'regression to infancy' and 'search for emotional security', but after thinking about them I don't find they are really relevant.

In more neutral words what is meant seems to me to be an attitude of willing co-operation with the dynamism that is behind evolution. The Mother embodies on the human level the aspiration towards fulfilment, the development towards the highest we may be capable of attaining. And she also mediates a power that moves people who have contacted it towards realisation and perfection. Some say she is that power, the Divine Shakti, the conscious creative energy in Nature. I have not yet the experience or level of consciousness to talk about that. I can see, though, that without doubt there are people here who are aware of her presence and feel her working in them. That is a psychological fact.

Talking to other sadhaks, I am told that the Mother, having regard to the difficulty that westerners have in surrendering to a guru, often advises them to find the Guidance and the Presence in themselves.

*　*　*

23rd May

After working with Vallabhdas this morning, I borrowed a bicycle from Harpagon, the Ashram foundry, and set off, at about 11.30, to go to lunch with Ananta on his island.

It seemed the hottest day ever, but I felt quite fit, and followed the southerly road out of Pondy between palm-bordered fields and past villages of keet-thatched huts. The cactus lane was so soft with dry sand and dust that one couldn't ride any more.

Coming at last to the water's edge I called across to the island, but with no result. Seeing an old man standing by his hut in a little coconut grove, I asked if Ananta was at home. The old man said yes, and sent his little daughter, aged about 11, to shout. Almost at once a boat pushed off from the island and a Tamil servant came to punt me across.

Ananta was feeling sick. He was resting in a long wicker chair with a footrest, by a shady tree on the lawn, outside his house. He explained that he'd been to a lunch party with the French Consul, and that the wine had upset him. 'But I enjoyed it so much' he said. 'I enjoyed being with those people much more than I enjoy being with the Ashramites – no that's not true, but they were so civilised. Only very spiritual people indeed can get to that stage of delicacy and tact and wit, my goodness ...' He went on about part of him being a socialite and another part being a solitary. He foresaw a struggle between them, and a difficult future for his sadhana right ahead.

He called a servant and had him prepare a lunch for me: fresh vegetable salad and chips, bananas and curds, with bread and jam and tea.

After lunch he suggested, as it was so hot, that I lie down for a siesta in a small hut at the other end of the island. I went down the sandy path, which scorched my feet, past the paddy fields and the

87

temple, to a wood of tall casuarina trees. It was shady and still, with now and then a high soughing in the tops of the trees as they bent lightly to the wind. Near the end of this wood was a small hut made of woven palm-leaf. Its door and front window faced the water, which lapped the shore beneath the trees only a few feet away. The palm roof projected a foot or two in front over a cement floor, and a row of shrivelled bamboo-leaf decorations hung in an old garland under the eaves. A few weeks earlier a former guru of Ananta's had stayed there some days.

I went in and sat on a reed mat on the cement floor. Outside the heat shimmered and glared off the water and reflected a white light among the brown tree-stems. On each side of me there was a square window criss-crossed with an open lattice of bamboo, and each had a door-like shutter of palm-weave opening outwards. Opposite the door was a wooden bed, and by the front window a small low table. I closed my eyes and became quiet. For perhaps 15 minutes the silence absorbed everything.

*　*　*

24th May

Tea with Ravindra Khanna. He talked of a tribe called the Gudis, who lived high in the Himalayas, and were truly noble and simple in their way of life – no litigation, no quarrelling or cheating – everything unadulterated, pure butter, pure ghee, and the women soft and gentle and full of kindness. He said that many retired British generals and officers had settled there and married these beautiful women – especially in the Kulu valley. An Englishman had become famous as a fruit-farmer there, winning many prizes. He had become a sanyasin.

Apart from this utopian tribe R.K. was pessimistic about human nature. He said India would not be able to learn the lessons of the industrial revolution in Europe quickly enough to save herself from much suffering. Nor would people learn family planning quickly enough to check the rise in population, which would offset industrial expansion for a long time.

Communism, he said, would grow here in the South, inevitably, because of the extreme poverty, and because only the Communists could make the unscrupulous promises they did make, such as the promises to confiscate property and distribute it. He said they were strong in Pondicherry, and had proclaimed they would seize Golconde, the Ashram Guest House, and make it a maternity hospital for the people. In the North, in the Punjab and Uttar Pradesh, people were well enough off to see through the propaganda, but the starving man will try anything that offers quick results: food and shelter.

We discussed how Herbert Read's anarchism and D.H. Lawrence's trust in the inner gods were prophetic of the possibilities open to man, but he concluded that their view of human nature was unrealistic before the Supramental change, as envisaged by Sri Aurobindo and the Mother, had taken place. R.K. said Sri Aurobindo had all Lawrence's respect for the virility in man but urged that it be diverted from the animal functions to strengthen the higher powers of aspiration, feeling and thought. He added, 'I can assure you from my own experience that this leads to a heightening of enjoyment and appreciation of the beauty and richness of the world, and not a lessening of them'.

Mind, indeed, was at the end of its tether; thought and idealism could not save the world, and though its continued existence was a result of the power of spiritual men's lives, the old spirituality was not strong enough or able to work fast enough to meet the present situation. So, Supermind.

He said Mother had said that one of the impressive characteristics of the new race would be its power – obvious and manifest. These would be men whom death could not touch.

*   *   *

26th May

Yesterday Purani took me to meet Mrs Pinto. We collected Eric, the Californian artist, on the way. We found him sitting cross-legged by the Samadhi, back straight, head up, pale and locked deep in meditation. Purani tried calling 'Eric, Eric, Eric', in a high voice. At

89

length he came to and joined us. He told Mrs Pinto that he would come anywhere for a cup of tea — not an extraordinarily polite opening.

We went up on to a flat roof-top terrace, where Eric soon got his tea. Mrs Pinto's husband Udar came and joined us – a large open-faced Indian, beginning to grow stout, but full of energy. It seems that he met his wife in Poplar at a time when he was taking a course in aeronautical engineering in England. They came to Pondy, knowing nothing about the Ashram at first. Then Udar became interested in it, and, after their one child had been born, was accepted by the Mother as an ashramite and persuaded his wife to join him. I gather she did not think much of the idea at first, but she seems very happy now, reconciled by her love for the Mother – and for her husband.

Eric told us how he had lived on his farm on a mountain in California. One day his neighbour, down in the valley, began burning brushwood, and the wind set the mountain alight. Only Eric's house was saved. But the woods were insured; so, with the money, he had been able to come to India. He said he had come because he needed the oriental wisdom for his progress in painting. He had visited Japan before coming to India, and had a great admiration for Japanese art.

After tea we went indoors and the talk came round to Sri Aurobindo and the Mother. Purani said how he and another sadhak, Champaklal, would fan Sri Aurobindo all night, taking turns. Eric said, 'But why did he give you all that trouble when he could have bought an electric fan?'

'He never asked anyone to fan him' said Purani, 'but he let us do it as part of our sadhana, as service and devotion'.

Talking of the almost unbelievable hours that the Mother spent in work and in listening to people's problems, Purani confirmed that for many years she never had a room or bed of her own, but would relax in a chair for a short while each night, restoring her energies by going into a higher state of consciousness. But now, he said, she slept for some hours every night, and the ashramites had at last made her a lovely room, high up, overlooking the central courtyard.

Eric asked whether Sri Aurobindo ever passed into Samadhi. Purani said no. Sri Aurobindo, he said, only advised going into a trance or leaving the body consciousness to prove to oneself the separation of body and soul – that the body is not the self – but it was his whole emphasis that the higher consciousness must be brought down into the body, and the body be transformed and made a true and important instrument of spirit. So, although always aspiring to higher consciousness, he did not ever lose body-consciousness, but tried to raise all his being, including the inconscient body, to a higher level. He would even meditate with his eyes open, and while walking.

Purani also described Sri Aurobindo's accident in 1938. He had fallen, tripping over a tiger-skin's head, and had broken his thigh, suffering a multiple fracture of the femur. This happened the day before a Darshan, when thousands had assembled to see him. He had become conscious of a hostile threat to the Mother, and all his awareness had momentarily been concentrated on defending her – then in a moment when off his guard, he himself was thrown. He stumbled and fell down a step, and lay in great agony – the worst pain he had ever experienced. For a long time there was no doctor, but one was found at last among the Darshan visitors and the leg was set. All the time Sri Aurobindo remained detached and at ease, joking with the doctor and quite above the pain. (Norman has told me that the doctor set the bones badly, and that he never lost a limp). Purani said that for a man of 66 or so his recovery was remarkable. He did exercises, and could bend and flex his leg in a way that athletes of 25 who had had the same break never achieved. One of his shoulders, however, was permanently an inch or two lower than the other. (Norman says this made him sit for Darshan in a particularly regal and stately way, with one leg thrown out).

Purani also described how Sri Aurobindo was persuaded by the Mother to give up smoking. Apparently he used to smoke heavily – cigars and cheap strong cigarettes from the bazaar – at the time when Mother first came. She was worried by it, but never said anything to him. Instead she told his intimates how bad it was for people, causing lung-cancer, coughs and catarrh. Soon this came to Sri Aurobindo's hearing: 'What! Smoking harm a man?' he had said. 'How can it!' Mother then made sure that he got the very best tobacco (Spencer's from Madras) and said nothing. But everyone knew what she felt. Then one year, on her birthday, Sri Aurobindo said 'I'll stop.' And she said it was the finest present he could have given her – she was so happy.

Later everyone in the Ashram stopped. (Purani used to smoke 80 a day!) But there was no rule laid down. Mother just let it be known that no-one who was a smoker could come and meditate at her feet in the evenings. So smoking died out.

I like a story Norman told me about one of Gandhi's sons visiting Sri Aurobindo. The latter was sitting on his terrace puffing at a cigar. 'I see you are addicted to smoking', remarked the pure young man.

'I see you (puff) 'are addicted' (puff, puff) 'to non-smoking', replied the sage.

*　*　*

1st June

Dear Anthony and Mary,

Thank you for your letter, which was good to have.

I am writing to you in the relative cool of the Ashram Library – a beautiful neo-classical building, once lived in by a French Government official. Let me see if I can answer your points about the evolution of a new species. You suggest that the process may take millions of years to get anywhere. This ain't necessarily so. It took an immense time for the first varieties of life to develop from the protozoa, but, as consciousness has emerged more and more, the rate of change seems to have accelerated, with shorter time-gaps between the new and the older species. At last, evolution has, in man, become conscious of itself, and purpose and choice play a part in development, as well as the old factors of variation and natural selection. For the first time a species can collaborate with what it understands as the most fulfilling trend open to it. And this may speed things immensely. Just as Marx believed that one could co-operate with and hasten the movement of history if one understood its laws, so Sri Aurobindo believed that by having a true and comprehensive psychological theory and by practising an integral yoga one could hasten human evolution, and something significant could happen within two or three hundred rather than two or three million years.

About the overcrowding of the planet if people were to become immortal: I think Sri Aurobindo is not on his own in seeing Death as the last enemy. If medical doctors, now, could stop the wearing-out process in the body, they would surely do so. Can the coming of the Kingdom of God, the increasing expression of a divine life on earth, be reconciled with the pain and indignity of death, the cutting short of a life's development, the apparent loss of an accumulation of knowledge and experience, and the break-up of loving relationships? As far as I understand him, Sri Aurobindo envisages a superman who combines a consciousness of Truth, of Love and of Power, i.e. mental, emotional and physical surrender to the Divine. Such a person would be able to defend himself or herself, and would not be pushed around by hostile forces in the form of human enemies or mortal diseases; even someone on the way to but not yet fully arrived at the new species might be able to counter the effects of old age and live for centuries, and, if he or she died, might do so as a matter of choice, not compulsion, like the kings of ancient Ireland who were said to 'stop their breath' and die when they had had enough.

Sri Aurobindo speaks of 'gnostic communities' of the new race. These would live among the old unchanged 'mental' humanity – just as the higher apes continue to live alongside men. At the beginning there would not be very many of these Supramental beings on the earth, but their impact on civilization might be very great. The quality of life among people everywhere would improve because of their presence, and under the influence of their wisdom and leadership war and poverty could disappear. You might say that this would lead to a population explosion, but conceivably it could work in the opposite direction, and world numbers might begin to decrease, just as educated people tend to have smaller families. Sri Aurobindo would not speculate about what Supermind would do – but it would certainly encourage a better life on earth.

All this may sound a bit irrelevant to life on a farm near Nettlebed, but here, with people who knew Sri Aurobindo and who live in the presence of the Mother, it does not seem so strange or impossible.

I hope all goes on well with you and the family.

With love, Dick

*　*　*

4th June

Days pass with a surprising ease and speed ... on June 1st there was a Prosperity Darshan. Mother looked wonderful. She gave each of us a bunch of a grey-green herb called New Birth, with a scent like rosemary. I wrote a kind of poem afterwards: 'This is what time has led to.' Part of me is critical of its uncritical enthusiasm. Part of me says 'Let it be: it is an intuition of truth.'

Today I have tea with Norman. I read Pasternak and some poems to him. He shows me his note-book of 'original thoughts' – short aphoristic observations and verses, e.g. 'As much life-force may be used in killing a fly as in killing an elephant.' Norman remarks à propos originality that most thoughts come to one from outside, and in the yogic consciousness can be seen to arrive: very few are really home-made.

In the evening we watch and listen to recitations of 'Prayers of the Mother' and of poems by Sri Aurobindo, done in the Playground by Madame Pitoeff and a chorus of speakers, men and women. The prayers, read by different voices, are best. The poetry sounds over-emotional and exaggerated. One couldn't imagine Sri Aurobindo speaking in such a way.

After leaving the Playground I wait around to speak to Eric, and find him getting into a jeep to be driven to Ananta's island. Ananta had asked me to come too, but I'd given up the idea because of lack of transport. But they say 'Get in', and off we go. Another car, containing a French doctor and his young Russian wife Tanya, follow us. Also of the party are Madame Pitoeff and Sadhana, the girl from Canada, and an Englishman, Tom Wild, from the Anglo-French cotton mill. There are also three Indians whom I haven't met

94

before. We go out of Pondy fast, hooting and swerving among the crowds. We find the dusty track leading to the landing-stage and leave the cars in the coconut grove nearby.

There is no moon, but the stars are bright and the island shines over the water, with many paraffin lamps lighting up its hedges and lawns. Ananta stands, in his immaculate linen suit, to welcome us as we are punted over in two boat-loads to his landing place. One by one we pass along the narrow log bridge, through the high hedges, to shake him by the hand.

Eric is ecstatic. 'Isn't it wonderful? This will be something to tell them about back home – if they will ever believe it.'

We walk down the sandy path towards Ananta's two-roomed house. On the lawn to the right is a group of Indian musicians, beating on tablas and playing long bell-bottomed pipes. Eric goes across to them saying 'Isn't it wonderful? Did you ever see anything like it?' and stands over them, watching them play.

At the house we are introduced and stand around talking for a bit. Sadhana drifts off to look at the lotus pools. Madame P. admires the wavy lines drawn on the sand paths. People explain to her, 'Don't you know, every morning Ananta crawls on his hands and knees and makes those marks with his nose. It's a part of his sadhana....'

Ananta comes up, short, massive and abrupt. 'We will start the Puja now. It is a pity Anil and his friend are not here. They're both Mahakali bhaktas. But we can't wait.'

We follow him to the little white-painted temple, which stands like a small summer-house on one of the lawns. Ananta is brisk and serious: 'Here, spread these mats around. Come close'. We spread two or three raffia mats on the path and grass in front of the temple steps, and sit down cross-legged.

Ananta opens the small double doors of the temple, revealing an altar on which stand photographs of Mother and Sri Aurobindo, both garlanded and decked with hundreds of blossoms. A Brahmin priest, a thin youngish man, is also revealed. (Who knows for how long he has been shut up inside?) There is just room for him to stand between the altar and the threshold. On the top step a young Tamil boy beats monotonously with a hammer on a metal disk suspended from the roof of the porch, while behind us the group of musicians close in and start an ear-dazing din.

The priest moves hither and thither with a ceremonial lamp, holding it up now to one picture, now to another. There is a heavy smell of incense. Then he begins to chant, in Sanskrit. The musicians seem determined to drown his voice. The boy hammering the metal gong sweats, and the paraffin lamps flare and hiss.

I look at the guests. Tanya sits bolt upright, with raised chin, occasionally scanning our faces, curious but absorbed. Ananta sits hunched in the front, gazing at Mother's picture, not caring how we react or what anybody thinks. Eric sits in perfect Buddha posture, with closed eyes. Tom Wild is detached, uneasy, not taking part.

The noise is really shattering. It seems to break up all thought and memory and bring one into violent contact with the moment. I close my eyes, and focus on the Mother … Is her presence compatible with all this noise?

Insects of all sorts are attracted by the bright lights, and fly against us, falling and crawling over our legs. On the top step a large predatory beetle-like creature pounces on some smaller creeping thing.

The priest takes up in turn various brass objects: a heart-shaped symbol on a stalk, a little circular canopy on a stick, with metal pendants – like a sun-shade, and others, and moves them before the pictures. Without some explanation it is all too strange to participate in.

Finally the playing eases, and the priest comes down the steps and offers us sandalwood ash and red powder to mark our foreheads. Sadhana makes a red dot in the centre of my brow with her finger-tip, very solemnly. What does it mean?

We move back to the end of the island by Ananta's house. He is now the perfect host, arranging mats on a bank under a tree where we can sit, overlooking his fish-pond. There is a low table, stacked with food for a buffet supper. People begin to talk and laugh again, and some women start serving the food onto plates and handing them round.

THE MEETING PLACE

This is what time has led to -
A courtyard of sunflowers, zinnias,
And a queue of silent people
Moving past a petal-covered tomb.
Dawns, noons, sunsets.
Days, months, lives.

This is what time has led to -
A path that goes to a staircase
And men and women of different countries
Leaving their sandals at its foot.
Dawns, noons, sunsets.
Days, months, lives.

This is what time has led to -
A gallery behind mahogany shutters,
A picture of a man's head, life size.
They pass it and mark its gaze.
Dawns, noons, sunsets.
Days, months, lives.

This is what time has led to –
A chair set before a gold patterned cloth
And a still, frail woman
Who smiles and has the eyes of God.
Dawns, noons, sunsets.
Days, months, lives.

This is what time has led to -
See each figure before her
Is not what he thought, felt or looked like
But an inner immortal come through
Dawns, noons, sunsets.
Days, months, lives.

When I came into Prithwisingh's room he was bent over his desk with his face almost touching the wood, peering through a powerful philatelist's lens, which he had placed over what he was studying, and by the aid of which he can still read, with a concentrated effort, moving it along over the page as word after word comes into focus. Apparently at one time he was a very active man and a great reader.

Yesterday he had given me an offprint of an article by Dr Sanyal, a famous Calcutta surgeon, on the passing of Sri Aurobindo. Today we were talking about it, and he said various interesting things – that Sri Aurobindo planned leaving the body because he found his work was going too slowly. He said it would take a hundred years at least to establish Supermind at the rate things were going, so he decided to sacrifice life in the body in order to hasten the process, working from the subtle physical plane. The Mother had to stay, to look after the Ashram, and to continue the yoga. Prithwisingh said she would not always be as she is now, but would herself be supramentalised and renewed physically. Since going into retirement she had said that more had been accomplished in six months than in the previous ten years. 1967 was the date she had given, by which time some visible effects of Supermind would be apparent for all to see.

Prithwisingh added that the Mother had told him that when the Supermind had come she believed his eyesight would be healed. As it is, in spite of his near blindness, he never complains and is most cheerful.

*   *   *

Prithwisingh was talking today of old age in the Ashram. He said that Nolini knew the art of keeping fit; he was in his 70s. This is amazing as I have seen him at the sports ground going round the track at quite a good pace. I remembered seeing in his room a photo of himself sprinting tucked into the frame of a portrait of Sri Aurobindo. I mentioned another sadhak who looked fit, but

Prithwisingh was disparaging, saying he was for his age – also in his 70s – but spent half the day looking after his body, exercising and so on – too fastidious – not like Nolini who knew the art ...

Prithwisingh said he himself was 62. He could not run or anything like that, because of his eyes, but he was fit.

After work I called on Norman. He seemed very happy, and ready as always to stop what he was doing, and talk. He was saying, today, that the Supermind had descended into the Mother. It was now a question whether she could bear the force and power of this descent on her own until she could prepare others with whom to share it. Up to now if she had tried to impart it to people, they had been damaged, or unable to accept it. Sri Aurobindo had only partly and intermittently had the Supramental consciousness. He had forgone the opportunity to establish himself in it and supramentalise his body. But Mother had the Supramental consciousness as a realisation, that is, as a permanent possession as distinct from an occasional experience. In her, said Norman, the Supramental consciousness immanent in the stuff of the inconscient had been released and had risen up and met the descending Supramental consciousness, which had come down into the earth's atmosphere. I said I did not understand how consciousness could go up or down or what he meant by the 'earth consciousness' which he said was being changed by descending Supermind. However he just looked at me with laughing eyes and said, 'You will.'

The walk to the roof-top restaurant for lunch was quite an ordeal, through deserted streets, the sun burning with a glittering heat all around one, and everything still and drained of life and colour.

The secretary of the New Horizon Sugar Mills, Kanti Upadhyaya, sat next to me at lunch. He is not an Ashramite but has been called in to help supervise the building of a sugar mill that is being undertaken for the Mother by a disciple. He is a friendly man, and both of us having read 'Passage to India' we play Aziz and Fielding to each other.

Today I asked him why India took the science-fiction-like gospel of Sri Aurobindo so apathetically. He said that to begin with the spread of Sri Aurobindo's ideas was handicapped by his own political silence and retirement, and then by his disagreements with Gandhi, who overshadowed him in the national consciousness, and then, when Gandhi was assassinated, and he himself might at last have spoken out, he himself went and died. Kanti said, too, that his main books were not published until during the last war, and then in English, and in an English that was particularly hard for Indians. So, now, Indians listened respectfully, understood what they could – and waited to see what 1967 would bring!

K.U. also talked about missionaries, saying he admired the West's missionary zeal – India had no-one to compare with Dr Schweitzer – but he did not admire the exclusive and intolerant dogmatism of the churches, this 'only Son of God' idea, and the national character of the religion exported to the East on a take it or leave it basis. It was not a religion of man, he said, but of the West.

*   *   *

14th June

At the far end of the Playground are several small rooms and courtyards in which people exercise in the evenings by electric light – that is, those people who want to exercise but are not in the groups that are doing the rhythmic marching.

Last night I went there, as I often do. Ananta, ruddy in the face, was doing his weight-lifting; Pavitra, a Frenchman now in his 60s, who has been here longest of the Europeans, was flexing and bending himself about, and there were a dozen or so of the Ashram muscle boys, with immensely developed torsos, playing around with dumb-bells, clubs and weights, some of them in front of large wall-mirrors.

It was here I met Ambu. He, it seems, is a specialist in the purely Indian exercises of Hatha Yoga. He has a little room up an outside staircase where he demonstrates and coaches anyone who is interested.

He asked me to tea, and today I visited him in his large rather dark ground-floor room near the Playground. He wears only the narrowest of loin-cloths, his body lithe and supple and beautifully poised and proportioned. His eyes dance and shine as he looks at one, like some superdog about to gambol. His whole presence communicates lightness and something of Lila – the divine play. It is hard to believe he is 50.

Before we ate he unrolled a mat on the floor and showed me five āsanas or poses, for encouraging health of body and quietness of mind.

I asked him if these physical exercises were a part of Sri Aurobindo's yoga. He replied that Sri Aurobindo had experimented with every method himself and then finally declared Aspiration, Faith and Surrender to be all that were needed. Ambu himself thought, however, that until one's aspiration, faith and surrender grew sufficiently powerful, one might usefully supplement them with other practices.

Ambu's room is like a Victorian museum. He collects everything – coins, stamps, match-box tops, Indian bronzes, old currency notes, interesting stones, shells, snake-skins, pictures, peacock feathers, toy soldiers, beetles, butterflies ... He says he just takes what comes his way and what people send or give him, and if it were all removed tomorrow he wouldn't mind so very much.

He gave me a small bronze figure of Vishnu, and an open invitation to visit him when I feel like it.

*   *   *

17th June

Yesterday I saw the Mother again. A few days previously I had written to her saying among other things, that, since I had stopped thinking about staying or leaving, the problem seemed to have been solved subconsciously by the assumption that I would leave. I had asked if this was a decision of soul's need or of vital conservatism. Anyway I went yesterday to see her, expecting her to agree that I did not have the 'resolution' or inner imperative to stay. Perhaps I might stay another two weeks until the July Prosperity Darshan.

At 9.15 I collected a flower called 'New Creation' to give to her, and then sat near the samadhi to calm my mind. Small black flies settled on lips and hovered by ears.

101

At about a quarter to ten I met Nolini by the Meditation Hall and he took me to the stairs where a sadhak I did not know was waiting to take me up. At the top the lion-maned man Champaklal directed me into the room where the Mother sits, behind the door. She was not there, but I sat down and waited by her empty 'throne'.

Soon she came in, smiling. I gave her the flower, and some personal messages from friends of mine in the Ashram, in England and from Yehuda Hanegbi in Israel. She asked who Yehuda was, and I told her how he had been a kibbutznik, and had left his family to come to the Ashram, but had had to return after visa trouble and other difficulties, and now worked in Jerusalem. She said the name was familiar, and she thought Pavitra corresponded with him. She said travelling was hard nowadays.

Then she continued, smiling and with an intent look, 'But how about you?'

I told her I had been very happy, since I had stopped worrying.

She then said words that made my heart sink but also spoke to that part of me which watched it sink with irony. Because it was so unacceptable I have already forgotten how she said it – but the gist was this, that it would be good for me to stay at the Ashram, but that the part of me that was attracted by England and the past would have to be dealt with first. Either I must face it here and decide clearly against it, or else I might go back and gain strength of soul, and then return later. But, she went on, I could be sure that once I had left this place a very strong part of me would be pulling me back all the time, and I would not be satisfied away from it. She said that as long as the problem was not decided either way, both sides of the nature would remain fairly quiet, but that once I had decided for one or the other, then resistance would begin. The important thing was to see in advance what were the forces involved and what their likely reactions would be, and then to be able to say a firm NO to their movements, when one had chosen one's position.

'There is no need for you to decide at once' she continued. 'You can stay here until August. I can say that we are pleased to have you here. You have settled into the atmosphere of the place and have done some useful work. We are happy to have you. During this time you can present the question, whether you are to stay, at the feet of the Divine, above your head' and she pointed to the crown of her head, 'and leave it there quite dispassionately. It must be done sincerely, of course, and then you will be able to see the answer for yourself. It must be a question of vision, not an intellectual weighing up of this and that, which will only lead to confusion. You must try to stand back and look dispassionately at the situation – like looking at a picture'.

I found myself able to talk very easily with the Mother. There seemed to be all the time in the world. I remember we discussed my responsibilities at home, and she pointed out that these considerations were really side-issues and irrelevant. You must find what is your true being, and take your stand in that and live from that. 'All these other things can be taken care of by the Divine.'

Remembering old Mr Clarke, a friend back in England, who had recently fallen and broken some ribs and was ill, I started describing his physical condition, and asked Mother if she could help him at all. She asked if she should send him something. I said that would be wonderful, imagining she had in mind her blessings or the pressed flowers she sometimes sends. But she went on to ask what kind of man he was, so she could choose a book for him. I suggested he was too old and set in his ways to grasp Sri Aurobindo's philosophy, but she said age was no disqualification – many people stayed alert and open in old age. I showed her one of his letters to me, saying it might help to give her some idea of what he was like.

She took it, and read some of it slowly and carefully, and observed that he was losing his vitality and was of a logical rather than intuitive type of mind. But she would think of a book to send him.

Then I told her of the death of a follower of Sri Aurobindo in England, and asked if I might send her sister some message from her. The Mother leaned forward, looking at me, and asked, 'Who did you say is dead?' I told her, and she seemed surprised, enquiring when it had happened. 'Oh, quite recently – yes, I will find a message. There must be one suitable among those we send on such occasions. I will ask Nolini to give you one.' I thanked her.

Looking back I can see that I was surprised that she did not know what was happening to a devotee in England, as if she could hold a continual simultaneous awareness of all the destinies of those who looked to her. Such, however, are the expectations she arouses in one, and such one's own preconceptions about the nature of one living the divine life.

'So', she said, 'you will stay on until August. You have enough money to return to England – for your ticket?'

I told her that I had, but asked her about the matter of my expenses. Should I stay where I was, and let the Calcutta man continue to pay for my keep? She asked where I was staying, not knowing that I was still at Ganapatram's hostel. On hearing this she said I could continue there if I was quite happy – as I said I was. We could neither of us remember the Calcutta man's name, though she remembered I had shown it to her written on a piece of paper. However, she said, 'Yes, he can pay. He is a rich man, and money is a curse – you must know this – and if a chance comes to such a man', she went on with a humorous look, 'for him to get rid of some of his money for the sake of the Divine – you are doing him a great service if you help him take advantage of that opportunity. Let him pay. If he doesn't want to, after a time, then you can stay on just the same, and no-one will ask you any questions'. She smiled as only she can, with eyes as well as mouth.

'Voilà' she said, 'Voilà!' And I got up.

On leaving she gave me a golden champak flower, which stands for Supramental psychological perfection.

Both doors were fastened on the inside, and I fumbled at them unsuccessfully, until she directed me quietly to pull down the relevant bolts, 'Voilà', and I was outside, going down the wide staircase.

*   *   *

18th June

When I was with Mother, I also asked her about loyalty to Jesus. I told her how I was confused at times in my prayers – directed as they were sometimes to Jesus, sometimes to Sri Aurobindo, sometimes to 'Father', sometimes to 'Mother': that I had feelings of treachery to Jesus, yet that He might Himself have led me here. What did she suggest?

She asked if I had felt a turning to Jesus in my heart, or had just happened to be brought up as a Christian.

I said I had had some devotion to Him.

She replied that then it was hard. The mind tended to see these aspects of the Divine as exclusive of each other, but if one went above the mind one saw that it was the same Divine behind the different manifestations. It was difficult, she said, to realise this at first. The intellect could cause a lot of trouble and feelings of treachery, especially if one had responded from the heart to one particular manifestation earlier on, and then changed ... but the conflict was unnecessary.

* * *

19th June

Apropos the Mother's knowledge I find the following robust pronouncement made by Sri Aurobindo, in the 1930s:

Question: "In what sense is the Mother everywhere? Does she know all happenings in the physical plane?"

Sri Aurobindo: "Including what Lloyd George had for breakfast today, or what Roosevelt said to his wife about the servants? Why should the Mother 'know' in the human way all happenings in the physical plane? Her business in her embodiment is to know the workings of the universal forces and use them for her works; for the rest she knows what she needs to know, sometimes with her inner self, sometimes with her physical mind. All knowledge is available in her universal self, but she brings forward only what is needed to be brought forward so that the working is done."

Sri Aurobindo on Himself and on the Mother

* * *

105

Yesterday I did some of my proof-reading aloud to Prithwisingh because it was interesting and he can hardly read at all now on account of his eye-sight.

What I read was an answer by Mother to a question about the gods. She explained how it was possible, for one who knew how, to visit the different planes or dimensions of existence other than the physical, and see the independent existences of things going on there. She contrasted the gods with dream creations of the human mind – the former being powers existing before mankind existed, and living lives in their own right apart from our contact with them.

I asked P. if others in the Ashram had occult knowledge like the Mother. He said it was hard to say, because those that had would not speak of it, but he thought that few had the power to visit occult dimensions voluntarily, 'to keep appointments', as Mother had said was possible. On the other hand quite a number of people had probably had occult experiences, which had come to them at some time or other, unexpectedly or without their will.

He himself had once been ill, and dreamed that suddenly two figures had ridden into his room on great horses, which they had reined up at the foot of his bed. He had said to them, 'What do you want? If you have not come to me with Mother's consent I will have nothing to do with you.' At which the two had smiled at each other, and then come forward to him with some sort of herb which they took out from under their cloaks. He did not know what they did then; although he knew they did something to his body – he could not see what it was. And then they had mounted their horses and swept away. He said the two figures seemed identical, and gave an impression of great size and grandeur. He remembers their fine strong hands showing outside their cloaks. They wore something tall on their heads.

He had told this dream in a letter to Mother, who had replied that from what he had described the two visitors had been the Vedic Gods of healing, known as the Aswins or Aswini, who always travel together. He had soon recovered his health. Indeed, since this vision, his filaria had been better, and he had stopped having the fevers that had been regular with him before.

P. agreed that occultism had no essential connection with spirituality. He said the Egyptian civilisation had eventually fallen because it had concentrated too much on occultism and lost its sense of direction and spiritual values. The Indian civilisation, on the other hand, had lasted 5,000 years because the spiritual element had always remained dominant over the tantric and magical.

*　*　*

7th July

Dear Anthony and Mary,

I'm glad to hear that you have been having a better summer this year. You will be able to put the children out to grass, with an electric fence round them. How did that rick we built stand up to the winter?

As you see, my mind wanders... It has been hot in Pondy during June. All wise white sahibs would have gone to the hills during such a season, but we have survived, gliding from shadow to shadow in the streets, lying naked under a mosquito net beneath an electric fan hung from the ceiling, swimming, in the cooler late afternoons, in warm seas off the Coromandelian coast. Sleeping. Now it is cooler. The monsoon has not really come here yet, but it is in process over the west coast, and we get a sort of fringe of cloud and occasional showers here on the eastern side.

Ganapatram has now got an American ice-cream machine in his restaurant. It was a present from someone in America. For months it has been expected, and now it has come – after the hottest weather is over. But still it makes good ice creams. We had the first ones yesterday. They are made with buffalo-milk, which is supposed to be extra creamy, and are flavoured with coffee, mango, vanilla, pineapple or rose-water. This last is not so good.

I have got to know a brahmin called Kanti Upadhyaya. He has suggested some 'cultural exchanges', and has expounded one of the Upanishads very learnedly to me, as a beginning. Last evening I went and talked to him about Christianity, and afterwards he asked

107

me to stay the night, which I did, sleeping on a bed on his roof-terrace. It was quite good until the dawn chorus around 5.30, when a large neem tree close to the house 'exploded into song' – what a noise! The crows especially are very numerous and raucous. Kanti insists that all these Indian crows have only one good eye each. I keep trying to find if they have their blind sides, and certainly some do. I walked right up to one whose good eye was on the opposite side – but they vary.

No, I do not work as you suggest in Ganapatram's incense factory. Every morning I go to do proof-reading in a room at the Ashram. Quite often, though, Prithwisingh, whom I work for, says, 'Again no proofs today', and then I get on with altering the page numbers of an immense index to suit a new edition of one of Sri Aurobindo's books. Lately, while doing this, all sorts of images of England have risen up in my mind – rivers and hills and greenery – as in dying Falstaff's. Very odd. I'm not usually nostalgic, and I don't think I'm dying.

At times I am still surprised to find myself here. In spite of your amusing eulogies it seemed simple enough to come. When the first step was taken all the others took themselves. After all, once one has bought the ticket it is unthinkable to stop until one has used it, and one is hustled along by the processes of travel as inevitably as when one has a return to Paddington. One likes to romanticise, but that is a misleading tendency of the ego! Where does free will come in? Perhaps in aligning oneself with one set of tendencies rather than another, like stepping on a moving staircase or refraining. Anyway I'm very glad to be here.

With love, Dick

*   *   *

22nd July

This evening I finished a book lent me by Kanti: Stefan Zweig's autobiography, 'The World of Yesterday'. It is an elegy for the Europe before 1914 and for Vienna in particular.

Zweig was fortunate – or cursed – in being the child of millionaire parents. He could travel and live how and where he liked, without anxiety, and seems to have enjoyed life and all that it offered him, without inhibitions. Though falling short of the spiritual in Sri Aurobindo's vocabulary, he was an ethical man, and had a noble passion for supranational 'European' ideals. He was one of those enlightened Austrians who were truly cosmopolitan under the old Hapsburg empire. He could lecture in German, French, Italian and English, and, like Rilke, spent much of his time in foreign capitals, with an international circle of friends among the artistic elite. When the First World War came he was one of those who refused to be swept away by hate-propaganda, and, with Romain Rolland, did his best to work for a movement for reconciliation and amnesty, to be brought about by the intellectuals of the opposing nations, whom he held should be above the conflict. Rolland he called 'the conscience of Europe'.

Zweig's Vienna is that of Freud, Mahler and Reik and the Secession and, later, his Europe is that of Koestler and Isherwood. In his optimism and final pessimism he is like H.G. Wells, who was a friend of his. Both were aware of far more that was happening to them than their contemporaries would believe.

In this book Zweig is reticent about his first marriage, and his second wife he persuaded to commit suicide with him after one and a half years together. He ends his farewell letter, 'I salute all my friends! I, all too impatient, go on before'. (This was in Brazil on 22nd February 1942.)

Norman remarked, on my describing his life, that he had probably failed through too much sex. 'At 50 he should have sublimated all that long ago instead of trying to start all over again. Sex and ego' he repeated, in a diagnostic tone.

*   *   *

7th August

In the morning there was a page-proof from Sri Aurobindo's 'Essays on the Gita' to correct, after which I did some work on the index to 'The Life Divine'. Prithwisingh controversial about the pronunciation of 'Ilion' – the title of an epic by Sri Aurobindo. Dictionaries unhelpful, and contradictory about 'Ilium'. We decided that the I should be long as in I, since it comes before a single l.

Read magazine article, in Library, by Verrier Elwin on 'Administration on the Planets by Terran Settlers' – a witty survey of science fiction, demonstrating from many accounts how Nehru's policy of allowing tribal differences to persist and subject peoples to develop along their traditional cultural lines paid off in outer space too.

At lunch Kanti was silent, except to deny the possibility of communist infiltration into his sugar factory. 'That cannot be.' Yesterday we had a heated discussion about the Ashram. He said the ashramites were lazy and stuck-up and unbusiness-like, that such people could not be the material for a new race – that one needed first class material for a first class piece of construction. These people, he said, worked for half an hour and thought because they did it for the universe that they were superior to him who worked 16 hours a day, (also for the sake of God, but without needing to mention it) – and he did not live in such a flabby sheltered condition either ... I reminded him of a saying of Mother's about what was possible if only 12 men of goodwill got together.

After lunch I read a book on Romain Rolland that Kanti has lent me. Slept. Went to tea with Norman and Lena, and then on to a class that Norman takes on 'The Life Divine'. Had long talk with him afterwards, about staying or leaving the Ashram – being a man before trying to be a superman, etc. He said that he himself had a deep conviction that he was living for the 'hour of God', the time of emergence, and that this feeling was growing stronger.

*　*　*

8th August

On the next corner of the street past the hostel is a villa where K.D. Sethna lives. He is a writer, and the editor of an Ashram monthly magazine in English, called 'Mother India'. He has a great interest in English literature and lectures on it at the Education

Centre. Sometimes I hear him, from my room, declaiming 'Paradise Lost' or Sri Aurobindo's epic 'Savitri' in a fierce voice from his terrace, behind a row of banana trees. Every day he rides to morning Balcony in a light stylish rickshaw, as he has a bad leg. Sometimes we meet on the way, and I walk along with him and we talk a little. Today he has lent me an 87-page typed essay on Blake's 'Tiger' poem. It looks interesting.

• • •

At lunch Ganapatram and Kanti talked of Jains, the non-violent sect of people who wear pads over their mouths and nostrils to filter the germs in the air, and eat only 'dead' vegetables such as pulse and dahl ... G. said that if they get bugs in their clothes they will persuade them all on to one garment, and then pay a beggar 4 or 8 annas to sleep on that garment, to feed the bugs! (The beggar will lie down where he is told, but when he has been punctured a few times will probably move off.)

• • •

The friendly man who came and talked to me at the Guest House the day after I arrived, has died. It seems he came here five years ago, having turned radically to the spiritual life – a very fine conversion, but the physical had been unable to change as swiftly as the psychic part of him. He had developed pernicious anaemia and diabetes, 'all his digestion was rotten', and now, still not past his fifties, he is dead. I shall miss him. However, his friends tell me he had taken a decisive step in this life, and so his next may be a more blessed one.

• • •

I visited Ravindra in the afternoon, and we read and discussed Hopkins' 'Wreck of the Deutschland'.

On leaving his house I sat in a catholic church for a while, and, later, on the roof of the hostel. A crow was teasing a kite in a very amusing way, on a neighbouring roof. It would settle behind it, cheek it until it turned round, then fly to its other side or hop down below the level of its perch and try to take it again in the rear. Finally the kite flew off and the crow after it, very triumphant.

In the Playground there was a British Information Services film: 'The True Glory'. This was an account of the defeat of Germany

111

in Europe, told by many narrators picked from among the fighters. Any work that can make such a war psychologically impossible in the future will be justified indeed. 'The True Glory' of the title, as in the Church collect, was to continue until the victory was really complete, and the work begun brought to a true conclusion.

*　*　*

9th August

In the morning, after balcony, Upadhyaya and I swam in the sea. He insists on wearing khaki shorts, a vest and his thick brown-rimmed spectacles, and swims slowly through the water, head well up, very solemn. Sometimes he stands and recites prayers in Sanskrit, or floats on his back with legs folded, meditating. I left him and swam quite a way out to sea, beyond the sandbank.

On the way back to Ganapatram's we argued about democracy. He said he had no use for majorities – pirates could rule if there were enough of them, on such a basis. He believed in government by an elite. I said 'Fascist!' but he replied, no – they would be rishis, really enlightened and wise men. I insisted that even so, they should be elected; otherwise the country lost its right to choose and make its own mistakes. Democracy should educate itself through trial and error, etc. We were neither of us convincing.

At 10 o'clock Mother distributed sarees to women and a kind of waist-cloth to men, and gave her blessings. It was a beautiful morning with everyone very clean and happy-looking. Only the crows were annoyed, as there was too much incense smoke rising into the air under the Service tree in the central courtyard where they sit.

It is true, by the way, that crows dislike church bells. Tanya says that on Sunday they all move away from the Catholic church, and come and sit in her garden and caw. Anyway, today I was sitting in this church when the sexton or verger or someone put in a bout of bell-ringing. When he had finished a crow flew into a tree just outside an open window, and cawed furiously, peering into the church. He then flew in, perched on the moulding of a pillar, gave

112

several resounding protests and flew fast up the aisle and round the choir, cawing as if greatly annoyed all the while, finally flying out of another open window.

After 'Blessings' I called on Norman. He said that the coming Darshan, on Sri Aurobindo's birthday, the 15th of August, marked one of the most significant days in the Ashram's year. The pressure to be felt before it was so great that some ashramites became irritable and strained. He suggested being quiet, and not mixing with too many people.

SEASCAPE

Alone under so vast a sky, borne up by so timeless an element,
The swimmer feels his solitude, his lonely setting.
Lifting him on its swell a comber passes
Breaking beyond him in a long encroachment,
Its swirling surf liquid on the sandy beaches,
Hurled by a habit formed in earth's first distant ages.
The swimmer feels a stripping and wide land-forgetting,
Small, in the sea surges.

*   *   *

12th August

The sea-shore curves away northwards in a sickle of pale sand. It is blurred in the distance by the fine mist of spray in the air. Dense groves of palms stand back above the limit of the tides, their grey trunks rearing like snakes, criss-crossing each other below their tufted feathered crowns. Tamil fishermen live in mud and palm-leaf huts among these trees. The children run across the trampled sand towards one, shouting Sahib! Sir! and pointing and patting at their bellies, but I have no money on me. Some men stand spinning, with a weight hanging from their right hands. Others make palm-leaf baskets or mend nets.

On the foreshore lie the long beams of palm-tree wood which are lashed together and used as a kind of catamaran; also the uncouth

113

boats made of wide planks sewn together and caulked with coir. Black pigs wander delicately among the flotsam and nose round the pools of stagnant water.

Returning from a long walk, the hiss of the surf still with me, I called on Ambu. He welcomed me in and began to prepare tea and toast, and to tell me of another Englishman he had known called Chadwick, later given the Indian name of Arjava, who had come here to live (perhaps in the late 1920s). He described him as a small man whose nerves had been all broken to pieces in the first world war. He had been a dispatch rider 'carrying secret messages', and in constant danger, and had been wounded in the leg. After the war, apparently, he had become a Cambridge philosophy don, and then got a post in India as a lecturer. While attending a philosophical conference at Madras he had been told about Sri Aurobindo. He had come to Pondicherry, seen Mother, gone back to England for six months, given up his post, and then returned to India to live in the Ashram until his death, around 1940.

Ambu said he had been a close friend of this man and liked him. He said he had had a brilliant mind, but withdrew very much into himself. At first he would mix with all kinds of people, later only with those on his own level. He would sometimes fly into a rage – even with the Mother – because of his English sense of time. She would say 'Come and see me at 11.30' – then she would be ready to see him at 10.30, and send for him. He would not go, but would sit in the Reading Room, complaining. At last he would go, in a great rage, but when he got to the stairs up to Mother's room he would change and become a different being, and go up and talk for perhaps an hour and a half – about all sorts of things.

Chadwick apart, Ambu said he was not impressed with Europeans. (He couldn't tell which were English or French or Polish; when he saw a white skin it meant 'European' to him.) He said they were dirty, and that the soldiers in the war ('Thompsons? Toms? – yes, Tommies') and their officers had been arrogant and unpleasant.

About staying here he said, 'Don't hurry. Slowly, slowly is the way. Go back to London and help the Sri Aurobindo Circle, and practise devotion to the Mother. There is nowhere in the world where you cannot contact her. There is no need to be here'.

He told me about an American lady who came, against his advice, and after staying two years in a pleasant flat given her by the Mother, had had to go back home, to keep sane. 'Please write' she had said to him, but he had said No, because then the thoughts would have started all over again, about the Ashram and coming back and all that.

'But you can take a plunge of course' he said, 'if you don't mind what happens, even if you hit your head ...'

* * *

20th August

Today I saw Mother, for a short interview. I had thought this would result in my leaving, but no, I am to stay until December, when again Mother will see if I have a clearer understanding of where I should be.

We talked a little about the nature of sleep and 'being conscious in sleep.' Sri Aurobindo writes, in 'Bases of Yoga', 'Sleep, because of its subconscient basis, usually brings a falling down to a lower level, unless it is a conscious sleep'. Many people, I think, can change the course of a dream they do not like, or wake themselves up, and this is because they know they are dreaming. It is this inner awareness and detachment even in sleep that is developed in yoga, it seems.

Norman was very happy for me when I told him of my reprieve until December.

We went swimming together. On the beach we talked to an elderly ashramite, who told us how, once, soon after he had come here, he saw a white lady apparently drowning. Before coming here he had been a strict Brahmin, and Brahmins must never touch strange women. He had quite a conflict of conscience as he stood on the beach and watched; but at last the teaching of Sri Aurobindo overcame his conservative habits, and he went into the sea and pulled the poor female out.

* * *

115

Dear Anthony and Mary,

Thanks for your letter which was good to get. But I'm sorry to hear about your father's heart-attack and the circumstances, which must have made a most impacted shock. From his point of view there's something to be said for a sudden exit, with no gradual deterioration or long illness. They would say here that his inner being was ready for a change and that what happened was best for him. Sri Aurobindo, in a published letter, says 'Things happen that seem unfortunate to the human mind, and a sudden accidental or violent death cutting short prematurely this always brief spell of terrestrial experience ... seems to it especially painful and unfortunate. But one who gets behind the outward view knows that all that happens in the progress of the soul has its meaning, its necessity, its place in the series of experiences which are leading it towards the turning point where one can pass from the Ignorance to the Light ...' (He is not using Ignorance in any insulting sense, but as the state of the mass of people who are unillumined, unrealised, etc.) I do hope you are feeling less depressed.

Your remarks about my lotus-life made me smile. No, unfortunately or fortunately, there are no naked ladies to hand in Ganapatram's hostel – that would be definitely inconsistent with Ashram life. They insist, here, that it is only by the sublimation (not repression) of the sexual energies that progress can be made. The ones who have won through say, moreover, that the bliss and joy of the love of the Divine is more real and overwhelming than any human love, and fills them in turn with a great love for everyone and everything. Many of them have been married or have formerly led quite rich experimental lives, so they give the impression of knowing what they are talking about.

For the last few days I have been feeling poorly, with a sick stomach. I have a frugal diet of buttermilk and rice, and sit a lot in my room (alone), reading the plays of Sri Aurobindo. Four have been published – one just recently, which I have been asked to review for a magazine called 'Mother India'. It is a lusty oriental story, full of slave-market scenes, harems, intrigues between bidders, etc. – from Sri Aurobindo's pre-Ashram period.

The reason for my indisposition was a picnic. A friend called Kanti Upadhyaya (I think I mentioned him) who is secretary of a nearby sugar mill and has lunch every day with me in G.'s restaurant, said he was organising a little jaunt into the country on Sunday – would I come? So on Sunday I reported at his house at 10 o'clock, as arranged. We sat and waited for the others to assemble, listening to Indian songs on his gramophone. By 12 o'clock we were more or less set, and went off in a fleet of cycle rickshaws to the bus station. There we waited perhaps 20 minutes and then seven of us, and a young child aged about six, jolted away in an aluminium-coloured bus.

The country was pleasant – paddy fields, shishir trees, cows and pasture, water-buffaloes, banyans. Someone even saw a monkey. After a while we came to Cuddalore, a town about 14 miles from Pondi. There was then a debate as to where to go next – as our connection had left by then for the place where the original picnic was to have been. However, we got on a bus to Chidambaram, 36 miles further on.

At about 2.30 we collected our bags of food and got out near a massive seven-storied stone Gopuram, gateway to a huge temple to Siva, covered with dancing and posing statues. We went in and came to a big enclosure littered with broken masonry, sleeping beggars, sadhus, etc., where we were asked to take off our sandals. There was a bit of an argument, as the ground was very hot and covered with small pieces of stone and brick, but we complied and limped towards a long building looking like a temple. Going up steps we came into a hall filled with hundreds of square stone pillars. Here we tried to make ourselves inconspicuous, and the women began to unpack the picnic. Soon they found that the essential bag containing buns, butter and the hostess's spectacles had been left on the bus. Four volunteers went back to try to find the bus.

I escaped and began to explore the precincts, taking a few cautious photographs of carved elephants and of a huge open-air tank like a monster swimming pool, lined with black rock steps, where pilgrims dip and bathe for purification.

Finally we had lunch, with much laughter and gusto – raw carrot, cucumber, onion and some nasty farinacious foods called sheo, chivda and gauthia, some of which I managed to feed to a chipmunk that came out from behind a pillar. They had not been able to find the bun-bag. After lunch we drew water from a large and deep well in the forecourt, washed our hands and filled our water-bottles. I think, now, that this was a mistake.

Kanti then said he would show me the famous golden statue of Siva dancing. We went through court after court, past shrines where huge carved bulls or coiled cobras sat, past ugly squat black elephant-gods, shiny with grease and lamp smoke, some grotesquely dressed in little plastic aprons or girded with towel-like cloths. At last we came to a small golden-domed shrine where K. said the image was. But it was so dark that though we peered in at the door I could see very little, and the statue seemed draped in garlands and obscured. Priests were waving lamps in front of it and conducting a 'puja' or worship. K. took me round to the side to get nearer, but an ugly fellow came at us and said we must not come in without taking off our shirts. K. was indignant, and apologised to me about this, and we came away. The atmosphere was not pleasant, so dark, dirty and squalid – though some of the carvings we saw were marvellous.

We left the temple about 5.30 but there was no bus until 7.30, so we sat by the road, near a café, and watched the crowds, and were investigated in turn by beggars, goats and sharp-looking dogs. We drank a lot of temple-water from our flasks and interrogated every bus we saw. One result was that we got back the bun-bag when our original bus came again on its next round.

Eventually at 7.30, we set off, and by 9.30 or so we were back at Cuddalore – in the dark. There we were told there were no more buses to Pondy that night, so there began a long bargaining with a small taxi-driver who wanted about 25/- to take us home. After about two hours we actually settled for £1, and the taxi came. It was an open Ford of about 1920 – with room for about six, doors held shut with string. The eight of us got in, and then the driver, while his mate stood on the running-board.

I was silent by now, but the others were still uproariously buoyant – and became even more ebullient when at midnight the left front tyre burst with a noise like a rifle-shot. Again we sat by the road in the white moonlight, and the wheel was changed. By 1 o'clock we got back to K.'s house in Pondi, and they said, 'Now you must have a meal' – and a horrible one it was.

Ever since then I have felt jaded. But I have a bottle of quite pleasant pink medicine from the Ashram clinic. Maybe I shall feel better soon.

With love, Dick

*   *   *

11th September

The still courtyard is lit by a few electric bulbs at the centre. Overhead the Service tree is dark and huge, its trunk rising at a slope at the head of the Samadhi, a simple massive flower-covered rectangular solid. Girls and men come and go, shedding their sandals by the side of the court and moving into the light to kneel or stand by the Samadhi. Some take a flower from the tomb before going home for the night. Others touch the blossoms with their hands and silently carry the contact to head or heart before leaving. Near the edge of the circle of light, a few sit cross-legged on the paving, meditating with closed eyes.

I see Prithwisingh, the white of his hair and shirt and dhoti showing up in the dark entrance to his room, and I go over to talk with him. He turns back before I reach him, and I follow him into his office. He is pacing slowly up and down, declaiming some Sanskrit verses. I greet him; we sit down, and he starts telling me of the past and of the future.

'The manifestation of the Supermind in the subtle-physical took place in 1956, but it has still not emerged into the body. Changes are already happening – you will see – the political situation will change, great alterations will take place. After all, only a few years have

119

passed since it came down. But it will begin to manifest more fully on the earth-plane in 1967. Then even those outside will see, and a great many people will come to Pondicherry. Mother has said that my eyes will be cured when the Supramental power is manifested in the physical – she told me so herself'.

'Will she supramentalise her own body suddenly, or will it change gradually?'

'Gradually. You see, Mr Dick, the process will take time, and we may see nothing at first, until the cells on the surface of the body and the nerve-endings become affected.' He pauses, and then continues, 'Did I tell you the vision I had one morning at Balcony Darshan?'

'No.'

'I was standing there – my mind was not particularly quiet, but what had to come made its way – and I saw a rosy light, shot through with gold, and it enveloped me right up to the neck. And then in this light I saw Mother like a young girl, but full of the experience of age. She was so wonderfully beautiful, like no-one I could have imagined; like a girl, but at the same time so pure that no bad thought could have lived for a moment in her presence, and yet although there was this power she was also radiating love and happiness. And this vision stayed with me for seven or eight minutes, until the crowd began to disperse ... I asked Mother about it and she said it was a true vision of a spiritual reality that was being realised. Also a girl in the Ashram saw a vision of many stars coming together, breaking up and then coalescing into one large radiant body. Mother said this represented the new action of Supermind on matter that was taking place, and that such visions appeared only when the actual manifestation was near at hand'.

Prithwisingh also told me how, three days before the passing of Sri Aurobindo, he had appeared to him and said, 'Prithwisingh, I am going down, but I will come again in a more glorious form.' He said this vision came as a dream. He seemed to receive a page of typewritten explanation from Sri Aurobindo, in which he had read with excitement and understanding why it was necessary for Sri Aurobindo to leave the body, and what work he was doing, but that on waking he could not remember anything of this – perhaps he was not meant to – except for the beginning, which said he was to continue with his work and trust always in the Mother, and the final phrase, 'I am going down, but will come again...'

Prithwisingh told the Mother, and she said how glad she was that he had had this vision, and that she had had the same experience. He said this was her kind way of saying things – she had surely had some far more intimate message.

I asked Prithwisingh if he thought we should live to see these things. He replied that for himself he was not sure, but that I would surely live long enough.

*　*　*

12th September

'I will come again'. Prithwisingh, Norman and many other sadhaks I have talked to have the hope, not a dogmatic one, but, in the words of an article by K.D. Sethna, the 'hope that sees the future pregnant with a particular most heart-soothing possibility ... that Sri Aurobindo who has already a divinised subtle physical sheath may employ the Supramental mode of manifestation for the purpose of presiding in the domain of Matter itself over the new humanity which the Mother will initiate.' That is to say that Sri Aurobindo may by soul-force alone fashion a new body, as an instrument for renewed action in the material world.

This hypothesis is based on the following passage written by Sri Aurobindo about possibilities consequent on the descent of Supermind: 'In the theory of the occultists and in the gradation of the ranges and planes of our being which Yoga-knowledge outlines for us, there is not only a subtle physical force but a subtle physical Matter intervening between life and gross Matter, and to create in this subtle physical substance and precipitate the forms thus made into our grosser materiality is feasible. It should be possible and it is believed to be possible for an object formed in this subtle physical substance to make a transit from its subtlety into the state of gross Matter directly by the intervention of an occult force and process whether with or even without the assistance or intervention

121

of some gross material procedure. A soul wishing to enter into a body or form for itself a body and take part in a divine life upon earth might be assisted to do so or even provided with such a form by this method of direct transmutation without passing through birth by the sex process or undergoing any degradation or any of the heavy limitations in the growth and development of its mind and material body inevitable to our present way of existence. It might then assume at once the structure and greater powers and functionings of the truly divine material body which must one day emerge in a progressive evolution to a totally transformed existence both of life and form in a divinised earth-nature.' (*The Supramental Manifestation*)

*   *   *

14th September

Ravindra told me how shortly before the passing of Sri Aurobindo the Force was coming down so powerfully that for days and nights he went without sleep. One did not need it; one was so alive and invigorated.

• • •

Norman said yesterday that the atmosphere of the Ashram was the nearest he had known it to that of 1946 when he had first come here. At that time the presence of Sri Aurobindo and the Mother seemed to fill the Ashram courtyard, and particularly the Meditation Hall – like going into water when you came there – but that now the atmosphere seemed all over the place, wherever you went.

It is certainly most concrete and pervasive, like the living silence of a really centred and 'gathered' Quaker meeting.

• • •

Ambu, on being asked about any change in the atmosphere, replied that he cared nothing for talk about such things. Of course there was an atmosphere at times in such a place where one's thoughts and aspirations were directed towards spiritual things – but what mattered was 'What are you doing with it? Could you assimilate it, or were you just the same when you went away as when you came?' A donkey could live in the Ashram, but it would remain a donkey.

122

He had known great men, apparently saintly and advanced souls, who had talked of 'atmosphere' and impressed everyone. But where were they now? When the test had come they had gone away in rebellion.

Even of those living in the Ashram, in perfect conditions, with every kind of help and grace poured out on them – even of these, how many really accepted Mother fully? He himself accepted her internally. There was a small but strong bond which had held him here with her for 31 years. But still he admitted that his outer nature – his surface mind, etc. – did not fully accept her.

*　*　*

GOD HAS CARED

The brown dog, seen for so many months
Sleeping with the naked street-boys on the path,
Has been run over – still, now, in the gutter.
Children are tormenting a crow that cannot fly.
'Ma, Ma' – Mother – the beggars cry.

    Pass by, traveller, pass along there,
    There's not enough for everyone.
    So keep your own fat share.

A child is lying outside on a dirty cloth,
Its legs and arms like yellow chicken-bones.
Old crab-fingered women sit picking each other's hair,
And the man on another's shoulders shouts 'No legs'
Waving the stubs.

    But all these hearts are bitter,
    All these minds closed up.
    One cannot help the truly poor
    But only wish them luck.

123

Does God care? Or is life too short to be seen?
Alone in his room, with no money to help another,
One man pledges his life to change the nature of things.
His fulcrum in other worlds, he works to perfect mankind,
His will given to the Divine.

The growing-point of evolution
Breaks the habits of the past.
Poverty, sickness and the mass inertia
Slowly give way at last.

Do men care? Little known, the leader passes,
Near his 80th year. Oh his body is radiant.
Do men see the work accomplished? None can take up his gift;
But God has cared. The true revolution has begun.

For something new
From behind the sun
Has broken the repetition
Of suffering, sleeping man.

Can you not see the dawn's annunciation?
Have you not heard the music of the earth reply?

*　*　*

15th September

Ravindra was relaxed and smiling as ever. There is never any
'news' and he is always well and happy, and 'going on as usual'. The
main topics we talked of, before reading some of Stephen Spender
together, were freedom in the Ashram and 'living in the Mother's
consciousness'.

Here, he said, the Mother allows complete freedom, once the four
rules are accepted and kept. If he asked her what to do in a certain
situation she would never tell him the answer explicitly, but let him

learn it himself, perhaps through trial and error, giving him an inner guidance and pressure. Other gurus might become possessive or attached to their disciples. Mother and Sri Aurobindo have shown absolute detachment.

Ravindra recounted how a man, who had attended Sri Aurobindo in his later years, had told him that whatever was reported to him (Sri Aurobindo) was received with complete equanimity. If one told him, 'X has been stabbed through the throat', he would reply, 'Oh, I see,' and if, later 'X has died,' again, 'Oh, I see'.

'Might that not be interpreted as indifference?' I asked.

'No', said Ravindra, 'because his consciousness was at that height where he saw that everything that happened was the will of God.'

With the Mother it appeared to everyone that each was her own particular care and concern, and yet the whole weight of the responsibility of the 1,200 people in the Ashram rested on her as lightly as if it did not exist, and no doubt if the Ashram were to disappear, Mother would not be affected in the least. Yet who could say she did not love? Daily, before she went into seclusion, she would meet people and hear their problems and difficulties, see their boils and their bruises, and cheer and help them, from dawn until breakfast – when she would go up to give Sri Aurobindo his meal. In time this became so continuous a series of interviews that Sri Aurobindo's breakfast got later and later – 9.30, 10.30, 1.30 … until it came to the point when she could not get away until 3.30. And his last meal, too, grew later and later, until it was at half past midnight. During the whole day she would not have even an hour to herself. But she had said, 'I cannot refuse them if they come to me'.

I commented that people must miss this contact with Mother very much, and he said how, after she had stopped coming out of her apartment, a girl had written to her saying what a deprivation it was not to have the blessing of seeing and talking with her. Mother had replied, however, that now she was with ashramites in a far more real way, acting on them constantly from within. They should not feel separated from her because she was no longer visibly present for their vital feelings.

This led me to ask, 'What does it mean that ashramites live in the Mother's consciousness?'

Ravindra's answer implied that Mother was able to be aware of each sadhak and his condition: that she could extend the focus of her consciousness at will. She might not know the particular causes of people's conditions without their telling her, but she would know the effect. Thus she might know that such and such a man was being troubled by sexual desire, though not for whom, and so on.

He told how a girl had been reported to the Mother for some misbehaviour. She had written to Mother, begging her not to believe the report. Mother had replied, 'Why do you fear that I may think wrongly of you? I do not believe all that is told me. I listen to everything that is said, but then *I look, myself, at what really happened*'.

*   *   *

16th September

Today, while swimming in the sea, I literally bumped into Yusuf, the American Buddhist, whom I had met on board the 'Laos' in the 3rd class. He had been on his way to Colombo.

We chatted a bit on the beach. He is only staying a day or two in Pondicherry. He's an architect; likes Golconde. Said he thought the success of the building had grown from the happy relationship between client and architect – that is, between Mother and Antonin Raymond.

He's struck by the sense of beauty shown in the Ashram, especially in the arrangement of the courtyards: the modesty and attention to detail, and the use made of the potted plants.

He also said that he had heard that the Ashram did not offer a religion, yet it seemed to him that it had its sacred books, a calendar of special days, and that the Mother had become an object of worship.

*   *   *

126

Why am I not shocked by the 'idolatry' of the people here in the Ashram who worship the Mother and Sri Aurobindo?

Sri Aurobindo himself has written, 'It is far from my purpose to propagate any religion, new or old, for humanity in the future. A way to be opened that is still blocked, not a religion to be founded, is my conception of the matter'.

There is a booklet called 'Sri Aurobindo and his Ashram' which has a chapter that begins, 'The teaching of Sri Aurobindo starts from that of the ancient sages of India that behind the appearances of the Universe there is the Reality of a Being and Consciousness, a Self of all things, one and eternal. All beings are united in that One Self and Spirit but divided by a certain separativity of consciousness, an ignorance of their true Self and Reality in the mind, life and body. It is possible by a certain psychological discipline to remove this veil of separative consciousness and become aware of the true Self, the Divinity within us and all.'

For the Christian from the West, however, there is a strong feeling that any such attitude to the immanent Divine in people takes away from the uniqueness of Jesus Christ, and is therefore dangerous.

There may be a reconciling doctrine in the pre-Athenasian one, that the Incarnation is true, not of Christ only, but of God and man everywhere and always, and that Christ uniquely revealed this universal truth, demonstrating the holiness of man's psychic being and the light it sheds on our life of thought and feeling. Since the seventeenth century, the Quakers, too, have spoken of 'That of God in every man' and of the Inner Light, the Christ within.

If I responded to certain qualities in Christ with reverence and devotion as if to the Divine, then surely I must also revere them if I meet them again elsewhere. Did not Jesus himself say, 'Before Abraham was, I am'. I should not limit the presence or power and love of God to one manifestation, according to an a priori theory. And if a person has genuinely surrendered himself or herself totally to the Divine – then it must be the Divine who acts and speaks through him or her.

The Divine Love has, perhaps, sent us forerunners in the evolution of man, people who have embodied the truths they taught, and demonstrated new possibilities. Idolatry happens when their images are revered by people who do not take seriously the challenge to become like them.

But who is the Mother?

Sri Aurobindo writes, 'If you follow your mind, it will not recognise the Mother even when she is manifest before you. Follow your soul and not your mind, your soul that answers to the Truth, not your mind that leaps at appearances; trust the Divine Power and she will free the godlike elements in you and shape all into an expression of Divine Nature.'

There is a story that a child asked the Mother if it was true that she was God.

The Mother replied, 'Yes, my child, and so are you. The difference is that I have realised this potentiality that is in every human being, but you have not done so yet'.

*   *   *

18th September

When people here worship the Mother, each one does so in his own way, no doubt. Some seek her blessing and health, others ask for nothing, but trust that she will be the mother to a second birth in them. They strive for surrender, and then their worship is an attitude of openness and silence before her, that her grace may act in them to alter all that hinders their inner progress. Some may not think of her as westerners think of God, but they know that she is able to help them and to hear appeals made inwardly from miles away, even in material crises such as danger or illness. In this they are not superstitious but realistic. And when they give her thanks that is not misplaced either.

• • •

To be one in thy spirit and with thy understanding and in thy heart and in all thy members with the God in humanity, this is yoga.

Sri Aurobindo

I and my Father are one.

Then the Jews took up stones again to stone him. Jesus answered them, "Many good works have I showed you from my Father; for which of those works do ye stone me?" The Jews answered him, saying, "For a good work we stone thee not; but for blasphemy; and because, thou, being a man, makest thyself God."

Jesus answered them, "Is it not written in your law, 'I said, Ye are gods'? If he called them 'gods', unto whom the word of God came, and the scripture cannot be broken; say ye of him, whom the Father hath sanctified, and sent into the world, 'Thou blasphemest; because I said, I am the Son of God?' If I do not the works of my Father, believe me not. But if I do, though ye believe not me, believe the works: that ye may know, and believe, that the Father is in me, and I in him."

John X: 30-38

For as many as are led by the Spirit of God, they are the sons of God.

Romans VIII: 14

*　　*　　*

19th September

In an old number of the Ashram's Bulletin of Physical Education, for February 1958, I have found the following question addressed to the Mother, and her answer. It is, to me, so remarkable and so moving that I am copying it out.

Question:

'I am with you.' What does it exactly mean?

When we pray or struggle with a problem within ourselves, are we really heard, always, in spite of our clumsiness and imperfection, in spite even of our bad will and our error? And who hears? You who are with us?

And is it you in your supreme consciousness, an impersonal divine force, the force of yoga, or you, the Mother in a body with your physical consciousness? A personal presence that knows our

129

each thought and each act and not some anonymous force? Can you tell us how and in what way you are present with us?

Sri Aurobindo and you, it is said, form one and the same consciousness, but is there a personal presence of Sri Aurobindo and your personal presence, two things distinct, each playing its own role?

Answer:

I am with you because I am you or you are I.

I am with you, that signifies a world of things, because I am with you at every level, on all planes, from the supreme consciousness down to my most physical consciousness. Here at Pondicherry, you cannot breathe without breathing my consciousness. It saturates the atmosphere almost materially, in the subtle physical, and extends to the lake 10 kilometres from here. Farther, my consciousness can be felt in the material vital, then on the mental plane and other higher planes, everywhere. When I came here for the first time, I felt the atmosphere of Sri Aurobindo, felt it materially, at a distance of ten miles, ten nautical miles, not kilometres. It was very sudden, very concrete an atmosphere, pure luminous, light, light that lifts you up.

It is now a long time since Sri Aurobindo had this reminder put up everywhere in the Ashram that you all know: 'Always behave as if the Mother was looking at you, for she is indeed always present'. This is not a mere phrase, not simply words, it is a fact. I am with you in a very concrete manner and those who have subtle vision can see me.

In a general way my Force is there constantly at work, constantly shifting the psychological elements of your being to put them in new relations, defining to yourself the different facets of your nature so that you may see what should be changed, developed, rejected.

But that apart, there is a special personal tie between you and me, between all who have turned to Sri Aurobindo's and my teaching – it is well understood, distance does not count here, you may be in France, you may be at the other end of the world or at Pondicherry, the tie is always true and living. And each time there comes a call, each time there is a need for me to know so that I may send out a force, an inspiration, protection or any other thing, a sort of message comes to me all of a sudden and I do the needful. These communications reach me at any moment obviously, and you must have seen me more than once stop suddenly in the middle of a sentence or work; it is because something comes to me, a communication, and I concentrate.

With those whom I have accepted as disciples, to whom I have said 'yes', there is more than a tie, there is an emanation of myself. This emanation warns me whenever it is necessary and tells me what is happening. Indeed I receive intimations constantly, but all are not recorded in my active memory, I would be flooded; the physical consciousness acts like a filter. Things are recorded on a subtle plane; they are there in a latent state, something like a piece of music that is recorded without being played. When I need to know with my physical consciousness, I make the contact with the subtle plane and the disc begins to turn. Then I see how things are, their development in time, the actual result.

And if for some reason or other, you write to me asking for my help and I answer 'I am with you', it means that the communication with you becomes active, you come into my active consciousness for a time, for the time necessary.

And this tie between you and me is never cut. There are people who have long ago left the Ashram in a state of revolt, and yet I keep myself informed of them; I attend to them. You are never abandoned.

In fact I hold myself responsible for everyone, even for those whom I have met only for one second in my life.

Now remember one thing; Sri Aurobindo and myself are one and the same consciousness, one and the same person. Only when this force or this presence, which is the same, passes through your individual consciousness, it puts on a form, an appearance which differs according to your temperament, your aspiration, your need, the particular turn of your being. Your individual consciousness is like a filter, a pointer, if I may say so; it makes a choice, fixes one possibility out of the infinity of divine possibilities. In reality, the Divine gives to each individual exactly what he expects of Him. If you believe that the Divine is remote and cruel, He will be remote and cruel, because it will be necessary for your ultimate good that you feel the wrath of God; He will be Kali for the worshippers of Kali, and Beatitude for the Bhakta. And He will be the All-Knowledge of the seekers of Knowledge, the transcendent Impersonal of the illusionists; He will be atheist with the atheist and the love of the lover. He will be brotherly and close, a friend always faithful, always ready to succour for those who feel Him as the inner guide in each movement, at every moment. And if you believe that He can wipe away everything, He will wipe away all your faults, all your errors: tirelessly, and at every moment you will be able to feel His infinite Grace. The Divine is indeed what you expect of Him in your deepest aspiration.

And when you enter into this consciousness where you see all things in a single look, the infinite multitude of relations between the Divine and men, you see how wonderful it all is in every detail. You can look at the history of mankind and see how much the Divine has evolved according to what men have understood, desired, hoped, dreamed, and how He was materialistic with the materialist, and how He grows every day and makes Himself nearer, more luminous, according as human consciousness widens itself. Everyone is free to choose. The perfection of this endless variety of relations of man with God throughout the history of the world is an ineffable marvel. And all that together is only one second of the total manifestation of the Divine.

The Divine is with you according to your aspiration. Naturally that does not mean that He bends to the caprices of your outer nature – I speak here of the truth of your being. And yet, sometimes He does fashion Himself according to your outer aspirations, and if, like the devotees, you live alternately in separation and union, ecstasy and despair, the Divine also will separate from you and unite with you, according as you believe. The attitude is thus very important, even the outer attitude. People do not know how important is faith, how faith is miracle, creator of miracles. If you expect every moment to be lifted up and drawn towards the Divine, He will come to lift you and He will be there, close, closer, ever closer.

*　*　*

At tea today, in his room Ravindra and I had been talking about the work of the Nobel prize-winner Jagadish Chandra Bose, and his experiments concerning the sensitivity of plants. He went on to say how the Mother had a great sympathy for trees. Whenever a new building had to be put up, and the ground had to be cleared of trees, he said, Mother would be very slow to give permission for them to be felled. She would refuse at first, saying, 'No, don't cut down the trees – they feel such pain', and only if the whole project became held up would she reluctantly give her consent.

He said that the trees themselves would communicate their apprehensions and fears to her, that she would converse with plants.

When the Sports Ground was being laid out the contractors wanted to cut down several large old trees, but the Mother refused absolutely, saying she would rather not have a sports ground than that they should be destroyed.

Norman once explained the size of the Service tree in the Ashram central courtyard by saying that Mother used to meditate on it every morning at one time, giving it love and encouragement. It is certainly the largest tree of its kind in Pondicherry.

Ravindra told me that in the evenings, after her attendants had left her, Mother would care for the bowls of flowers in her room, changing the water and arranging them, before she herself would rest.

THE TREE OVER THE SAMADHI

My shield is on every high branch;
My trunk leans, guarding my Lord.
All over this courtyard I extend my limbs,
I am the rusty shield-bearer, the Copper Pod.

The devotees sit below me in cool shade.
I harness all air and earth and the fiery sun
To make good wood and dark green leaves,
So my shield is strong, my pod well made.

My reach covers the pilgrim and the sadhak.
I hold in my twigs the black crows and their nests
And I let the squirrels chase up and down my bark.
All under my shield are welcome guests.

Through my foliage the incense rises,
And in the season I make my own offering
Of gold flowers, letting them fall about the Samadhi
That I shield. And so my vigil passes.

Men in their envy plotted my downcutting
But I appealed in my danger to one who knows me,
And she sent away those men with their saws and axes,
For I am of service though my shield is rusty.

*　　*　　*

22nd September

Massive and beaming, Ganapatram came and sat down by me while I had supper tonight. He told me that Nirodbaran had been to the restaurant for the first time, that afternoon.

I mentioned that I'd been reading his correspondence with Sri Aurobindo, and said how humorous Sri Aurobindo's replies had been.

"Yes", Ganapatram agreed, "and Nirod was very direct and open with him, too. I remember one day he wrote and said to Sri Aurobindo, "You say that you have *selected* all the people who come here to live in the Ashram, but how is it, in that case, that there are so many fools? Today, do you know, I met a man and asked him … and he replied …, and he was no better than a donkey. Why are there so many donkeys here?"

"Nirod told me," went on Ganapatram, "You see I have written this to him, and asked him. Now we will see what he says." Next day he had a reply dealing with other parts of his letter, but at the end Sri Aurobindo had written, "There is a place in this Ashram for donkeys. They too are needed."

"Well, we laughed over this together at the time, but then one day Udar found a real donkey – a young one – somewhere in the town, and brought it to the Ashram. He told the Mother that he had a donkey, and could it be kept? And she said, "Bring it to the courtyard and I will see it."

"So one morning Nirod comes to me where I work in the Reading Room and says, "Hey, Ganapatram, come and look. That fellow's come that Sri Aurobindo needed. He's going to have an interview with the Mother." And there was the donkey, standing where the Samadhi is now, under the service tree. And the Mother came down and looked at him, and then stroked his chin and took his head in her hands and said, "Look how beautiful he is. What a fine mouth". And we were standing laughing and laughing, five or six of us, because a donkey, you know, in India is a byword for being ugly and stupid. But the Mother said Yes, he could stay, and at once wrote out chits saying he was to be supplied with this thing and that thing and where he was to live, and she gave instructions to Udar to look after him.

"And you know some years later there was a donkey race organised in the town. All the town donkeys ran and our donkey ran – and ours won. He won and was given a prize."

Some children came onto the roof-top to buy ice-cream, and Ganapatram got up to serve them. "There are so many funny stories about things that have happened here," he said, "that one could sit and laugh about them for hours."

*　*　*

23rd September

Ambu, alive like a light flame, warns, "Before you decide to take the plunge and stay here all is even and happy, nothing serious raises its head. The Mother is all love and kindness, and your psychic being is prompting you all the time. But once you decide to be a permanent sadhak, for life, then, oh then, it is all different. The psychic being retires. It has done its job. It has brought you to the Mother's feet. Now its work is over and the Mother's work begins. But the Mother leaves you alone – she pays no more attention to you. She has let

135

you know unmistakably that she has accepted you, that you are her child. But now her work is inward. You are apparently dropped and left on your own. And now all the fear and revolt of the vital nature expresses itself – all the dirt and the lust and bitterness come to the surface. You can hardly believe you are the same man, that you will ever be happy again. Perhaps you are ill; no-one comes near you: your friends never bother; your work-mates don't get on with you; you have a dark hot room … This is the time and the test that shows if you really want the Divine or any easy life!"

He seemed to think that Godfrey would either leave or go mad. I asked why no-one warned him or remonstrated. But he said, "The Mother knows which way he is going. How do we not know that it is perhaps the quickest way to teach him some lesson?"

Godfrey is a Scot who fought in the Burma campaign. He has been here four years and is now very withdrawn and intense, and speaks to no-one. But sometimes he will sternly put some Indian in his place, or lose his temper in a white-hot denunciation of some insincere or immoral behaviour.

Ambu said he had seen many like him during the years he had been in the Ashram, and that he would go down – and he made a gesture as of something being dropped.

*　*　*

26th September

I have been talking with Ravindra about the study of occult laws. There seems nothing intrinsically wrong about such study. It merely extends the frontiers of knowledge and of human control. The motive of the student is the important thing. If the motive is pure, and the will surrendered to the Divine, then the more knowledge the better the instrument and the service. As Evelyn Underhill has said, the Magi were led, through their wisdom, to the heavenly child.

The attitude of Sri Aurobindo and the Mother seems to be that the time has passed for esotericism in these matters, that mankind is ready, fearlessly and openly, to test and experiment with his hidden potentialities, and that what has been for so long the secret

136

knowledge of adepts and yogis should now become available to all who look for it, just as the knowledge of physical science has become universalised.

Ravindra said that when the Mother had been living day by day with the Ashramites there had been numberless opportunities to see occult laws in action. For instance, the weather. Once there had been a great drought. No rain for months. The Mother heard that the local farmers were in despair. She collected a number of children and made them dance in a ring, invoking rain. Within two hours the clouds began to form, and soon afterwards heavy rain came down. Later the Mother heard a report that the farmers had said, "If we'd had another three inches we would not have needed any more this year." "So they want some more rain?" said the Mother, "All right then, they shall have it." And they did.

Again, when the Playground buildings were being painted, it was essential to have a few dry days. But rain was gathering. The Mother was told, and she assured the contractor it would not rain. Nor did it.

Similarly on a Darshan day it was raining hard and someone told Sri Aurobindo that the visitors and sadhaks would be finding it very inconvenient queuing up to receive Darshan in the wet. "I see," said Sri Aurobindo, and gazed out of the window. The clouds cleared and the sun shone and everyone had Darshan dry and in comfort.

A boy complained to the Mother about how it always rained on a certain sports day. The Mother guaranteed that this time it would not rain, and it did not.

People would notice how on meditation nights the clouds would seem to hold off until all was over, and then, as if by permission, drop their rain.

An engineer, a disciple of the Mother outside the Ashram, decided to ask Nehru to attend the opening ceremony for a project of his, and fixed the date for it on the Mother's birthday. The local people warned him that on that day there would be heavy rain in their district. He informed the Mother, and asked for her help. That day there was no rain at all.

Sometimes the Mother would say, "No", when asked for particular weather, "I don't like to interfere."

Ravindra said he had the feeling that she could demonstrate weather-control to the scientists of the world any day, but that they were not ready for it.

He added that there were conscious beings in control of the forces of nature, and that an occultist of the Mother's greatness could employ their co-operation.

*　*　*

27th September

This morning Prithwisingh said that the Mother had astounded the Russian visitor who has been here for a few days. This woman had read a Russian poem to the Mother who had then given her a résumé in English of what it had been about. Prithwisingh said the Mother knew no Russian, but could tell by yogic power what the person was intending to communicate. He said that true yogis could understand the language of the beasts, of birds, plants and trees.

I asked him if he could understand what the birds said.

He laughed and said, "I? No, one has to be a first-class yogi – perhaps only the Mother has the occult knowledge, here in the Ashram."

"But one can tell when they are happy, for instance after a shower of rain?"

"Yes, that is true, Mr Dick, because then the air is fresh and everything has been made clean, and they have washed their plumage – and with trees, too – it is possible to tell when they are happy, when their leaves are bright and glistening in the sun, or when they are depressed and gloomy after heat and dust. But the language of these things is something else."

• • •

At lunch Kanti said that the Russian lady had been very much impressed by the Mother – had had all her questions answered before she had asked them. He said that she had come to make enquiries about yogic methods of breath- and heart-control, with reference to space-travel. Already, according to him, the Russians had Indian hatha yogis in Moscow, engaged in training men in preparation for rocket flights.

138

Behram, the Parsee at the Guest House, said this Russian lady was very eccentric and troublesome, complaining about the food, the lighting, the time of meals and so on. He was pleased she had left.

*   *   *

28th September

Prophecies, miracles, wonders … A westerner may come here and be either fascinated or repelled by them. Living in the atmosphere of this place they have become less suspect for me. They no longer seem the arbitrary expression of omnipotence, but the occasional exercise of a special vision or force in answer to need, prompted, as with Jesus, by compassion. The followers may treasure the tales, but Sri Aurobindo and the Mother have discouraged all such gossip, knowing that signs and marvels are peripheral and not essential to the work, nor evidence for the truth of the teaching, nor of spirituality.

I hear that some fakirs came here once who actually walked on the sea – but the Mother was not at all impressed.

A lady once sent a request to the Mother that she would make some demonstration of her power, to convince a visitor. The Mother declined, adding, "Who does she think I am, Madame Blavatsky?"

No, the real marvel is something else, for which the people who live in the Ashram are never tired of expressing their gratitude.

*   *   *

29th September

What does Sri Aurobindo mean by 'the psychic being'? In his writings he speaks of a divine element, a spark, in all living beings. In humanity it has evolved and become individualized into a definite being – the psychic being – but this is veiled by the ego's surface consciousness of sensation, emotion and thought. Very few people are aware of their psychic beings, except, perhaps for an experience or two in a lifetime.

This psychic being is the secret soul in us. Sri Aurobindo is careful to distinguish between it and the Divine. He says in a letter,

139

"They (the psychic being and the Divine Presence in the heart) are quite different things. The psychic being is one's own individual soul-being. It is not the Divine, though it has come from the Divine and develops towards the Divine." It is the representative of the Jivatman, the soul in eternity, whose envoy into space and time it is. If the Jivatman is already perfect 'in heaven', the psychic being can be seen as aspiring to create that perfection 'on earth'. It is the indestructible part of us that comes back again and again, each time with a new instrumental nature, learning and developing from life to life.

Again, he writes, "In this yoga, one can realise the psychic being as a portion of the Divine seated in the heart with the Divine supporting it there – this psychic being takes charge of the sadhana and turns the whole being to the Truth, the Divine …" "Its function is to offer all things to the Divine for transformation." It leads the evolution.

Concerning its quality, Sri Aurobindo speaks of it as "deeply conscious of truth and beauty because truth and good and beauty are akin to its own native character". It brings a flavour of light, simplicity and sweetness into life.

The influence of the psychic being is there behind all great art and noble action. It is secretly prompting the best in human achievement.

I remember Norman saying that the Madonna and Child theme in western Renaissance painting and sculpture represented the psychic being as the infant Christ in the lap of the Mother, and that Sri Aurobindo had spoken of a Vedic image in which the psychic being is spoken of as the Divine Child.

• • •

It would seem, in contrast to the ideas of Christian evangelism, that for Sri Aurobindo, the soul is about the only part of man that does not need saving, since it is closest to the Divine. It is its clothing in matter, life, the emotions and mind that needs to be changed. The psychic being is the agent for that, with the support of the divine Grace.

* * *

NOMINAL RHYMES

What is the gold in this imaginary rain?
It fills the pools where angels stir the waters.
The beggars must leap in to heal their sores,
But wounded kings who fish must fish in vain.
Among the beggars you may find kings' daughters
While in the palaces are perfumed whores.

O come from the past, come out of the dead seed,
The sun-flower knows no parents, cares for no sister plants;
It turns all day, when grown, towards the sun
And never counts its generation from the weed.
So now let go the previous incarnations' dance,
Let be what you have been, being now new begun.

Or, if dark ladies and still centres,
Sources of power between one day and another,
Figures of beauty mothering their times,
Passive channels, where the Shakti enters,
Seem perennial symbols, like a father, lover,
- Look to the Numen, not the nominal rhymes.

*　*　*

1st October

There is a small grey-haired man here with a noble face and profuse beard, about whom Norman told me an intriguing story.

It seems that he came here, first, with his wife and seven children, a few years ago, while on a holiday tour of South India. After staying some days, two or three of the children refused to leave. They said they were so happy that they wanted to stay. So determined were they that the parents were at a loss what to do, not wanting to carry them off by force. They decided to ask the Mother's advice, and when she gave blessings in the Playground next day the family approached her, and the father explained the situation; would she speak to the rebels?

141

The Mother said, "So they want to stay here, do they? Let me see them." And she took each child's face in turn between her hands, looking long into their faces. Then she said, "They can stay."

Their father, aghast, said, "But what about us, Mother?"

She looked at him and said, "You too can stay."

The man was speechless, and for some days seemed bewildered. But they stayed – all nine of them, and the children are among the most brilliant in the school.

The father comes to Norman's weekly study class on 'The Life Divine'.

*   *   *

6th October

Today Godfrey came to breakfast at the roof-top restaurant. He seemed fairly lively and cheerful, but I noticed that the middle fingers on his right hand were bleeding, and one was bandaged up.

As we ate our idlis and toast, it came out that he'd had a fight with a brother sadhak. Early in the day, about 6.30, he had asked his servant to get him some tea. The fellow had refused, not to G.'s great astonishment, but later on he had teased him, saying he wouldn't give him any more bread, and, having some water in his hand, he had splashed some over the fellow's back, because he looked so insolent. The servant had run off, to a young sadhak who lived nearby, and complained.

This person had come up to G. and said, "What have you been doing to your servant?" in so aggressive and unpleasant a way that G. had felt, so he said, that he would have to make a stand, and so he had answered him back angrily.

Before he knew much about it they were both fighting on the floor, the man having attacked him as an arrogant imperialist.

"Not very dignified for a contributor to 'Mother India', said G. ruefully.

Anyway the man got G.'s right hand in his mouth, G. felt his teeth grating on the bones, and there was blood everywhere. He did not know what to do at this point, as he could not use his right, but

142

he pulled the man's head down onto his blood-soaked shirt and said, "Stop it, look what you are doing," and the man let go.

G. said he preferred a fight to the secret guile and intrigue which also went on. But all the same he was talking of asking to go to the Ashram's farm up in the Himalayas – "Where I won't get my poor fingers bitten."

At lunch Charupada loomed up. "Godfrey's been bitten, and the other man has his head broken," he said, rolling his eyes.

*　*　*

8th October

Ravindra said, today, "Godfrey has done a bad thing. He has hit a boy so hard that he has had to have four stitches."

He went on to talk about the Indian attitude to the British. In his opinion it was time to forget the differences and wrong-doings, and to remember the similarities and the good qualities on each side. Indians, he thought, should remember that the British were imperialists in an imperialist age. It was a phase of history when Indians too might have been imperialists if they had had the power and the opportunity. Also the very ideas and ideals of freedom and democracy, with which the Indians fought the British, had been imported by them from the West.

He said that Indians forgot that most of their grandfathers were enthusiastically pro-British, because Britain had brought peace and good government, so that people were no longer afraid to go out after dark. He remembered that even when he was at school the boys would still say to a bully or some-one who was being unfair, "You can't do that – it's British rule now!"

I mentioned Rammohan Roy and the Brahmo Samaj as having been pro-British, and he replied, "Yes, and not only them. Many people felt that British rule brought western civilisation and much that was progressive and good to India. Why, for instance, did Sri Aurobindo's father send his sons to England for their education, with special instructions that they were not to come into contact with other Indians?"

143

There was no doubt, he continued, that the British did much good, for instance William Bentinck's suppression of compulsory suttee in Bengal, and the stopping of Rajput child murder. Did I know that in the better families the Rajputs, whenever a baby girl was born, would dash its brains out on the ground? This was because they were so proud that the idea of a son-in-law was intolerable to them. His father had met an old Rajput who boasted quite openly of having killed six baby daughters. But the British said this would be treated as murder.

Again, there were the Thugs, who used to paint their faces and then climb up into trees by the road-side, and at night, when travellers rested underneath, would scream and howl like ghouls or djinns until the travellers ran away and left their belongings. But Bentinck came with a gun, and said, "Come down, or I'll shoot you down!"

* * *

16th October

S., travelling in a train to visit the Ashram, met a man also on the same pilgrimage. This man told her the following story.

His mother, a very old woman, was in the habit of sitting silent, and, as everyone thought, dozing for long periods. It seemed now that it was more a state of peace, silence of the mind and contemplation. Anyway, one day this old lady breathed a prayer for some money that she needed for a particular purpose. The answer came – into her lap – in crisp new Bank of India notes.

This had happened often, whenever money was needed for the grand-children. But the old lady never abused the power, and they never talked of it except in the family and with a few close friends. Now, however, someone had told her son, "You must tell the Mother at Pondicherry, and ask what this means," and so, when S. met him, he was on his way.

Norman said that stories of this kind would increase in the coming years, as examples of the action of the new forces. At first

144

they would seem arbitrary and chaotic, but later people would want an order, an explanation, for these things, as this man had done.

The natural explanation, it seems to me, is that the old lady has a source of money she wishes to keep secret; she sells her jewellery, perhaps. However, this is a story to 'hold', and certainly to enjoy.

*　　*　　*

27th October

"Even a maxim such as 'Pride goes before a fall' is in a sense an occult law", observed Ravindra, and he went on to describe how if a sadhak prided himself on being free from some particular fault or temptation then it invariably came back and gave him a bad time.

He instanced his having once said to someone that he now believed his subconscious was becoming purified, because he had had a dream in which one of the most beautiful of the Ashram girls had come to him and said she was in love with him, but, in his dream, he had reasoned with her, telling her to love the Mother, and that she would find more happiness in that than he could give her. Soon afterwards he was attacked by the most continuous and persistent sexual desire and lost all peace for a period.

● ● ●

Talking of illness in the Ashram, R. described how there was a sadhak who had terrible ulcers in his intestines, and daily grew weaker. R. used to bring him flowers from the Mother, and would talk with him. This man, although extremely weak, did not give up hope of getting better because he felt the presence of the Mother with him whenever he called to her. However, the doctors could do nothing, and one day when they came to see him he was unconscious. The Mother was informed, and for half an hour she concentrated on that man. From then on he began to improve, "And now," said R., "he is in perfect health and you've probably seen him walking on the sea-front."

R.'s own son was brought here as a child when he was dying of dysentery. He was having over twenty motions a day, and passing clots of blood. The doctors had said they could not help him.

145

However, the Mother was told about his condition. She concentrated for some time, the motions stopped – and he rapidly recovered.

Another person he knew was suffering from a prolapsed womb when she came here. Medical opinion was that an operation was essential, but the Mother saw her and told her. "I can cure you completely, only it will take about a year – and only if you believe it possible. Can you believe me?" The lady said Yes, she could. For a year she stayed indoors, with her feet up, resting completely. At the end of that time she was cured.

*　*　*

29th October

On my birthday I had another interview with the Mother. I had not expected this. On the day before, while talking to Ravindra, I had happened to mention that it would be my birthday the next day, and he had at once said, "Does the Mother know?"

"No," I told him, "Should she?"

Yes, indeed, he insisted. It was very important. Maybe the Mother had prolonged my stay just for this thing, that I should spend a birthday in the Ashram. "You must send a note by Nolini, telling her about it," he said, "and then she will concentrate on you, and put some special force on you, and it will be a very significant day in your life. She will send you a flower, with her blessings. There is something of special occult importance about a man's birthday. What time were you born?"

I did not know. He proposed that we should meditate together for a while, which we did in a fine atmosphere of peace. Before I left he recommended that, on the day itself, I should keep as quiet as possible, and not mix too much with other people, so as to be open to the Mother's influence.

That evening I wrote a note to give to Nolini, but next morning, just before setting off to deliver it, a messenger arrived at the hostel from the Ashram, to say that the Mother would see me at 10 o'clock, and would I be ready at 9.45. Apparently a friend had told Purani, who had told Nolini, who had already told the Mother.

Having collected two posies which the gardener had left for me, I went and sat in the Meditation Hall. At about five to ten Champaklal came down the stairs nearby and indicated that I should come up with him. He showed me into the long rather dim room where the Mother sees people. No-one was there. It smelled of sandalwood.

For about twenty minutes I stood there holding the two bunches of flowers. At first I concentrated on becoming aware of the room. There were pictures of Sri Aurobindo, that rested on lion-skins with incense-sticks in front of them. There were Kwannon-like figures carved out of bone, standing on metal lotus flowers, under glass bells. There were cases of ivories and a Japanese picture of a rough green sea. By the door was the Mother's high-backed arm-chair, while at the opposite end of the room was the double throne on which she and Sri Aurobindo used to sit when giving Darshan. Now it was covered with skins on which rested the photograph by Cartier-Bresson of them both sitting there.

I stood by a picture of Sri Aurobindo and gradually became still in mind and body. I felt once more the possibility of giving myself – that everything was practicable and all right.

Then, quietly, the Mother entered from a door out of sight in the ante-room between Sri Aurobindo's room and the room I was in. She stood, small and stooping, by Champaklal, choosing some flowers from a bunch which he was holding, then came towards me, lifting her head suddenly to give me a smile and a greeting with her dark, brilliant eyes.

"Bonne Fête," she said, giving me a rose. "We always wish a person Bonne Fête on his birthday, as I expect you have found out."

I gave her the flowers, which she handed over to Champaklal who took them and left us. Then she gave me a copy of Sri Aurobindo's 'The Mother', in the de luxe edition, and showed me that she had signed it, 'To Dick, with blessings'.

"It is a good little book," she said "and the only one I still sign for people, now."

She handed me the other flowers which she had chosen, with her blessings for the coming year, and said she hoped I would find what I wanted.

I asked her if I might find my Psychic Being before my next birthday. She looked up into my eyes with a very piercing, serious look, and said, "Yes, that is what I am hoping for you."

I asked her the meaning of the flowers she had given me, and she explained: the tallest ones at the back of the bunch were like fruit-blossom – thick green woody twigs covered with small white flowers with golden stamens. "This is Peace, in the Physical. It has a rather nice scent," she said. The next, in front of them in the bunch, were zinnias; these she said, were Endurance. Finally, also enclosed by the blue silk ribbon, were gaillardias, which stood for Joy in Artistic Creation. Separately there was a small red rose.

She asked how old I was, and I told her.

"To me that is nothing at all," she smiled, "Voilà!"

I thanked her for seeing me, and came away.

Since she had come in we had stood in the centre of the room together. She looked small and frail, but nevertheless radiated power, and created an atmosphere of great lightness and happiness. There was, too, a stillness and peace, and a complete relaxedness about her, and a real love, as if she was entering into the birthday spirit for one of her children. I felt I had known her always.

• • •

In Prithwisingh's room they were eager to know what had passed. I told them, and Prithwisingh insisted, "Anything else she said …?" He was greatly struck by the Mother saying I might find my psychic being within the year. "That would be really remarkable progress for you," he said.

In the evening I went to Norman and Lena's for supper. We, together with Norman Junior, had a special English meal – fried egg and chips, with tinned peas and cauliflower-sauce, followed by bananas and tea! Then we sat and talked until about 10.30.

Back in my room I meditated in front of the flowers given me by the Mother, and felt an enveloping atmosphere of love and peace slowly flood my consciousness.

After half an hour I felt overwhelmingly sleepy and had to go to bed, but before then it had been like contacting a deep current of spiritual power … The next day I could not recover the experience.

But while it lasted it had been definite and real, showing again what is possible – an encouragement and a foretaste.

*   *   *

3rd November

This morning, after some proof-reading, I called on Norman. I was surprised to find him reading a fat Modern Library edition of the Basic Works of Freud.

He said that Sri Aurobindo agreed that one's surface consciousness and behaviour were greatly influenced by what he called 'subliminal forces' of which one was normally unaware. He had compared the conscious mind and ego to the crown and dome of a temple rising from the waters, while the great body of the building which supported them lay submerged below the waves.

However, Sri Aurobindo had disagreed with the practice of many psycho-analysts who concentrated on bringing the lower vital subconscient into consciousness without first contacting and establishing their patients in the peace and light of the superconscient. The latter, he had emphasized, was the true foundation of things, and a component of the subliminal which Freud and much of western psychology had tended to ignore.

Norman went on to talk about Sri Aurobindo's description of the true or inner mind, the true or inner vital and the 'subtle physical' consciousness behind the surface ego personality – opening above to the superconscient and below to the subconscient ranges, both individual and universal, and all, together, composing the subliminal.

He said that the inner mind, inner vital and inner physical parts of us were responsible for works of genius, and for genuine paranormal happenings such as precognition, clairvoyance, telepathy, far-memory and so on, when they occurred.

I asked Norman if Sri Aurobindo included the psychic being in the subliminal part of one's nature. He said that as one is not conscious of it directly, until one has made 'the great discovery', it is certainly subliminal. It lies behind the inner faculties, which are its potential means of expression in the world – once the ego has

149

abdicated and it is able to come forward. Meanwhile it exerts its influence secretly on the surface life. It is the true person.

On the topic of psycho-analysis, Norman concluded that without some access to the higher levels of human nature it was dangerous to stir up the lower regions. It could result in a fouling up of the consciousness, rather than in healing or transformation.

All the same, Norman was enjoying reading Freud for the first time, because of his personality and the force of his writing.

Did Sri Aurobindo comment anywhere on C. G. Jung?

*   *   *

4th November

At supper tonight an old man with a laughing face, Major Ramachandra, told, with some sense of occasion, an incident from his youth – in 1919, to be exact. At that time he had been teaching in Madras, and was also running a Boy Scout group. He had taken a party of forty of these boys to Pondicherry for a fortnight's change of scene, and they had spent much time on the beach.

One evening, on their way back to their camp, he had said to one of the boys – a bright, keen lad who later became India's Ambassador to Norway – "Go to that house there and you will find Sri Aurobindo sitting on his terrace. Ask him if we may come and see him."

'Well, the boy ran off, and we waited, and then he returned and we said, "What does he say?" and the boy replied, "He says, 'Come'".

'So we all went in, and there was Sri Aurobindo sitting on his roof-top, with a chaddar over his shoulders, enjoying the cool evening air.

'Well, I asked him all sorts of questions, chiefly on the liberation of India – when it would come – but also about the relations of labour with capital, about the international situation after the war, and many such things, and Sri Aurobindo answered everything for perhaps half an hour, and then we went away.

'But after we had all gone down and left him, I ran back up the stairs and said, "I have one more question." Sri Aurobindo smiled and asked me what it was. "How may I become a better teacher?"

150

"By helping the souls of your pupils to develop."

'But then I had another question: I said, "I can help the minds of my pupils to develop, and I know how to help their emotions and their bodies to grow – but how can I know about their souls?"

'He answered very seriously, because my question was a very serious one, "You must first study your own soul."'

* * *

5th November

Norman mentioned this morning that a young Frenchman, known as Satprem, was living in the Ashram. This man had been in the Resistance during the war and had been captured by the Gestapo. He had spent a year and a half in the Camps. On his release, he had first come to India as a junior member of the French Administration in Pondy. Here he had discovered Sri Aurobindo, but had gone on, in search of adventure, to Guiana, Norman thought, and then to the forests of Brazil. Later he had returned to India and become a wandering sannyasi. But his wanderings returned to Pondy and the Mother, as to a magnet, and now he was staying here and teaching some classes in French literature in the Ashram School.

I think it must have been Satprem that I saw the other day sitting on the beach, wrapped in his orange cloth, meditating. As I walked by, he got up and we greeted each other, but he was withdrawn and concentrated and we did not talk.

* * *

6th November

A tall, very pale young man called Baber has come to stay at the hostel. He is from Bihar, where he is a university lecturer in English poetry. He is one of the few Muslims I have met here.

He seems to be at some kind of turning point in his life, saying he has felt many times that there is some special destiny in store for him, but that he has not known yet what it may be. Now he feels he may find out, here.

151

There is something both distinguished and youthful about him. He sums people up with much insight and confidence – most often unfavourably.

He says the aim of the good Muslim is to remember the Divine at all times, wherever you are, "Even when you go to the toilet."

*   *   *

7th November

Dear Anthony and Mary,

Thank you so much for your interesting letter. I am sorry to have missed such a splendid summer, but glad you and the family have enjoyed it.

You ask if one is able to keep in touch with the news, here in the Ashram. The answer is yes, if one wants to. There is a small room in the main group of buildings where a selection of the national and local papers in various scripts and languages, are laid out on the floor for anyone to read. The Mother calls this place 'La Salle du Mensonge'. Also, once a fortnight, there is an open-air film programme in the Playground which combines news with a documentary about some interesting Indian person or place.

The Playground is a large oblong sandy court surrounded by Ashram buildings, all surfaced with colour-washed plaster – grey and white. People come in and sit cross-legged on the sand or on raffia mats, but there is a row of chairs at the back where Norman and I sit with other stiff-legged or superior people. One lovely film we saw recently was about a visit Nehru made to the Kingdom of Bhutan, in the North-East. One saw Nehru riding on mule-back through wild and mountainous country, with his daughter and about a dozen companions. They crossed through Sikkim and, after changing onto yak-back, made their descent into the valley of Bhutan. Nehru was very vigorous and evidently enjoyed the journey immensely, though he limped a bit after the yak. The party was welcomed by the King and Queen of Bhutan, and exchanged silk scarves. Then Nehru addressed the people and the King translated his goodwill message, saying how India was keen to lend them technical experts

152

and advisers if needed. After this there was a kind of pageant, with dancing, and a display of archery. The King joined in this and hit the bull's eye with his first shot. Finally one saw them all saying goodbye, and the children looking sadly after Nehru as he rode off with his little party, against a background of distant Himalayan peaks.

We all like films with Nehru in them – he is so obviously sincere and seems to enjoy things. He is often shown riding a splendid white horse.

The Playground is also the scene for other evening entertainments. There has been a performance in French of a play by Molière, and another in Bengali by Tagore. The latter was prefaced by a summary in English, so we could follow the plot. Last Saturday some of the Ashram children presented a play. No-one under ten years old had been allowed to come to the Molière show, so this time the children said no adult over 25 could come to their play unless personally invited. Unfortunately it was in Hindi, and not very easy to follow – but the performers were quite free from stage-nerves, and everyone went away happy.

With love to you all, Dick.

*　　*　　*

10th November

Baber tells me that he read English at Liverpool University for three years, and that he actually *enjoyed* Liverpool. He says that its ugliness made him determined to get out of it and see England, but that after two or three weeks away he always wanted to be back there again. He found the people friendly, and would like to return to England if he can. It is amusing to hear him trying to imitate a Lancashire accent.

I shall miss him when he leaves, tomorrow.

This morning he had an interview with the Mother, about which he is reticent, except to say that while they talked he suddenly felt his consciousness leave his body. It was as if he was looking down on the room from somewhere up by the ceiling, and he saw himself, for

153

a minute or two, from outside, sitting with the Mother. Afterwards he told her what had happened, and she had nodded and said it was not an uncommon experience.

*　*　*

11th November

Sri Aurobindo writes of three possible approaches to the Divine. He may be found within the individual; He may be found in the world around us, or by a merging in the Transcendent, beyond the universe.

However, the distinguishing aim of Sri Aurobindo's yoga is, ultimately, not to achieve individual enlightenment, cosmic consciousness nor a breakthrough to Nirvana, but rather to change the waking consciousness of mankind, and transform life on earth.

The great realisations achieved by the old yogas are still necessary if the new yoga is to be integral, but only as preliminaries to a bringing down of the Supermind.

This is why Sri Aurobindo's yoga is said to start where the other yogas leave off.

*　*　*

15th November

Norman told me the following story, about an episode in his sadhana.

I woke up suddenly one night after a dream, which had taken place in the higher vital, and I can remember exactly how the half moon was lying low in the sky, shining in at the window, and in the distance I could hear someone ringing a hand bell.

I knew in advance what was going to happen: that the bell was coming into the house. It came nearer and nearer and then it was outside in the street. I heard it come into the courtyard, and then it came over the balcony, across the room and stopped with a kind of final double ring, right at the foot of my bed.

I could see nothing at all, but could feel a definite person there in the room. I was sitting up cross-legged at the head of the bed, and I

154

faced it with the mental query 'So? What about it?' It stood there for a bit, and then there was a kind of chuckle, and it was gone.

This happened for three nights running, each time with a growing sense of positive bad-will. Then it stopped. I mentioned it to the Mother, and she listened very seriously and then said, "You *must* protect yourself," very emphatically. But nothing happened then for about a year. No more recurrence of the bell-ringing, and I thought no more of it.

Then one night it began again. I knew well in advance what was going to happen – the Mother must have given me warning. The bell got louder and louder. It came into the room and I felt the evil presence coming right up to me. As soon as I knew what was coming I had put a circle of light round myself – the Mother had shown me how to do this a long time before. But whatever it was came right up to me, and was so close that I felt it almost stifling me. And then it gave a puff of breath, straight into my face, that was as putrid as if one had put one's head down into the rotten flesh of a corpse, unbelievably horrible. Corruption. And then it was gone.

Next day I met the Mother in the Playground and very briefly explained what had happened, and told her that I was afraid that if it came again I might not be able to save myself.

She said, very intensely, "If you need help call on me at once. You must call for me".

That night I woke up again and it was coming into the house. I cast a ring of protection round myself and waited. But I must have been insufficiently pure, or have harboured some evil thoughts during the day, because there was some gap or chink in the protection, and whatever it was came close up to me and suddenly reached through and grabbed my left leg. I felt it – a hard fierce grip. I pulled my leg away and let out a gasping sort of cry, and called to the Mother for help. Immediately the creature was gone. The Mother's power had completely broken up and swept the formation away, and it never came again. But it had touched me, just above the ankle.

I told the Mother about it, and she said again "You must be more careful, and learn to protect yourself." After that I thought no more about it.

Then, about a year later, when the new swimming pool was opened, we all had to have a medical examination. When my turn came the doctor found me fit enough, as I had expected, until he came to a rough patch of skin on my left ankle, a small area which looked sore, rather like a spot of eczema. He said "How long have you had this?" I told him I'd not noticed it before. He said "Can you feel anything there?" and he rubbed the spot with his finger, and I couldn't feel anything. It was as if the place was anaesthetised. "You see, it's dead, isn't it?" he said. Finally he arranged for me to see another doctor at the Hospital, and I came away – without being allowed to use the swimming pool.

Later I had further examinations, but the doctors were unable to make up their minds definitely. Then our Ashram doctor said I had better have a specialist opinion, and arranged for me to go to a medical institute some distance away in the country, with a letter of introduction to the Director.

I still had no inkling as to what he suspected – right up to the moment when the car drove up to the building and I saw, written up on a board 'Institute for Leprosy Research'. You can imagine what I felt, when it came home to me what I had got.

Well, I saw the doctor there, and, after he had looked at my leg, he said "Were you in the Far East as a child?" I said "No, I came out here during the war for the first time." He was puzzled at this, and said again "Are you sure you were not out East when you were very young?" I told him I had definitely never been anywhere near the Far East, or the Near East before I was 30. He said he couldn't understand it, since I had a leprous infection of a type which always took 20 years to manifest itself after the first contagion. He said it was definitely this kind that I had, but that so far it was in its early stages, and that I should be cured within 3 years, if I followed his instructions. These involved taking a particular drug once a day, and keeping the spot covered up.

I was assured that there was absolutely no danger of infecting other people, and that it would be quite safe to continue my usual work, and the specialist gave me a letter to that effect.

That evening, back in the Ashram, I went to the Playground feeling pretty miserable. But at the march-past the Mother gave me such a smile of encouragement and blessing as I shall never forget. So much light and radiance passed into me from her look, that I could hardly contain it, and felt that other people must be able to see it shining from me! I had to go and sit down by myself somewhere quiet to assimilate it.

Later, when I saw her, to tell her about the result of the examination, she said that I had better stay in my house, in case people became nervous, and get on with my reading and private work.

I did this, and took the prescribed drug, which had very unpleasant side-effects, by the way, and, to cut a long story short, within 18 months I was passed as completely free from infection.

The doctors, though, could never understand two things: firstly, how I could have developed that kind of leprosy at all, and, secondly, how I could be cured in so short a time.

• • •

Talking about this story Norman said the attack he suffered had been a definite move on the part of 'hostiles' to interrupt his sadhana, but that the shape it took was determined by his own particular personality. What had happened had corresponded to something dramatic and violent in his make-up. The externalisation of the whole conflict had resulted in a kind of catharsis, and eventual purification and strengthening of the being. He said that frightening though it had been, it had not been – and such things never are – more than he, at that particular stage, could bear.

He had asked the Mother to enlarge on the experience, but she would make no comment at all, saying that he had all the elements of the situation before him, and had felt them personally far more vividly than she. So he ought to be able to draw his own conclusions.

* * *

An Englishman from South Africa, called Gilchrist, has come to stay at the hostel, in one of the small rooms across the landing from mine. He is a man in his late forties, tall and rather angular. When he goes out he wears white shorts and a peaked tennis cap that make him look very like Monsieur Hulot on holiday.

At first he seemed puzzled by the lack of any organised programme for visitors here – the absence of guidance and instruction, timetable, rules or discipline. But he tells me that he had come to the Ashram almost by accident, and knew nothing about the place before he got here.

He works, back home, in the Johannesburg Municipal Service, which allows its employees to accumulate their leave over several years. He had about six months' due to him and had planned to spend it in a Burmese monastery, about which he had read in a book written by an American admiral. This man had visited the monastery and been subjected to an intensive course of what sounded like brain-washing. I asked Gilchrist if it had led to anything, and he replied, "Well, not very much, because unfortunately just when he seemed on the verge of a breakthrough the admiral was recalled to naval duties, but he did have some sort of an experience afterwards, in Venice, I think, while looking into a glass of red wine."

However, the sound of this place appealed to Gilchrist, who felt that drastic measures were needed to get out of the rut of the common life, so he had written and asked if he might go there for a visit of some months. He had had no reply. Meanwhile, in Johannesburg, he had been attending classes on yoga-exercises, run by a lady who later married Sir Paul Dukes – himself a populariser of hatha yoga for westerners. One day Gilchrist mentioned to this teacher his disappointment about receiving no reply from Burma. She had said to him, "Well, if you want that sort of thing, why not visit the Sri Aurobindo Ashram at Pondicherry?" So he had written another letter which was answered at once, and here he was.

He was particularly sad that the yoga exercises and āsanas which he had learned very painstakingly at home were apparently not held in any esteem here at all. So I took him to see Ambu.

Ambu, lithe as an ancient Greek athlete, spread his little mat on the floor and suggested Gilchrist showed what he could do. And Gilchrist did, doing some most strenuous contortions. I looked hopefully at Ambu for some encouraging word, but he remained grave and silent. Finally, rather red in the face, Gilchrist came to a halt and also looked up at him from the floor.

"You are too tense," said Ambu. "You must learn to do each of these exercises in a completely relaxed manner, breathing evenly, without effort. I will show you."

Ambu then did some of the same āsanas, but as calmly as a cat washing, smiling and bathed in peacefulness. The movements were the same, but the difference was considerable, though hard to define.

Gilchrist was impressed, and they agreed that he should come and practice with Ambu whenever he liked while he was here.

*　*　*

24th November

It has been dull, the sun obscured by cloud, and with rain in the air at times. Thirty three years ago Sri Aurobindo achieved 'a permanent realisation of the Overmind in the physical consciousness', so I am told. This was a major step forward, preparatory to the bringing down of Supermind, and today it was celebrated with a Darshan.

I went to the Ashram at about 9.30 and, sitting on a stool at one side of the main courtyard, watched for about an hour and made an effort to prepare myself. The court filled up until every available sitting-place was occupied, and a queue formed for the Darshan that was so long and involved that it was a puzzle to find the end of it. The Ashram girls had new white dresses and the women wore their best sarees. Many of the men carried garlands and bunches of flowers – roses and ixia and croton – to offer to the Mother.

Rising murmur of voices, rising clouds of incense from sticks burning by the Samadhi, then conversation dies away, a drizzle of

159

rain, greetings briefly breaking the prevailing silence ... the slow movement of the looped queue, the running of children ... With what attitude should one approach the Mother once again, and see once more those eyes? If it were Christ ... If it were the Divine ... How go to meet her having already determined to leave and return to Europe? Such a confrontation, what did it demand of one but perfect candour, self-offering and deepest gratitude? But these are not there for the giving. If one could give oneself perfectly one would already be a realised and illumined being. As one is, one can but approach, quieten the thoughts, reject anxieties, be aware at every sense and pore of all the situation ...

Once more the green stair-carpeted ascent, the involuntary pounding of the heart, the heavy stillness of the air, and the queue moving it seems faster and faster like a river nearing a waterfall. We pass through the small ante-room into Sri Aurobindo's room. His bust gleams with a greenish silver light; there are his books, his desk, his lion and tiger skins, and a Japanese painting. Once again the queue turns, back through the other end of the ante-room ... a cheetah's head snarls and flares. We go forward into the Darshan chamber, past carved wooden chests and cabinets of objets d'art, past an alcove where a transparency of Sri Aurobindo is illumined from behind with a golden light ... again one hastens, counting the people in front of one – be still and know, oh soul – then she is there, small, steady, smiling, her eyes looking straight into one's own. She hands one the message, already her gaze has dropped and is seeking the next person ... "Thank you, Mother," I murmur inaudibly, and in a moment, it seems, am at the bottom of the staircase again, light, happy, without a care, with, for a rare moment, a mind at ease and still.

*　*　*

25th November

It is cold all of a sudden, and I've been wearing a pull-over for the first time this year. There's been a north wind blowing for days. In the mornings this wind carries dozens of large black and red butterflies with big fat scarlet bodies. Most of them fly high and straight over the town and go off to the south.

After the Darshan yesterday, in the afternoon, there was a prize-giving in the Playground, for the athletes and school-children. It rained very heavily, so the programme was rather disrupted, but the Mother came and distributed the prizes in the gym. There was too much of a squash for many of us to see what was going on. The Ashram band played 'Love Divine' and part of Beethoven's Pastoral Symphony. Gilchrist was much moved, and surprised to hear such western music.

There was also a march-past, with all the various groups in shirts and shorts, each group wearing its distinctive colour – red shorts, green shorts, khaki and so on. They were soaked by the rain but it didn't matter.

The hostel is crowded, now, since a boy of 19 arrived leading a party of nine people, including a doctor, a mill owner and an astrologer, from his home town. They say he is a marvellous boy, a Child of India, a spiritual prodigy, who has had visions since the age of six. I do not feel attracted to him myself.

*   *   *

26th November

This morning, coming back from Balcony Darshan, I was crossing the bridge over the 'canal' to go to the Hostel when I heard shouts and a woman screaming. By the canal-side a rickshaw-man was beating a thin tousled-looking woman. Several other rickshaw-men were looking on.

A powerful feeling of anger rose up in my body and I shouted at them. The man looked uneasily at me, but went on.

Coming up to him I stepped between him and the woman, shook him by the shoulder and said, "No!" very loudly.

The woman broke free, and, running off, disappeared under the bridge. The man turned away, muttering something.

I told Norman about this, later, and he was amused at my 'English fair play' reaction, but he said it was usually best not to interfere

161

on such occasions; that according to their customs the woman may have deserved what she was getting. I was lucky, he said, that they, including the woman, had not turned on me.

Today Doris, the Secretary of the London Sri Aurobindo Circle, has arrived. She has been dreaming of visiting the Ashram for years, and has now made it – "Before I get too old and decrepit, my dear."

It will be quite a change of routine for a 65 year old who is used to South Kensington. However, she has a beautiful room in Golconde, with pleasant Ashram-made furnishings. The whole external wall of this room is made up of concrete slats, about a foot wide, like a large Venetian blind, which can be opened or shut by moving a rod. The opposite wall is a sliding partition so that if the room is too hot one can slide it back and have a through draught from similar shuttering the other side of the passage outside.

When I went to see her Doris was reading, rather incredulously, a notice requesting visitors not to spit through the shutters – a difficult feat, we thought.

Udar's wife, Mona, has helped Doris to dress in an Indian saree, and she looks very distinguished, though I don't think the old-time mem-sahibs would have approved.

*　*　*

27th November

Yesterday I had tea with Ravindra again. We did not read any of Cleanth Brooks's 'Understanding Poetry' as planned, but talked for the whole time.

He said it was perhaps good to go back to England and then come again with the definite resolve to do yoga – not to plunge after having come with the idea of only a two month visit. One thing he said he could tell me, as a friend, and that was that Sri Aurobindo's yoga worked. It gave what it promised. He himself was now a happy man. Before, he had suffered much, owing to his sensitivity. He had gone for long periods when he could sleep for only two or three hours a night – his father had been very worried by his condition. He would brood for months over some sight or happening. Once he had travelled in the same railway compartment as a condemned murderer. And this man was weeping. Some-one had offered him an orange, but he had refused ... What was the use of an orange to him? For weeks he had been haunted by the memory of this man's face, and by imagining how such a one would be feeling. Then, after reading in the paper of the declaration of war in 1939, he had paced all night on his roof, unable to shake off the thoughts and pictures that rose up in his mind of all that this meant. He had been very interested in a girl at this time, but after that he could never look at her again nor bring himself to think of family happiness in a world of such suffering ...

Dr Johnson, when asked if a man could be happy, replied, "Never, but when he is drunk." But this was not so – he had proved it. Happiness was real and possible in this life. He himself did not need to stir out of his room all day – the inner life became so interesting. He did not depend on books, although one could learn useful things from literature and enjoy good books, yet he had so prepared himself that if he became blind tomorrow he would still be happy and absorbed in the yoga.

*　*　*

28th November

The lack of 'instruction' for visitors or new members of the Ashram is certainly rather baffling to a westerner. There is a complete absence of exhortation, preaching and any obligatory forms of worship or belief. It is hard to discover just what is going on. Although there is a stronger sense of purpose than in any other community I have come across, it is an individually motivated purpose, not imposed from above – though everything, one realises in time, is linked as by invisible threads to the guiding will and presence of the Mother. Indeed it is recognised that each person must 'find his own way', since no two are alike, and ready-made formulae are a hindrance rather than a help to growth.

One sadhak told me that if at times he became depressed or troubled by problems then he would turn to a volume of Sri

163

Aurobindo's, perhaps to his Letters – which were a superbly rich mine of spiritual direction – and he would invariably find help and be encouraged. Always, too, practical points of difficulty could be referred to the Mother for advice, and though she might not always give an answer in so many words, a solution would be found.

'The sadhana of this yoga does not proceed through any set mental teaching or prescribed forms of meditation, mantras or others, but by aspiration, by a self-concentration inwards or upwards, by self-opening to an Influence, to the Divine Power above us and its workings, to the Divine Presence in the heart and by the rejection of all that is foreign to these things. It is only by faith, aspiration and surrender that this self-opening can come.' (Sri Aurobindo. Letters.)

I asked Norman about 'self-concentration inwards or upwards.. What did it mean? He said these were basic processes in Sri Aurobindo's yoga. Normally, people lived in a very limited state of awareness, in the superficial ego-consciousness, but it was possible to break through or out of this in two ways – inwards, by a concentration in the heart-centre in the middle of the chest, or upwards by concentrating in the head-centre between the eyebrows. The first led to the discovery of the psychic being, full of love and aspiration, and the second led to a realisation of the Self above, and to levels of spiritual knowledge, peace and immensity beyond the normal range of the mind.

Sri Aurobindo had recommended the search for the inner Divine, within the individual, as generally easier and perhaps safer than the breakthrough into the cosmic or transcendent Divine, but both approaches could be used, or whichever was most congenial to one's nature. First, however, he was emphatic that one should work for purification and peace, otherwise a premature influx of power and sudden experiences of one's inner being could be dangerous and unbalancing. He, Norman, had become friendly with a young Irish visitor to the Ashram who had 'pulled' impatiently on the Force, and had had a breakdown and been advised to leave. He had not prepared himself by learning detachment from his ego-nature.

I asked which, then, came first, the Force which would transform one, or the transformation that would enable one to receive the Force without going mad.

Norman replied by reading a passage from one of Sri Aurobindo's letters to a sadhak who appears to have asked a similar question. "It is a mistake," he writes, "to dwell too much on the lower nature and its obstacles, which is the negative side of the sadhana. They have to be seen and purified, but preoccupation with them as the one important thing is not helpful. The positive side of experience of the descent is the more important thing. If one waits for the lower nature to be purified entirely … before calling down the positive experience, one might have to wait for ever. It is true that the more the lower nature is purified, the easier is the descent of the higher Nature, but it is also and more true that the more the higher Nature descends, the more the lower is purified. Neither the complete purification nor the permanent and perfect manifestation can come all at once; it is a matter of time and patient progress. The two (purification and manifestation) go on progressing side by side and become more and more strong to play into each other's hands – that is the usual course of the sadhana."

We also talked about the importance of psychological attitudes rather than mentally formulated beliefs. Norman got up and went to where some flowers stood in front of his pictures of Sri Aurobindo and the Mother. He picked out a thick-petaled cream-coloured blossom, and gave it to me. "That is a champak flower – you will have seen some champak trees growing near the main entrance to the Ashram. The Mother has given it the name 'Psychological Perfection'. It has five petals, each one standing for one of the attitudes that make up the total perfection, and they are surrender, sincerity, faith or trust, devotion – which includes gratitude – and aspiration – which includes courage. If one aims to develop these qualities, and is persistent in one's efforts – if one does what Sri Aurobindo has called some 'enabling sadhana' – then it is safe to be open to the Force that is here, and one will grow, sooner or later, to the point when the 'reversal of consciousness' happens, and one is born into a new world – an amazing adventure."

I remember, now, that it was a champak flower that the Mother gave me on the 17th June.

*   *   *

30th November

I told Ravindra that in Ambu's room I had seen a photograph of a hatha yogi who was said to have been 350 years old. What about that?

R. said it was quite possible. He had seen such a man himself – a man called Nagna Naresh, or 'the Naked Prince', who used to live outside Amritsar in the barren countryside thereabouts, walking around and living in the fields: a man of very great robustness and physical health, who throughout the year wore only a light muslin cloth round his waist. And this man would never talk of the past or of his age, but said that people who did so were all 'dead men' – that death was behind one, but that in front was only life, and that life was coming to him always out of the future – new forces of health and energy and immortality.

This man said, too, that all men were only 'dead men' because they thought of the past, and reckoned their time according to how many more years they had to live, whereas he rejected death. "Give me your death," he would say, "and I will give you my life". When someone mentioned a great general to him, and how this man had won battles and so on, he had said, "Huh, what is great about killing men that are already dead? If he had killed 10,000 such dead men, what would be the sense of it?"

Ravindra went on to say that 'the Naked Prince' was interesting to talk to, and that he and his brothers would often go out and listen to his conversation. His youngest brother eventually became one of his disciples. He had first discovered him when on a walk. He had noticed water falling from overhead, and had looked up and seen this man high up in a tree, urinating – he would often climb trees. And when he was hungry he would just pluck a handful of leaves and munch them.

166

In the 1930's, when the nationalist movement was very strong, and people talked to him of the poverty of the country and how it was being exploited and so on by the British, he would say, "Poverty? I see no poverty" and point to the trees and the fields and the bushes, which were enough for him to live on!

He used to say that life came to him from the basic elements, but that men who were 'dead' cut themselves off from these sources of health. Thus they would wear clothes to protect themselves from the air, and shoes to insulate themselves from the currents of earth, and they would shelter from life-giving rain, and so on.

He would not let people do pranam or bow before him, but would shout out, "Why do you do that? Why not reverence the life in yourselves. Come, I will show you how to be immortal!" and his disciples certainly seemed healthy, and happy too. They would only eat 'live food'. All cooked food or things made from flour he called 'dead food', so they ate fruit and vegetables and leaves and roots of all sorts … and these people, some of them quite old women, developed such heat in themselves that they could sleep without any covering on the banks of canals in midwinter, when the nights were bitter with frost.

If the guru got a fever he would welcome it, as, he said, the heat was good, and burnt up all sorts of impurities in the body.

As to his age – nobody knew it, because he refused to talk of the past. But the oldest people living in those parts said that he had been just the same when they were small children.

Ravindra said that he himself had not felt greatly attracted to this man because he never spoke of spiritual things, and his way of life was so dull and unproductive – like an animal's – and seemed fully filled up with keeping fit. He never did any work.

*　　*　　*

1st December

Gilchrist and I went this morning to Anilbaran's weekly lecture on the Gita. There were about ten people there, counting ourselves.

Anilbaran came in, tall, bald and stern, looking rather like Goethe in his 'aged eagle' period. He made pranam to us and we to him, seated himself, and asked if we had any questions.

Mr Grunwald, a visitor from Germany, in the front row, asked about 'the Divine as the worker' and 'not doing work for the fruits'.

A. sat plunged in silence, frowning, with eyes closed, then said quietly that these were fundamental questions. If we understood these points we understood the Gita. Slowly he amplified his theme. The Gita did not emphasise karma yoga, nor gnana, nor bhakta, but taught all three equally. However, the Gita's commentators stressed the one of these most suited to their times and opinions. The present age was one when the element of Karma yoga was being emphasised. It was this aspect of the Gita that appealed to the West, and, because the West seized on it, Indians too were looking at the Gita in that light. Indians now followed the West, and it was necessary that they should in this, since the West had much to teach them about the doctrine of work. Western civilisation had this to teach India, for Indians had to learn to live and work in the world, abandoning the apathy and indifference which had so strong a grip on them. Only then could they go on to learn the Life Divine, and, when that was learned, they could teach the West – not before.

Someone then asked if it was the Divine Worker who made mistakes. He replied that in the divine perspective there were no mistakes. It might be necessary for actions to fail in the short run, but ultimately all worked for success. A chess-player might lose a pawn or two, but by that very loss he might win the game. What one had to do was to work for the object set before one: do one's best, but without having any attachment to the result, meeting success or failure with equality. The idea of duty for duty's sake, he went on, also had its place in the West. Did we remember Nelson's signal at Trafalgar? Not 'England expects this day that we shall win this battle', but simply 'England expects this day that every man shall do his duty'. Each man must play his own part and not worry over the success or failure of his own or other's causes. For instance he, when he came first to the Ashram, could not simply get on with his sadhana, but was full of worries about the freedom of India. Sri

Aurobindo had pulled him out of politics but could not pull the ideas of political work out of his head. He would ask Sri Aurobindo, "Is it true that Independence will come?" and Sri Aurobindo would say, "Yes. It is already assured. The decree has already gone forth – nothing can stop it. It is as certain as tomorrow's sunrise." "But *when*?" he would persist, "when will it be?" But then Sri Aurobindo would say, "I do not make prophecies". ... "But give me some hint so that I may know when it is getting near." Sri Aurobindo, though he knew these things, being able to see the whole pattern, the past and present and future, would not be concerned with anything but his own work – but he did say this, "I saw in a vision two eagles meet in the Brenner Pass. When this happens India will soon be free." That was in 1926. During the war Hitler and Mussolini met in the Brenner Pass ...

But Anilbaran wanted something more concrete, so he went to the Mother, and said, "Mother, Sri Aurobindo says India will be free, but he will not say how soon – tell me, so that my mind will be at rest."

The Mother looked at him and said, "The English came to this country because they were asked to, and they will leave in the same way, and when they go they will not be able to go fast enough. And it will happen peacefully." And then she lifted her eyes and looked into space and said, "When you see the Japanese fleet in the Indian Ocean that time will be near".

When India did become free after the war Anilbaran told the Mother how she and Sri Aurobindo had foretold it. She mentioned it to Sri Aurobindo, and he said, "Did we say these things? Have you got it written down? Give that writing to me."

Talking with Prithwisingh, after Anilbaran's lecture, about Sri Aurobindo's prophecies, I commented that he had spoken with equal certainly and emphasis about the victory of Supermind.

Prithwisingh repeated what he had said once before, that Sri Aurobindo had left his physical body, sacrificing this and his personality and foregoing his own full supramentalisation, in order to save time and shorten the sufferings of humanity, and that he had taken up the work from the subtle physical world, from which he was helping the Mother towards her transformation. When this became evident, in 1967, all the world would see and believe that what Sri Aurobindo had taught was true.

The Supramental yoga, meanwhile, was as great an act of faith as the attempts to release energy by splitting the atom. Who could believe, before it happened, that so minute a particle could destroy a whole city and lay waste the country around it?

"I must remind you that I have been an intellectual myself and no stranger to doubts – both the Mother and myself have had one side of the mind as positive and as insistent on practical results and more so than any Russell can be. We could never have been contented with the shining ideas and phrases which a Rolland or another takes for gold coin of Truth. We know well what is the difference between a subjective experience and a dynamic outward-going and realising Force. So although we have faith (and who ever did anything great in the world without having faith in his mission or the Truth at work behind him?), we do not found ourselves on faith alone, but on a great ground of knowledge which we have been developing and testing all our lives. I think I can say that I have been testing day and night for years upon years more scrupulously than any scientist his theory or his method on the physical plane. That is why I am not alarmed by the aspect of the world around me or disconcerted by the often successful fury of the adverse Forces who increase in their rage as the Light comes nearer and nearer to the field of earth and Matter.

"If I believe in the probability and not only possibility, if I feel practically certain of the Supramental Descent (I do not fix a date), it is because I have my grounds for the belief, not a faith in the air. I know that the Supramental Descent is inevitable – I have faith in view of my experience that the time can be and should be now and not in a later age…"

Sri Aurobindo, in a letter of 30.8.32

'No, the Supramental has not descended into the body or into Matter – it is only at the point where such a descent has become not only possible but inevitable; I am speaking, of course, of my

170

experience. But as my experience is the centre and condition of all the rest, that is sufficient for the promise."

Sri Aurobindo, in a letter of 14.11.33

* * *

2nd December

Ravindra said that Anilbaran had been much respected by Sri Aurobindo, that he had been away from the Ashram when Sri Aurobindo had gone into seclusion, but that Sri Aurobindo had made a special exception for him when he came back, giving him an interview and explaining to him why it was necessary for him to retire.

Anilbaran, said R, had a very powerful will. He had made a Buddha-like resolution not to leave the Ashram buildings until he had achieved some goal he had set himself, and as a result had not come out of the Ashram gateway for 23 years, that is from 1926 until 1949.

Similarly he had started doing physical exercises, and nothing now could make him miss these. He had started attending French classes, and although many others had dropped out, because the classes were late at night, Anilbaran was always there. Five years back he had started learning German. He was still carrying on. He would go on with whatever he had begun until he had seen it through to the end.

The Mother had once said that she had seen a vision of Genghis Khan riding furiously towards her and, as he got near, suddenly the face changed and it was Anilbaran. Perhaps, if not a reincarnation, he embodied a similar intensity of will.

R. added that A. was a very intimate friend of his, and that he was always most loving and helpful to him in any time of crisis or difficulty.

He had all his life been a great student of the Gita, and had come originally to Sri Aurobindo for a really spiritual interpretation of it.

* * *

171

Last night Kanti took Gilchrist and me to visit two friends of his, living in the Ashram, to hear some records of Indian music, songs and poetry.

Kishor is about 18 years old and has just begun to train as a photographer. He lives with his widowed mother, a shy, kind-faced lady who knows little English and so left most of the conversation to us, after seating us on wicker chairs in the inner courtyard of the house, and giving us a kind of onion batter or fritter to eat. Kanti told us how she was one of those on the roster of life-guards, who kept watch on people swimming in the sea. This was part of her sadhana.

"All life is yoga," quoted Kishor, smiling.

The first record we heard was one of Tagore reciting one of his poems in a shrill, old man's voice which was, all the same, penetrating and forceful. Next we heard Dilip Kumar Roy singing 'Sivo ham, Sivo ham', followed by another Bengali singer, then some songs of Mirabai, and finally some snake-charming music. This last was most haunting, and of a great complexity of rhythm and variation, with a kind of drone to it.

Kanti said that when this music is played snakes come from every side. Black cobras drop down out of the thatch. Pythons appear ... When this particular recording was included in a film it had caused much trouble because snakes had come to many of the halls and cinemas where the film was being shown – very large snakes some of them – and the audiences had had to leave.

Looking round rather uneasily, I asked Kanti about snake charming. He said that charmers would play their music with one hand, and as the snakes danced in front of them they would seize them by their necks and put them into the basket, without stopping playing. If the music stopped the snake would strike. Of course, he added, most of the snakes used had had their poison removed first.

Kishor then told a story about a boy who had bought a record of the very music we had just heard. He had gone into the jungle, thinking he would play it and attract snakes, like a professional charmer. He put the record on his portable gramophone and played it. A black snake appeared and wove and swayed in front of him, but the record came to an end – the music stopped.

"And then?" we prompted him. Kishor looked solemnly at us through his thick glasses, "The snake bit him and he died."

*   *   *

4th December

"Many are called but few are chosen," said Jesus, and Sri Aurobindo added, "They who choose the Divine are chosen by the Divine."

Last week I picked a strange tulip-like flower growing by a wall and kept it in my room. One day I asked Norman what its Ashram name was, and he said, "The Divine Call."

It seems that I have had this call – but still try to forget that I have heard it, and wish to go home to take leave of my parents, or bury some dead that should bury themselves.

Some say, here, that Sri Aurobindo decided to give up his body because the world was not ready for him, and his disciples were so disappointing …

The other morning, while washing on the open-air landing of the hostel, I felt that I could stay here. The 'block' vanished. I sensed the release from all tension, the freeing of all creative energies, the spring-like joy of true abandonment.

I dressed and at once wrote home explaining how I must stay here. But I could not post this letter.

Later I wrote to the Mother describing what had happened and saying I had to return to England, until I knew more certainly where I should be. I asked if I might postpone leaving until after the special Darshan on 29th February.

In the evening of that same day I received a note from the Mother, which by its simplicity and compassion cancelled much distress.

It will be all right for me to stay until March.

*   *   *

173

Today Eric, the Californian artist, turned up at Ganapatram's again for breakfast. He has brought his wife, Betty, with him this time. They are back from a stay in Japan, where Eric has been learning to paint in the traditional way, with a block of solid ink, a little water and a pointed brush. Every brush-stroke must be clean and faultless, expressing an intuitive understanding of the object, and to be proficient an artist must be in a highly sensitive condition and have developed his technique until it needs no mental effort at all. Eric says, of course, that he has only got a little way, but he is enthusiastic about what he has seen, and about the small successes he has had so far.

After breakfast everybody in the Ashram assembled for a special meditation to commemorate the passing of Sri Aurobindo on the 5th December, 1950. The Mother sat upstairs in the large room where she interviews people, and the sadhaks sat round her on the floor and in Sri Aurobindo's room and in the small connecting room between. Others sat on the stairs down to the Meditation Hall, which was also full, and so on, right into the main courtyard, around the Samadhi and on the verandahs and steps of the buildings that enclose it. Everyone had been told in advance where to sit, and by 9.45 they were all in their places.

Norman had explained to Gilchrist and me that during the half hour of meditation the Mother would gather each person present, one by one, into her consciousness and then raise herself and them to the Divine in an act of offering and surrender. During this time, he said, the Divine became very close to all those so gathered.

At 9.35 Gilchrist and I went upstairs, with many others, and found a place on the floor where we could sit. I could not see the Mother, but it was not too crowded a position. Eric came wandering in, late, and could not find a space, but finally he went into the Hall where the Mother was and people made room for him right at her feet.

The stillness and heaviness of the atmosphere were intense. No-one moved or coughed or made any sound. At times all thought seemed to be silenced, drowned in the Mother's presence. Norman had advised us that it would be unnecessary to make any effort to establish a contact with the Divine by one's self, but that it would be best to adopt a quiet attitude of surrender, physical relaxation and peace, so that the Mother could raise one up herself.

The half hour passed quickly, in an atmosphere of extraordinary concentration. Then a bell from an alarm-clock rang, and people began to stand up, and the Mother left the hall.

For some time people waited in their places. Then they formed a moving queue which circled through Sri Aurobindo's room and then back through the Mother's hall and down the stairs. At the bottom many people were standing, silent and attentive, as if they hoped to see the Mother come down, but she was gone.

This half hour of intense concentration by the Mother was unforgettable, though what effect it has had on me, beyond a slight headache, I don't know. Perhaps the seed within has been helped to grow a little, or the shell around the psychic being has been thinned. Or, more significantly, it was the raising of the consciousness of the group to a new level.

*　*　*

6th December

Recently I was talking to Karl Christiansen, a visiting journalist from Denmark, who I'd met in the Playground. He asked if there would be a meditation there that evening.

"No," I told him, "there are only two a week, on Thursdays and Sundays."

"And then Mother comes, yes?" he queried.

"No, she never comes, now, since she has gone into seclusion," I told him.

"But she is surely there, in the background, in the little room where the photographs are?"

Again I said No. She never came to the Playground for meditation now, ever.

175

"Well, then, I have seen a vision," he exclaimed, "because last night when there was meditation, and I was sitting here, I looked up and saw her in that room. But I never guessed it was a vision. She must have been there for quite a quarter of an hour, and during that time I noticed her whenever I looked into the doorway of the room. That is strange."

*　*　*

7th December

This morning Norman was describing the interment of Sri Aurobindo's body. Udar Pinto with his team at the Harpagon workshops had made a coffin of rosewood, lined with silver and satin, and a deep vault had been excavated under the Service tree in the main Ashram courtyard. The burial had taken place in an unforgettable silence. After the vault had been closed with concrete slabs, the sadhaks, led by Champaklal and Nolini, had each added their portion of earth to fill the space.

Norman also mentioned a visitor, staying in the Ashram at the time, who was known to have a serious criminal record. This man had asked if he might help the group of devotees who were digging the vault. The Mother had accepted his offer, and he had worked with great concentration and devotion, helping to hack out the hard impacted sand.

Afterwards, people had asked the Mother if she was aware of what sort of man he was. She had replied that on this occasion the best side of his nature was uppermost, and that he had contributed a fine energy, and his offering was very acceptable. It was not his past failures but his psychic being that she had seen.

*　*　*

8th December

Godfrey was talking tonight about the Cross. He said that when he looked at one it gave him some kind of deep inner satisfaction. Before coming to the Ashram a crucifix had struck him as something rather morbid, but now he had one on his desk

176

always – a cross with a skull and bones at its foot, which had been blessed for him by the Mother. He felt that so much of life was an effervescence, vital or mental, a matter of superficial interest and attachment, but that the Cross stood for something profound and permanent and serious; it was not tragic, because death was not something fearful or final, but triumphant because it was the prelude to resurrection.

He also told me that the longer he stayed here the more Christ meant to him, and he did not see how this could be otherwise. The fact that Christ meant more to him did not imply that Sri Aurobindo and the Mother meant less, but that he was growing in his capacity to respond to the greatness and divinity of all three. People who asked him if he was a Christian or not were missing the point. He did not know or indeed care – such categorising was unhelpful.

He sat for a time every day in a Catholic church, because he found the Mother there, and because it was widening his horizon beyond the Ashram. He didn't like the 'frog-in-a-well' mentality and felt that to become a member of a sect was to be avoided; here it could lead to 'Ashram egotism'.

Godfrey said that year by year, since coming here, he had felt his consciousness had been heightened, not by his own efforts but by the Mother. It was up to us to keep right with her, that was all, and she did the sadhana for us. When he had first come to the Ashram his had been a normal materialist consciousness, concerned wholly with outward things. Now it was more inward, but even outward things were richer – for instance colours and flowers.

*　*　*

9th December

Today there was a collective meditation to mark the anniversary of the interment of Sri Aurobindo's body, on the 9th December, 1950.

The Mother came down and sat in a chair at the foot of the stairs opposite the Samadhi, in the Ashram courtyard. She looked pale and bent and unsmiling, but, after she had sat down, a silence descended which one could feel. Thoughts seemed to be cut down to a few slow stragglers. Attentive, one sensed a revelation imminent – that the clouds obscuring one's consciousness might roll back, to disclose an unimaginable dimension. This did not happen, but at one stage it felt as if the whole key had changed and one was 'centred down' into a wider, deeper level of being. The mind was active still, but with periods of vibrant silence between its voices, and there seemed to occur a concentration of one's energies more in the heart than in the head, which remained but as a remote and superficial talker, no longer dominating the stage.

After half an hour the small alarm clock broke the silence, and the Mother was gone again, upstairs. Slowly people dispersed, and the crowded courtyard emptied. A Chinaman remained crouched on his mat, for a long time, his head dropped far forward and his hands hanging limply from the wrists, his long narrow feet folded under him. On a seat, near the corner of the court by the garage, a small American lady sat with eyes closed, oblivious, her face pale and faintly smiling.

*   *   *

10th December

This afternoon I had tea with Godfrey. He lives near the Ashram main buildings, in a small room that opens on a flat roof-top or terrace. He seems better, more relaxed.

He showed me some short stories he has written. They stay in the mind, leaving a flavour of mystery and wistfulness.

Talking about writing, he said, "One must be able to put things simply, in a language that everyone can understand – no long learned words". (pause) "Though a big word in the right place is a very fine thing."

Later he spoke about the Mother: "I have no use for those people who go looking for the Divine in human beings. Sometimes one may see this, this miracle – I have experienced it myself several times – but it is a Grace, and it does not come by looking for it.

178

Once I remember seeing Satprem radiant as a god, after having had an interview with the Mother – and of course I have seen this thing in the Mother herself more than in anyone. I remember her coming down the stairs towards Amrita's room, behind Nolini. And she must have been recently in a state of communion, in Sat-Chit-Ananda, because her face was flecked with the gold-dust of ecstasy – with flakes or pearls or drops of the divine light. And Nolini was talking to her about furniture, the disposition of this or that table or chair. And she was giving him a portion of her attention – even in that state she had to come down and listen to what he was saying…"

And in Vinoba Bhave he had also known the transparency – the shining through of the inner divinity.

*   *   *

12th December

This week, Purani went off in an Ashram car on a short lecture excursion to the south. He asked Doris and me to go with him. One of the places to which he had been invited was Gandhigram, between Madurai and Tanjore.

We arrived in the afternoon, turning off the road up a track that led through small bushes and trees to the scattered houses of the settlement. Here we were met by Purani's friend Chandrishankar, who welcomed us with quiet pleasure and took us to the guest-house, a small bungalow overlooking a paddy field.

After a cup of tea there, we went on a tour round some of the community's departments. Chandrishankar introduced us first to a woman with a strikingly noble face who looked after the small foundling hospital. She showed us about ten babies lying in their cradles, each one under a kind of meat-cover. Some were only a few weeks old. We were told how they had saved one baby found lying on the nearby railway lines; another had actually been thrown from a passing train; a third had been discovered half covered over with earth in a local burial ground. To such desperate behaviour had their mothers been driven by their poverty. In other rooms we saw older

179

children, aged from two to four, sitting on mats having tea. When we entered they all stood up and greeted us, in a most disciplined way.

Our woman guide, we were told afterwards, was a high caste Keralan, who had entirely renounced her previous life so that she could work here, refusing many offers of marriage, some of them made to her since coming to Gandhigram.

We next saw several cottages in which men and women were learning village crafts such as the manufacture of soap from the nuts of a tree, the extraction of oil from seeds, the making of paper from waste-paper and rags, weaving at hand-looms and, of course, spinning. In one room we found from thirty to forty people sitting on the ground, men on one side, women on the other, hard at work, each with a special spinning apparatus.

The aim of the settlement is to help the villages in the surrounding area. Villagers come and stay for a period of training and then go home having learned at least one craft or trade, and also it is hoped, having absorbed something of the Gandhian ethic and ideal of service. 'Basic education' is stressed – the relation of learning to practical work. For a part of every day each student works in school and for a part he works at a craft or in the fields. The school is growing in size and improving in standard, and soon the Principal intends to extend it to more advanced levels. Buildings for this higher education are being constructed, again, of course, by the students themselves. In time the settlement may become a rural university.

Purani asked a lot of questions concerning the economics of the place. We were told that each department aims to be self supporting. Many of their products are bought by the Government, so they have, to a certain extent, an assured market. Purani thought this 'feather-bedding' a bad thing; he was also critical of the messy disorder of some of the workshops that we saw, and compared them unfavourably with the economy and organisation of the Mother's running of the Ashram … We did not have time to see the agricultural, medical or rural hygiene departments, nor the 'rehabilitation of fallen women' which we understood they also had in hand. Instead we were taken back to our rooms for more tea.

180

We sat in a part of the library where, besides works by Gandhi and Gandhians, I was surprised to see a case containing the writings of the great American democrats – Jefferson, Franklin and others, while balancing each other, on either side of the door, were large framed photographs of Gandhi and Lincoln.

When tea was over we were hurried to the prayer-hall for the evening service, after which Purani was to speak. He had been unusually silent and rather uneasy since his arrival, pondering this talk he was to give. Sri Aurobindo had differed from Gandhi in many ways, notably over the doctrine of passive resistance, and Purani's audience might, I imagined, be a critical one. He had asked Chandrishankar what subject he should take, but Chandrishankar had insisted that he should speak on whatever aspect of Sri Aurobindo he liked, which did not make things easier.

Arriving somewhat late at the prayer-hall we were hustled in and guided to sit down on mats near the front. Doris was shepherded to the left of the hall with the women; Purani and I to the right. Ahead of us stood a brass ceremonial lamp, surrounded by a design done in coloured powder on the floor, and on its left, facing us, were three young women and two men. These took turns in conducting the meeting – reading prayers, singing devotional songs and leading the hymns. Readings were chosen from the writings of Hinduism – the Gita and Vinoba's comments thereon – from the Koran, and from the missionary Stanley Jones, representing Christianity.

The service over, Purani was invited to come and stand at a microphone in front, and was introduced by Chandrishankar: "We are indeed fortunate today in having in our midst a very great man… For many years I have been asking him to come. Now he is here…"

Purani asked what language he should speak in, Hindi or English. The Principal said English would be best, and that there would be a translation into Tamil afterwards.

First, said Purani, squaring his thick shoulders, he would make clear what his relationship with the Mahatmaji had been. They had both been in the freedom movement in Gujarat in the early days, and he, Purani, had agreed to co-operate with Gandhi and work for him wherever their aims were the same. But he had always made it clear that for him non-violence was not an essential part of the movement. He had always said that when a man went to fight for his country there was a fifty-fifty chance whether he would *suffer* or *inflict* violence, he might *die* for his motherland, which was a noble thing… (At this point I sensed a muttering and restlessness among the Gandhians behind me). But, Purani went on, Gandhi had entrusted many difficult tasks and missions to him and his group as a sign of his faith in him, and they had worked together until the time came when he had finally come to Pondicherry and stayed there at the request of his guru, Sri Aurobindo.

Purani then launched into a critique of true and patriotic citizenship: it depressed him, he said, when he travelled about India, to see how many people, all these years after Independence, did not seem to know that they were free, and how there were others who wanted to separate, and split up their own country which they had struggled so hard to liberate. "But", and he raised his voice, "India is *One*, and India is *Free*!" When he saw a tap on a railway station left running it made him sad. Did people not realise it was their own water that was wasting, not someone else's? And he had heard that Indians now stole the light-bulbs from railway compartments … Did they not realise they were stealing their own property? These things were their own, not belonging to the British or anyone else anymore. Indians must realise these things – develop a sense of their responsibilities, group, civic and national, and realise what a heritage they possessed … "India is *One*, and India is *Free*!" He lifted his fist and stamped his foot, and his listeners became silent, watching him.

However he grew quieter, himself, after this, telling us that not only must we wake up to a hard-working dutiful life, but that we must be satisfied with nothing short of a Divine Life on earth, and he went on to develop this theme: a man must find out what is God's will for his life; he must be continually asking God to tell him what is his work; as he walks and as he works he must say, "Show me what is your will for me, and what I am to do," and then the knowledge would come to him and he would begin to grow.

He concluded by quoting a Vedic scripture to the effect that there are three kinds of men – those absorbed in the ordinary life; those who through effort grow out of this, the vibhutis; and thirdly the avatars, who are the Divine Himself living the Divine Life. And he implied that this last was what Sri Aurobindo had been, and why he, the speaker, was his disciple.

The Principal translated some of the address, and then, as it was getting late, said that the heads of departments were to tell people the rest. Getting stiffly to our feet we went back to the guest-house for supper.

By now we were feeling weary after a long day, but no sooner was supper over than eight teachers and senior students came into the room and asked Purani to talk to them on the philosophy of Sri Aurobindo. Puraniji seated himself cross-legged in the centre of a large divan and the eight sat in a crescent around him. He talked fast and well, starting with the evolutionary side of Sri Aurobindo's thought.

Doris, sitting at one end of the divan, fell asleep after about an hour and a half, but the students seemed interested and towards the end managed to ask a few questions. Finally, they left, thanking Purani respectfully, and we went to bed.

Next day, at about 5 a.m. Purani got up and walked off by himself to the foot of a nearby range of small mountains. What energy he has for a 65 year old! I remember someone telling me that up to a year or two ago he would still join in bouts of Indian wrestling in the sand-pit, as well as give instruction. In his revolutionary days he had run a physical training club.

After breakfast we were told it was time for the daily parade, and we were escorted at a brisk pace to the saluting base and given places on the raised platform, alongside the Principal and heads of departments. In front of us, by the flag-pole, stood a very upright and efficient young woman who gave ringing words of command to the groups of students and workers drawn up on the parade ground. She brought them to attention for prayer and for the singing of 'Bande Mataram' and 'Jana, Gana, Mana,' and then, having stood them at ease, approached Purani, saluted, and asked him if he would speak to the assembly.

Purani stepped smartly to a microphone and in a stirring voice began, "*Soldiers*" – at which I groaned inwardly – but then, "Soldiers of *Peace*!" (dramatically). "You are engaged on a great work. Peace is sorely needed in this world, not only between individuals, and between groups, but between parts of the nation, and between nations themselves in the world community. Last night I was very glad to hear you sing of the Bharat Shakti – the vigour and strength of the Motherland – for it is indeed strength that is needed for this peace we work for. For peace is no negative thing, peace is not merely an abstention from violence, not a passivity, not inert or supine. Peace is a positive power, and to build it in the world we must have the power of God, for true harmony can only come when we belong to the Divine and live in the power of the Divine Life – and that is my message to you today."

• • •

At Annamalai University, our next stopping-place, we called on Prof. T. C. N. Singh. We caught him just as he was cycling away from his house to go into town. Purani said we needed a wash and a cup of coffee, and he replied that we must certainly come to his home. He dismounted and came back with us, and was altogether most hospitable and friendly.

Having washed, we sat down with him in his front room and drank our coffee. He is a botanist, and the walls of the room were hung with many dried plant specimens – root, leaf, flower and seed. I had heard of him many times in connection with his experiments on the effect of music on plants – how he had made plants excel themselves by playing ragas to them. I had wanted to meet him, and now here we were sitting next to each other, and he began, himself, without any prompting, to tell us quite naturally about his work.

He explained how it was reasonable to suppose that sound waves had an effect on plants, since light waves and heat waves did. Darwin had played the bassoon to try and excite some sensitive plants, but without success, and no-one had seriously experimented until he himself had begun soon after 1950. Tests made since then had

184

shown that sound waves vibrate the cell walls in plant protoplasm and that this stimulates a faster release of oxygen, that is to say, the process of photosynthesis is accelerated and the growth of tissue goes ahead quicker.

Results had been quite spectacular, he said. It was possible to relay a tune to crops growing in the open, using a mobile sound-unit, and after doing this a farmer in Ontario, Canada, had reported a 66% increase in yield from a ten acre wheat field. Tests on paddy grown near Pondicherry had shown increased yields of from 40-60% compared to control plots of the same variety of paddy grown under identical conditions, but not musically treated. Tobacco grown near Annamalai had improved by 65%.

I asked him what made him begin this line of research. He replied that a South African concert pianist had told him that the roses outside the windows of the ground-floor room in which she practised every day had done much better than elsewhere in her garden. Also he had discovered that crops grown near a railway line grew better than those further away, presumably because of the vibrations made by passing trains. Indeed this fact was recognised by local farmers, who asked a higher price for land next to the track. Telephone poles or electricity installations, he said, also made their vicinity more productive, because of the humming they produced.

"What about bees?" I asked.

Yes, he thought the buzzing of insects helped plants, and probably bird-song did, too. Not all sounds were helpful, however. To excite favourable results they must be of a certain pitch. Ultra-sonic waves were bad, and a man's singing voice would have no effect, being too low. Women's voices were in the right frequency range, but his most successful experiments had been made with music produced by violin, flute and nadaswaram. He had also used tuning-forks, a harmonium and the veena.

The sound administered had to be rhythmic and harmonic, although it could be the repetition of just one, two or three notes. The plants must not be excited for too long – not more than half an hour a day – or else they got browned off, and, most strange, for the best results the *same tune* must be repeated every time. At one stage Professor Singh experimented with a plot of mixed vegetables, giving them half an hour a day of a radio music programme. The vegetables did not improve – indeed began to die – except for the potato which alone grew faster.

Plants which had the same Karnatic ragas played to them regularly, for half an hour a day, became very much more vigorous and sturdy, produced leaves of a darker green, flowered sooner and had more profuse root systems than the musically deprived control. Seeds were found to germinate sooner after being subjected to the ringing of an electric bell, and seedlings raised with music were more disease resistant …

Professor Singh's enthusiasm became contagious as he pointed out what the results of his research could mean to under-developed and hungry countries.

We asked him if he had had much opposition. He said some people were amused, some indifferent, but some had recognised the importance of what he was doing.

He then told us of a visit by Professor J. B. S. Haldane to see his work. Haldane had been sceptical at first. Then he, Singh, had told him, "There is no magic about it. You do the experiment for yourself. See, here are two plants under glass domes, where we can measure the oxygen content of the air. If you will shake this hand bell beside one of them, for half an hour, you will see for yourself how the oxygen content goes up". Haldane did this, and the oxygen release doubled. After this he was on his side, when he had seen the truth of the matter for himself.

Professor Singh had complained that being a university lecturer and teacher, he had only two hours a day – from 7 to 9 a.m. – in which to experiment. Professor Haldane had said that he must not try or expect to do everything himself. It was for him to start this completely new branch of study, but he could do no more. There would be at least a hundred years of research-work ahead.

Among the things which have to be discovered *for each type of crop* are (1) the optimum pitch of sound, (2) the optimum length of dose, (3) the optimum rhythm or time beat, (4) the best time of day for playing the music – cassava liked evening ragas – (5) the best length of harmony to be played before repetition, and (6) the loudness of the music.

Before we left him, Professor Singh showed us photographs of a dancing girl performing inside a circle of potted asters. He said that the rhythmic vibration of the ground, made by her feet, had resulted in the asters growing higher, by a third, than their less fortunate unstimulated fellows, and that they had bloomed from ten days to a fortnight sooner.

He also showed us a gold medal which he had been awarded for his work. He said he had been encouraged by the Mother, who had told him in advance that the field tests would be a success. When he had been given the medal he had taken it straight to the Ashram, and shown it to the Mother, and thanked her for her help.

By the time we left Annamalai the sun was getting low, but it was still light enough to see the damage caused by the recent monsoon rains. The road was broken by flood-water in places and we had to make detours. We saw where the water had cut deep gulleys in the sandy earth and removed tons of soil, eating into the banks on which the road ran, laying bare the roots of trees, and where it had left whole areas stripped of vegetation, so that they looked like the Crau in Provence. The papers say that in the Chidambaram district the flooding has rendered 10,000 habitations useless, and that whole villages lie water-logged, with their mud walls crumbling.

The paddy alone seemed to be flourishing, in spite of its having neither music nor dancing girls. Perhaps the sound of our horn was a help.

*   *   *

15th December

This morning there was a lecture in the School by A. N. Chubb, an Indian Professor of Philosophy on a visit from Calcutta.

He talked about the theory of knowledge. After outlining the difference between analytic and synthetic propositions, and the meaning of the terms a priori and a posteriori, necessary and contingent, he came to the matter of metaphysical propositions.

187

The scientist could check his hypotheses against sense-experience, but it did not follow that such verifiable propositions were the only ones having any meaning. Positivists were right in saying that metaphysical statements are literally nonsense, but did it follow that one should then agree with the early Wittgenstein that "What we cannot speak about we must pass over in silence"? He, Professor Chubb, thought not.

Certainly, metaphysics could not be explained by verbalising. Either one reduced it to terms of one's own limited experience, or left it unintelligible, by the use of equivalents. There was no problem for the naïve, nor for the mystic, but there was one for the metaphysician: how could one express the ineffable?

Professor Chubb suggested that the answer lay in the use of analogical notions and of words as conceptual symbols, not as literal representations. To do this, the symbols must have a point of contact with our normal experience, but without being reduced to the ordinary. When symbols have *no* contact with our experience then indeed the metaphysical statements that employ them are meaningless.

But metaphysical statements are unique in that they make a demand on the hearer. For example, the statement 'God exists' is an imperative, saying 'Realise God exists'. The person who would understand such a proposition must start with faith, and be prepared to listen, and have an impulse towards finding the full meaning of which so far he has only an inkling.

Professor Chubb saw the work of the religious philosopher as the building of a bridge from the phenomenal world to the noumenal world. For Sri Aurobindo, faith is not dependent on reason, but comes first, born of the soul's secret knowledge, which philosophy then attempts to make explicit. He quoted from one of Sri Aurobindo's letters: 'Faith is the soul's witness to something not yet manifested, achieved or realised, but which yet the Knower within us, even in the absence of all indications, feels to be true or supremely worth following.'

The professor spoke without notes, scanning the faces in his audience, observing whether or not he was being understood. At the end of his talk there were questions, and I found myself in an unexpected dialogue with him, which continued after the meeting dispersed. He told me he had studied at Oxford, before the war, under the philosopher R. G. Collingwood, whom he admired.

Traditional philosophy in the West has suffered the crippling effects of positivism, he said, precisely because it became separated from an askesis or practice for developing the consciousness of its practitioners. Because philosophy had become an architecture of words it had had to be undermined and demolished. He contrasted the objectified concept of God with the sense of an indwelling Presence 'closer than hands and feet, closer even than breathing'. He spoke of 'the integral existentialism' of Sri Aurobindo.

* * *

16th December

Today I talked with a German Pastor, Heinz Kappes, who is visiting the Ashram. He is a stocky, elderly man, who has retired after a long pastorate that had involved resistance to Hitler, and a stay in a concentration camp. He has begun translating Sri Aurobindo into German.

Soon after his arrival here he had had an interview with the Mother. He said he had come away with his eyes full of tears, that her presence was 'absolutely overwhelming', as if heaven had concentrated in her to meet humanity at every level. He thought she was different for each person who met her.

He said that the way to Sri Aurobindo for the West was through the Cloud of Unknowing, Meister Eckhart, Ruysbroeck, St. John of the Cross, St. Teresa, and through George Fox. He said Fox's experience was profound: his vision of the ocean of light and love and of the ocean of darkness and death, and his early sufferings which led to his finding for himself what he afterwards found in the Bible. But Fox did not have either the training or the inclination to articulate his experiences, whereas Eckhart did.

Heinz also talked about the mysticism of St Paul, and quoted the Greek for three types of body mentioned by him (vital, mental

189

and spiritual?). I must ask him again about these. He said that Paul foresaw 'the New Man.'

He described how, after Sri Aurobindo had taken hold of him (he had been in Palestine at the time), he returned to Germany and took up his work there again as a pastor, and he told how, before doing so, he went before his bishop and fellow clergy and explained to them what his position was. He had said how he had studied European mysticism, Hinduism, Buddhism, Taoism, Sufism, Hasidism, and, finally, Sri Aurobindo – and how all this had made him a better Christian. When he had finished, the bishop said he could not understand a word of what he had been saying but that he could carry on as a pastor.

The crux of Christianity to him seemed to be transformation. He said the Celtic church had had the secret of the New Man, and that it had learned what could be assimilated from the Druids and Celtic occultism, and that until it became absorbed by the Roman church it had had a life of power and spirit.

Talking of 'the New Man', Heinz Kappes said that he had been present when a specialist in psycho-somatic medicine had addressed a gathering of German clergy and theologians, and that this man, a sceptical and rather cynical fellow, had asked what were the characteristics of a man who had been reborn. When he, Heinz Kappes, had heard the lame and faltering reply that was given, he realized how much had been lost by orthodox Christianity. Was not this being born again central – the very crux of the matter? He did not feel that the kind of conversion preached by Billy Graham was the answer, at least not for all people. Some people were reborn slowly, some dramatically quickly, but for most they had to be born again and again, day by day.

I do not think his idea of rebirth is quite the same as the radical realization spoken of by the Mother. For instance, in a talk with the children in June 1958 she said:

"You become a new person, and whatever may be the path or the difficulties of the path afterwards, that feeling never leaves you. It is not even something – like many other experiences – which withdraws, passes into the background, leaving you externally with a kind of vague memory to which it is difficult to cling, whose remembrance grows faint, blurred – it is not that. You *are* a new person and definitively that, whatever happens. And even all the incapacity of the mind, all the difficulties of the vital, all the inertia of the physical are unable to change this new state – a new state which makes a *decisive* break in the life of the consciousness. The being one was before and the being one is after, are no longer the same. The position one has in the universe and in relation to it, is no longer the same: it is a true reversal which can never be undone again. That is why when people tell me, 'I would like to know whether I am in contact with my soul or not', I say, 'If you ask the question, that is enough to prove that you are not.'"

*　*　*

17th December

What distinguishes faith from credulity?

When I read Sri Aurobindo (or Swedenborg or Rudolf Steiner) how can I judge the truth of their experience when it exceeds my own by such a range of dimensions?

One's own experience must still be one's touchstone, as far as it goes. But if we find that the geography of the other worlds, when we begin to glimpse them, corresponds with the descriptions these travellers bring back, then we are encouraged to trust them and follow their instructions for the next part of the journey. If not, then we must be clear and honest about it.

The scientific attitude seems to apply to all areas of knowledge and experience. It implies an openness to facts, the rejection of beliefs based on superstition, a concern with truth, and the testing of theory where possible, involving the development of a method suitable to what is being researched.

For me, I have an intuitive response to the authority of Sri Aurobindo's writings, which gives me faith in what he is saying. However, the great empty words like 'The Divine', 'the Psychic

191

Being', 'Soul', and indeed 'Life' and 'Love', remain to be filled with meaning – more and more until we die, I suppose, and beyond.

*   *   *

19th December

At the end of the day, I hear, as in a dream, Godfrey's lilting Scots voice talking. He is recreating a mood, using words more skilfully than I can recall or record. He is the aboriginal story-teller, moulding his listeners' minds, and at the same time re-establishing in his own mind the reasons for his persuasions.

He is talking of the Mother, as usual. At first he was not impressed by her, not at all. Indeed he found things to criticise in her, and in the attitude of others towards her. But, then, within a month, he had realized there was something quite extraordinary about her. At first he was highly critical of those who knelt at her feet and worshipped her. After a month he was doing the same, because he knew that here was the Divine. And this in spite of his Presbyterian up-bringing.

He spoke of looking into the Mother's eyes. "Now, at first, I took them to be somewhat cold and impersonal and I didn't like looking into them. But one day I was kneeling before her and I looked up into her eyes and found I could not only look into them but go deep into them, too. With most people, you know, there is a barrier behind the eyes, made by that person's feelings or thoughts, and that stops you. But when I looked into the Mother's eyes I found this barrier was not there. Her eyes were truly gateways to the soul. And I found I could enter. There was a deep inviting territory behind her eyes, calm and joyful, and I could penetrate into that place and find myself there, by gazing. And this was a strangely delightful experience, you know," and he laughed, "and I would always be doing it when I got the opportunity – and I think she must have known all about it.

"But sometimes she showed a different aspect of the divine nature, and she would express the force of Maha-Kali – and especially on Darshan days. And one could describe what happened then as the transmitting of quanta of divine energy, like white particles which proceeded from her eyes to the eyes of those who passed before her.

192

A row of people would process slowly in front of her, on a Darshan day, and to each there would be this gift of a charge of the Divine Substance – like a white bead shot from her eyes... And for each person who came before her she had to decide or know intuitively 'Is this one open?' and then, 'How much can he or she take?' – for we can only bear a little of this immensely powerful substance. And, you know, it is never that the Divine is unwilling to give, but that He cannot, either because we are closed to Him or because we cannot sustain or utilize the gift. I remember once I was in a very devoted and pure mood, and I passed before the Mother and she imparted a charge of Shakti so powerful that I felt struck motionless. I could not move, and then I was shaking like a leaf, and what I remember above all was her look of apology and compassion for having hurt me unwittingly. For she is pure goodness and love.

"I remember kneeling before the Mother, one day. And one can never know what may happen on such occasions. She leaned forward and seemed literally to take something from my head – and throw it away. I believe she removed some obstruction, some karmic weight from my mind. Oh, I know I'm not a saintly or highly developed being or anything like that – but ever since then my consciousness has been lighter, somehow – not so moody or anxious.

"And I have seen the Mother take away grief from a person, too. There was a woman who came to her in an extremity of sorrow, an Indian woman who had lost her only child in a very tragic way. She was wild and distraught with weeping, but the Mother placed her hand on her head and she became calm and peaceful and went away quite changed. And here this is no uncommon occurrence. The Mother can actually take away grief and remove it from a person."

*　　*　　*

21st December

He is brisk and purposeful in his movements. He carries a black brief-case, and is full of an alert intelligence. He is a Fellow of St. Anthony's College, Oxford.

"You have been here nearly a year, you say?"

193

"Yes. How long will *you* be staying?"

"I shall only be here for two days, unfortunately. I have a rather full programme – but you, what are you doing here? I am fascinated by this place and the way it is run. Why don't you apply to your old college for a research grant, and you could write a paper on the funding and economic organisation of the Ashram. You are extremely well-placed. You know the people. I'm serious…"

*   *   *

5th January, 1960

Dear Anthony and Mary,

It is raining, so I am sitting in my room until my class begins at 10.40. Since Christmas I've being teaching in the International Centre of Education (i.e. school) belonging to the Ashram. I have eight pupils only, aged between 17 and 22, four m. and four f. I see them for 50 minute sessions on Mondays, Wednesdays and Fridays, to help them with their English. They are quite keen. We read a book called 'Achievement' – brief lives of characters such as the Great Mogul, Abraham Lincoln, Tsar Peter, Florence Nightingale and the like – and intermittently we resort to a grammar book. I've learned a lot. Some of the students have been going off to Madras to see the Australian test-match, this week, so the class has been smaller still. Next week I am to start reading 'The Merchant of Venice' with some senior students.

There is a visitor called Gilchrist, from South Africa, staying in the hostel now. He was a Londoner until he went to Johannesburg 25 years back. He is very quiet and puzzled by this place. There is so much freedom. He says that all his life he has been leading a regimented existence, organised by someone else… He hopes to stay here another four or five months. It will be an experience for him. He does yogic postures, or asānas, on the bed in his room. These keep one fit, being an eastern variety of P.E. without the snap and violence. The benefit accrues through being able to stay, without movement, in certain positions where some muscles are flexed and others relaxed, or some nerves or blood channels or guts are

194

subjected to pressure or released from it, i.e. it is not the movements that count, as in western exercises, but the static tensions and stresses – coupled with relaxed abdominal breathing. It has nothing to do with spirituality, except that a healthy body helps as a basis for anything. Also it is said to calm and control the nerves, so that if necessary one can sit for long periods without restlessness. It is not looked upon as important by most people here, which disappoints Gilchrist, as he has become quite proficient. There is one Indian called Ambu, however, who is a master of asānas, and we have tea with him sometimes, and he gives us demonstrations on the floor. He has a perfect body, like a boy of 18, although he is 50. He is a very lively fellow, full of vitality and laughter. One day he showed us a collection of photographs of himself in every conceivable posture, always apparently quite relaxed and at ease. A French doctor was so incredulous at some of the poses that he whipped him off to the hospital for X-ray photos, to see if he had a skeleton, and, if so, where the bones went. We saw some of these X-ray pictures.

There is also a tall handsome Frenchman staying here, from Madagascar. He barely speaks to Gilchrist or me, but reads and studies in his room, or stalks off to the main Ashram buildings. I went with him to the Ashram theatre, once, to see a modern Sanskrit play, put on by a visiting drama group – a very dreary sight. It seemed to last about four hours, and, apart from the language trouble, had no plot, no pace and no variety in it. I don't like Sanskrit plays. But perhaps the classical ones are different.

On Christmas Day the European visitors each received a Christmas card and a little basket of gifts chosen and packed by the Mother. I had a fine illustrated diary, a note-book in a plastic cover, a pencil, an orange, some nuts, a chocolate bun, a piece of soap and a tin of Heinz asparagus soup. In the morning there was school! (The only holiday the school has is about a month from mid-November to mid-December.) But in the evening there was a big gathering in the Ashram theatre, where a casuarina tree had been set up, hung about with coloured lights and decorations, and around 2,000 people – ashramites, children and many townspeople – were all given presents. These were distributed by Mona, an English lady, who stood by the Christmas tree and acted as Father Christmas. We were given bottles of aerated fruit drink, and a loudspeaker broadcast recordings of Ashram children singing carols. It was a memorable scene.

How go things with you? I hope you had some profit out of the farm last year, and that the family is fit.

Best wishes for the rest of the New Year.

With love, Dick.

* * *

7th January

Madame K. lives alone in a dark one-storey house in south-east Pondicherry. She has a garden shaded with mango, lime, palm and drumstick trees, with crotons in pots along the wall. And Tou-Tou the bitch watches under the trees for crows to drop odd pieces of carrion and bone. There is a pillared verandah, and inside the house two long rooms, each with an end window onto the street.

Madame K., aged around 65, stands upright and solid between two pillars of the verandah, and greets me in slow high-pitched French. She shows me the garden, the trees and the crotons and Tou-Tou chewing a bone. Then she begins to speak warmly of the Mother, whom she has known for many years, but she criticises the ashramites. She also opens a box of biscuits and pours out a glass of orangeade.

"Eat the biscuits quickly before the others come. I do not want them to have any," she says. "And drop a few pieces on the floor for Tou-Tou who will be most grateful."

Sitting down behind her powerful squat projector she shows colour-slides of Kalimpong. "I went there to stay with a friend," she tells me. "The Mother said I could check the Pali text of the Dhammapada for her, as I would not have much to do. So I did that and took photographs. This is a Tibetan lama, a refugee, with the possessions he was able to rescue. This is a hill woman, a Lepsha – see her necklace of gold rings. It is worth 300 rupees."

196

And so on. She has taken many very good colour pictures of people in the market, in temples, in shops and on the streets, and some fine views over the mountains towards Kanchenjunga, an aloof peak, covered in snow and sometimes partly obscured in mist.

Afterwards I have a cup of tea, stirred with a Tibetan silver teaspoon, and come away.

"Next Sunday I will show you Darjeeling," she calls.

*   *   *

14th January

A sadhak who had lived here for many years, was sad because he had had no 'experiences' – no visions, ecstasies, profound dreams or signs that he was on the right track. He wrote to Sri Aurobindo about it, and Sri Aurobindo replied, "There were two men travelling to Calcutta by train. One looked out of the window all the way, and saw many landscapes – hills, rivers, and plains. The other man leaned back in his corner and slept, and saw nothing. Both men got to Calcutta together."

*   *   *

16th January

After Balcony this morning I went swimming with Behram and Bapsie. They used to live in Bombay, where Behram had worked for the Post Office. As we walked back from the sea they described how, after attending the Sri Aurobindo Centre there, they had taken the decision to come here together to live a life of sadhana, and how the Mother had accepted them and put them in charge of the Guest House. They told me about it in the same happy, shy way that a young couple in the West might describe how they had come to get married.

After I had left them to return to my room I went along a side-street where there were impressive threshold patterns in front of the small Tamil houses. Each is done very early in the day by a woman or girl who, after cleaning a piece of road or path in front of her house, then takes a handful of what looks like flour and dribbles it through

197

her fingers into the most complex and often beautiful pattern. Some are geometrical, others full of baroque curves and movement; a few have flower motifs. They are produced quickly and unfalteringly, with no rubbing out, and no two houses seem to have the same design. Each day I try to memorise one, and reproduce it on paper in my room afterwards. So far I've collected about forty-two.

Before lunch, outside the Governor's Palace, near the Flame of the Forest tree that leans over the path, I met a bearded sadhu, who asked me where he could find Sri Aurobindo. He would not accept from me that he was dead. His eyes were peculiarly dark and glowing, as if he had a very high fever.

After tea I visited an interesting exhibition of photographs taken by members of the Ashram. There were some particularly fine studies of children, flowers and animals. Some had won awards in international competitions.

In the evening Gilchrist and I went to a sadhak's flat where, sitting cross-legged on the floor, we listened to music for about an hour and a half. The performers played the veena and the tabla, or small drums, and there was some singing. Incense was set burning before large pictures of Sri Aurobindo and the Mother, and the atmosphere became very pure and intense.

THE SANNYASIN

Do not speak to me of richness or poorness
Of how to wear my rags or of what to eat.
Do not ask me where I shall sleep,
For I live in the house of timelessness.

Men count their properties and their possessions
But I count the sands of the sea-shore
And the handfuls of stones in the river-beds,
For I am in the house of timelessness.

The sun and the green earth, what are these?
I see the shining universe like a picture.
I speak to you – but what is speaking
For one who is in the house of timelessness?

Oh it is well furnished, the world has less.
But why do you look strangely at me?
It is so silent. Will you not talk with me
In the house of timelessness where I live?

*   *   *

18th January

On the ground floor of Golconde there is a cool, airy space, opening at both ends on the Japanese garden, like a wide passage. There are concrete benches down the side and in the middle a few round tables with chairs by them. Doris and I were sitting here, about to have tea in the shade with Mrs. Grunwald, a large motherly Dutch lady, aged about 60, with grey fuzzy hair and kind eyes.

Doris had produced some biscuits and a girl had just brought us some tea, when suddenly Mr. Grunwald, the Dutch lady's German husband, came in. He sat down on the fourth chair at our table and began at once to tell us about what he had been doing that morning. He was in an eager boyish state of excitement, full of his experience.

"I have zis morning been to ze last rites of a friend of mine, who yesterday died," he began, mopping his bald head.

He went on to tell us that the man had had a stroke and had been unconscious for some days. His family had been called and had been present when he died.

"Zey say zat as he passed away he vas for a moment bathed in a golden light – ze Mother's light."

He had been asked to the cremation ceremony, and had found it most interesting. He looked around at us with an alert seriousness, and proceeded to describe how the body was laid out at the burning-place, and the face anointed with a strong scent. Then the family had walked round it holding incense-sticks, and, as each had passed the head, he or she had held the incense to the nostrils of the dead man, as if to let him smell it, too. Next, the whole corpse had been covered with a thick layer of cow-dung cakes, then a layer of straw, and over it all a covering of clay. This was to keep in the heat of the cow-dung which would burn very hotly and steadily for a long time. The eldest son had lit the straw.

"Ze ceremony is most beautiful," he had gone on, "as all is carried through so to stress ze separation of ze corpse from ze person zat we all knew – to show ze corpse no longer ze man was, but only ze empty shell, for vich he had no more use."

"Have another biscuit?" I said to Doris.

She was watching Mr. Grunwald with a look of barely controlled horror, very pale, her eyes staring. Mrs. Grunwald was looking at her husband in an amused, tolerant way, fascinated but not shocked, rather relishing the tea-time incongruity of his topic.

Doris made some remark to show she approved of the lack of sentimentality in Indian cremation methods, and Mr. Grunwald went on, "Zey tell me zat ze cow-dung vill go on burning until by tomorrow, ven zey vill again come to ze burning-ground, zere vill be nothing left of ze body but a few small pieces of bone and some ashes. And zese zey vill collect, and throw zem into ze village pond, because zey say, 'Life out of ze vaters came, and to ze vaters it returns.' He paused and drank his tea.

I wondered if Doris had realised that the man who had died had been our friend Chatterjee, an old man who had often talked to us in the evenings while we watched the marching in the Playground. Lately he had been suffering from a bad knee, and Doris had done her best to cheer him up and assure him it would respond to treatment in time. I don't think she realizes why he no longer comes to the Playground.

Suddenly Doris said she must get a letter for the post, and got up and left us hurriedly.

*　*　*

200

This evening, after supper, there was a meditation and then a few of us went to the library, where Niranjan played a programme of western music on records. Gilchrist, Sadhana (the Canadian girl), Godfrey, Kanti and I sat about on the steps of the entrance hall in the portico and listened to Bach's Double Violin Concerto and some of the Brandenburgs.

In the atmosphere of the Library, and with the great palms outside rising motionless in the mild still night, I have rarely been so stirred by music. Perhaps it was part homesickness, or the feeling that here was something from the familiar West which was of the same world as this eastern community, speaking the same language of aspiration and joy. But it was chiefly the music, the music itself.

I see that music can be a powerful aid to sadhana. Stendhal wrote somewhere that the only reality in music is the state of mind it induces in the listener – yet how indiscriminately I have listened, without integrating my listening to the general purpose of my life. I remember a friend of mind, who later became a Roman Catholic priest, startling me at school by telling me that his touchstone for judging a piece of music was to imagine Jesus listening to it. In the Ashram, the touchstone for all entertainment and relaxation is 'Does this raise my consciousness nearer to the Divine or not?"

There is a man here, from Czechoslovakia, who is a judo instructor and who also is very enthusiastic and knowledgeable about western music. He plans the programmes of records played once a week in the Library. He puts up a neat typed notice on the board near the entrance to Prithwisingh's room, announcing what is to be played, and giving short notes on the pieces, often with quotations such as:

> "The aim and final reason of all music is the
> Glory of God and the recreation of the mind."
>
> (J. S. Bach)
>
> "Music ought to create and fan the
> fire of the spirit of man".
>
> (L. van Beethoven)

"Music is an essentially spiritual art and
has always been associated with religious feeling
and an inner life."

(The Mother)

* * *

20th January

A small lady doctor has arrived on a visit from Saurashtra. I met her at supper in Ganapatram's restaurant, and afterwards we walked back together to the hostel. We had been talking about her work as a doctor, and she came into my room, seated herself on the spare bed and continued to explain, enthusiastically:

"When there is a patient, and he is lying there ill, I say to the relatives, 'Get away. Stand over there and pray. This is my business,' and then I go to him and concentrate and I do this and I do that. And there are two things about a man that one must keep active. There is the heart and there is the *shwas*, the breathing. If either of these stops there is no life. So I make sure that these are kept going both and then the patient is going on living, isn't it? And then one must just cherish him, and give him this pill and that pill and give him the smile of sympathy and it is all right."

She talked with much animation, in a staccato voice, looking at me now and then with bird-like glances to see if I was following her.

"I will tell you," she said, "of a baby that was born, that was only 2 pounds 14 ounces. It was born to young parents and was their third child. And the wife I knew, and I diagnosed that she was part mad. Not that she was not all right – she served food nicely and put the things in front of you, but she was not giving herself. She had something turned in, held back inside – you know? She couldn't help it, isn't it – that was how she was. And this woman had had three babies, each one after 9 months 9 days. But each one weighed only 3 pounds, 2½ pounds, and 2 pounds, and although I know many lunatic women give birth to their children in the street all right, I diagnosed that this woman, because there was this little lunatic part

202

in her, could not give herself to her babies, so they were so small, and they all died, in this nursing-home or that over the country.

"Now I have the first floor of our nursing-home in Nullapore, and on the ground floor there is a very clever man, a surgeon, and he has B.Sc. and M.D. and all big long degrees, and he uses his degrees to prescribe expensive cures and excruciate the people for money, you know? And the rich people they like it, and they won't come to me because I say 'Buy this for 2 annas and you will be well,' but they say 'What is this 2 anna woman?' – and they go to the big doctor downstairs and he makes them an expensive cure. And he takes all the patients, except for the poor people who come to me.

"But he has not got his Delivery, and so all the Delivery cases he sends upstairs as well, and he says he doesn't want these long cases, where the doctor is having to get up through the night and having all this 'Ma, Ma,' and crying. He has the quick-money cures." The lady doctor drew her orange saree about her with quick movements of her hands, as if to protect herself from the coldness of this man, and went on, "So this woman comes to me, and says will I take her case, and I say yes. And then she comes, and the baby is born after 9 months 9 days. And it weighs 2 pounds 14 ounces. It is so small and miserable a little thing – its buttocks are like these two knuckles of my hand. But I have a love for it, and I think what can be done for it to save this baby's life."

"And I have an elder sister who is a nurse, and she has a concentration on the patient, and she has not slept for 34 years, and her eyelashes and eyebrows are all gone, but she is huge – like the Himalayas – and strong and peaceful. She is a great nurse and has given her life to nursing babies. If you put a baby on her, on her arm or her stomach or her thigh, or anywhere against her, it will sleep. She is like your Nightingale, isn't it? But bigger. Ours is a massive Nightingale."

She looked at me, smiling at the aptness of her own description, and then pressed on with her story, breathless with the drama of it.

"And I get her and she comes, and we keep this baby warm with hot water packets and with our hands, and I give it more than 40 pricks in two months, and I give it saline and vitamin K and vitamin

C, and never any water because it can't take a thing internally – and then after 2 months it is big and lovely and shining like the moon, with a big moon-face. And all the people say "How is this?" But I say to them I did not give it life. That is not man-given. We can only concentrate and offer what we do up to God, and if He gives life that is not our thing. We are afloat on a great ocean and who can say where we shall come ashore?"

I asked if the surgeon knew what she had done.

"Ah, the big surgeon downstairs – and downstairs he has oxygen cylinders and machines and all the equipment, but upstairs we have nothing, no masks, no oxygen, no expensive cradles, but plenty of fresh air from the Nature – this big surgeon he asks me how we keep this baby of 2 pounds 14 ounces alive, and I tell him it was this *love* we had for it kept it alive, and he agrees with me. And you will see the life comes like that, isn't it?"

*　　*　　*

23rd January

The worship of the Vedic gods, said Anilbaran, was a worship of the powers of the Divine. And the Vedic rishis worshipped Indra, Amrita, Soma and Agni in order to become those divine powers, in themselves. They sought to bring them down into their own bodies. It was not a question of bribing or propitiating. Hinduism, since, had fallen into ways of ignorance. People performed animal sacrifice and perpetrated all sorts of cruelty with goats and buffaloes, but this was not the spiritual worship of the gods.

Sri Aurobindo had opened people's eyes to the spiritual meaning of the worship of the aspects of the Mother – Maheshwari, Mahakali, Mahalakshmi and Mahasaraswati. One was to worship these aspects of the Divine until one became them, until one's being was merged in the Mother's being, "until one felt her feet in one's body."

Anilbaran went on to say that the old yogas had taught that woman was the gate of hell, but now Sri Aurobindo taught that she was the entrance to heaven, the Mother was the love-aspect of the divine, and He prepared all men for entering into relation with Himself by

204

giving them the experience of Mother-love as children. There was also the Radha aspect.

Sri Aurobindo wrote 'The Mother' for Mother, and read it aloud to her as he did it. He himself became the learning of Maheshwari and the thorough painstakingness of Mahasaraswati. Even the smallest things he did with the utmost attention. For instance, when he fed his cats he would first boil the fish, and then take out every bone, and feed them with it himself. If a thing was worth doing, it was worth doing well, he used to say.

Anilbaran said we need not read 'The Life Divine' or the 'Essays on the Gita', but just this one book, 'The Mother'.

*   *   *

24th January

Today I visited Ambu. He talked about President Woodrow Wilson's eldest daughter, Margaret. It seems she came across a book by Sri Aurobindo, and then entered into a correspondence with him. She began to practise the yoga, and asked if she could come to live in the Ashram. At first Sri Aurobindo said, "Wait – not yet", but eventually, around 1938, he said she could come. He gave her the name 'Nishtha' which means 'One-pointed' or 'Focused on the Divine'.

He, Ambu, got to know her because the Mother asked him to look after her and give her any help she might need from day to day. Before she left America she had been told by her doctors that she had an incurable disease and could not expect to live more than a few months. However, she had adapted to the life of the Ashram, and lived very simply, for six years, until she died in 1944.

During her last year she had gradually wasted away. People had suggested she should return to America for specialist medical treatment, but she had refused, saying, "If I go back to New York the doctors there will care very well for my body. But who, there, will look after my soul?"

*   *   *

205

At the gym, yesterday evening, Pavitra came up to me while I was trying to lift a weight, and asked if W. B. Yeats had been brought up speaking Gaelic, before learning English. I didn't think so.

Pavitra was interested to know if there were people who had become famous writers in a language different from their mother tongue – as Sri Aurobindo had done.

We both thought of Conrad, but I did not remember Santayana or Nabokov until afterwards.

As it happened, Dr. Ghose, Sri Aurobindo's father, was so keen an anglophile at the time of Sri Aurobindo's childhood that I should think it likely that English was spoken in the family as well as Bengali, and, if so, then Pavitra's question rather loses its point.

*   *   *

This evening Godfrey came to have a meal at Ganapatram's. Afterwards he stayed and reminisced.

"The Mother knows what is going on inside us better than you or I do ourselves," he said, "because she is in all of us. When I am really up against it, in a tight spot, she comes to the rescue. It is really remarkable."

He looked at me across the table, half smiling, half absorbed in his search for the right words for his memories.

"Once, soon after I came here, I was attacked by the most overwhelming feeling of hate. It was like a force entering into me and taking hold of my heart and squeezing it."

He held out his fist and clenched it until the joints whitened.

"One is quite helpless, when something like this happens. One can witness it, and know what's going on, but one is powerless to do anything about it. Well, you know Judith, the tall American woman who works with Anderson? There was always something of the hoyden about her, she let herself go, though she's a sweet woman in herself and we are very good friends now. Well, one day she had told me to do something in such a crude and abrupt way – you know how the American vital behaves – that afterwards I was filled with hate. I could have committed murder. Everything lost its colour and delight. There was just the overmastering heavy black tension of hate filling my whole being… Quite disproportionate to its cause. It was some force from outside which had me in its grip."

"You may not believe me when I tell you this, but it happened. I remember I went to the Ashram Library. And I began to go up the stairs from the entrance hall, and on the half-landing there is a statue of Nataraj, Siva dancing. In my utter misery, I put out my hand and touched this figure. I could not speak a word – I just touched it. And then I looked up, to where there was a sky-light over the stairs. And then it happened. It was as if a sudden immensely powerful wind swept through me. It entered my body and released the psychic substance of Sat-Chit-Ananda that was in me – that is in everybody – and it rose like a column of liquid light through my body, and there was an empty cavity behind my forehead, and the wonderful heavenly substance entered this cavity and then shaped itself into the form and features of the Mother. She looked at me, and spoke, 'She too is one of my children.' And then the experience was over, and I found myself, you'll never believe it, the tears running down my face, weeping like a five-year-old kid."

"And the Mother knows what our questions are," Godfrey continued. "She gives us the answers to what we really need to know. My own mother died while I was in Burma, during the war – and in particularly distressing circumstances – in poverty and alone. And I felt bad about this. She was a good woman – and I would brood on it all, and wish I had been there to thank her and say goodbye …"

He paused, and gazed at the table, before going on.

"And then, one day, I was lying in bed, very early, and I was awake, but my physical being was not – you know what I mean? In myself I was fully conscious, but the connection had not been made yet with the body, which was still unconscious. And the Mother came to me, bringing my mother with her, and they were both there with me. And the psychic being, or the soul in a person, does not fill the whole body, you know, but is quite small – no bigger than my fist, it may be, and my mother's being was like that, but I knew it was her. One recognizes one's loved ones even though they have left their bodies. But do you know how big the Mother's psychic being was? It was immense, compared to ours. She completely filled the room. She is so powerful.

"Well, she brought my mother to see me, and I was able to speak to her, and say briefly what I wanted to, and then the Mother took her on her way."

"Most people leave the earth's atmosphere soon after dying, unless they are held by some attachment or earthly affection, when they may hang on – for about three years, I believe it is. This was nine years after my mother had died, but the Mother had found her, and brought her to me, and then set her on the path forward once again."

"I don't know why I tell you this. Maybe it's so that if I die suddenly of a fever these experiences which have been given me will not be totally lost."

*   *   *

1st February

For several days, now, bales of cotton have been accumulating on the sea-front, brought from some mill inland. Early this morning after Darshan I watched the fishermen from the villages north of the town taking these bales to a French ship which was anchored off-shore during the night. They ferry them out in their ungainly wooden rowing-boats, clustering round, waiting their turn at the derricks.

The launching of these craft from the beach is a strenuous affair, the crew running them through the surf, making desperate efforts to keep the bows head-on to the waves, then leaping on board and paddling furiously until they reach calm water. A man stands in the stern, steering with a long sweep.

The sea was brilliant with sun-glitter, the men naked except for loin-cloths and turbans.

Later in the morning I visited Norman. He put aside a poem he was writing, which made me feel a bit like the traveller from

208

Porlock, but he was most welcoming and we talked for some time until Lena came in and gave us bowls of 'soup'. His main theme was the collective nature of the sadhana and of the ultimate realisation. He said how the Mother had once spoken of her vision of the Ashram as a world community in a microcosm, in which, one day, people from the different countries would live in concord together – each nation with its cultural pavilion showing its distinctive character and contribution to human life. It would demonstrate multiplicity in unity, a harmonious richness of variety.

Norman stressed that such a community could not be fully realised without the attainment of the Supramental consciousness. Given this precondition, its members would act from the awareness and will of the Truth, from what Sri Aurobindo calls 'the self-achieving Truth-consciousness' in which knowledge and action spring from the same infallible source. Then as in an orchestra all the individual contributions would blend in concert.

He said that, since the Mother had shown it was possible to live in the Supramental consciousness, it was only a matter of time before a number of individuals would be able to share this state, and, when they did, they would lose the feeling of separateness and become a living collectivity. He quoted the Mother as having said that once the connection had been made between Supermind and the material being 'it must have its effect in the outward form of a new creation, beginning with a model town and ending with a perfect world.'

After visiting the Playground in the evening I walked along the sea-front again, where a number of the Ashramites promenade at this time when the heat is less intense. The ship was still off-shore, a twinkling configuration of lights, and the small boats were still bobbing out to her in the darkness to be unloaded.

"Have you ever thought," said Gilchrist, "how stupid it is of all those pigs to live in the streets of the Indian part of the town, where I suppose they are always getting killed off and eaten by the low-caste and outcaste people?"

"No," I said, "but what can they do about it?"

"Well," he answered, "today I was going to see Ananta, and where the town ends and the fields begin I saw a whole herd of swine making for the open country – big ones and little ones of all sizes and colours, grunting and squealing and trotting along at a fine pace. It was really as if some wise old pig had persuaded them not to be exploited any more and was leading them to freedom. They seemed full of glee."

As we walked on we noticed the ship was preparing to sail. The anchors were raised and soon she curved out to sea, a coruscating efficient little world on her own, passing away home to the West, with a hold full of cotton to show for her contact here.

EINE KLEINE NACHTMUSIK

All night's shadows play a tune
Round the ground base of the sea.
Monuments upon the shore
Stand in the dark
And chant the moon.

Rusted iron and concrete blocks
Bar the beaches, break the tide;
The past lies heavy on the sand
And sets the dogs
Howling among the rocks.

Clouds and stars across the sky
Dwindle the sea's horizons down,
Boats and fishes, bursting waves,
The candle light-house
Earth's faint sigh …

Only the Self can last the night.

* * *

Last night Gilchrist and I took Norman along with us to Ganapatram's restaurant. Ganapatram came forward to greet him and they hugged each other. He is always very happy to see Norman, and, while we two regulars were eating our supper, he brought him a dosa and an ice-cream and, sitting down at our table, began talking.

He told us about the preparations for the Darshan on 29th February – how it seemed that the Mother was making a point of asking her outside disciples to come for that day, a thing she had never done on any previous occasion. A film producer living in Calcutta had mentioned to the Mother on his last visit that he didn't think he could come for his birthday on 23rd February, and she had replied, "It doesn't matter, but I want to see you here on the 29th." Disciples were full of plans for celebrations, but the Mother, it seemed, wanted only a quiet peaceful atmosphere on the day. There would be some decoration with coloured lights, and the Meditation Hall was being altered into a temple, with a vaulted roof… People had suggested these things to the Mother, and she had said, "Yes, if you like."

"Mind you," said Ganapatram, "she said 'If *you* like.'"

There was also a plan for decorating everything with golden hangings, along the route from the Mother's room to where she would sit on the day – and in the Cottage Industries they were making a special gold silk carpet for the balcony, for her to stand on. Everywhere, too, there were to be golden sunflowers in pots. And so many people were coming. Already the guest-houses were booked up. Maybe there would have to be tents out at the Sports Ground, to house the over-flow. There had never been so great a gathering of disciples before.

Ganapatram also said how he felt a change in the atmosphere: in the last three or four days he had noticed several incidents which showed that something was different. For instance, a man, who is always cross and refuses what one asks, suddenly had agreed at once when asked for something, and been most helpful. "I think, from outward incidents, I can see something is happening to the atmosphere. Of course we cannot speak of what we see inwardly, but we can say this, that from outward signs something is changing."

The conversation then came round to Ganapatram's youth. He said that he had been reading many spiritual books, by yogis and sages, but only one by Sri Aurobindo, at that time, and that was a book of letters. An orthodox Brahmin pundit he knew had been very impressed with this book because of one thing in it. Somebody had asked Sri Aurobindo how many of the people in his Ashram had got beyond the sex difficulty, and Sri Aurobindo had replied, quite bluntly and openly, "None." And this Brahmin pundit had said this was a wonderful thing – so honest and frank, with no pretence about how advanced his sadhaks were, and he had said, too, that it showed he knew what he was talking about, since no-one who knew anything of the spiritual life would say that the problem of sex would disappear when one took to yoga.

Ganapatram went on to say how one had to be open about these things. Take, for instance, the school, and the children in the Boarding. Visitors sometimes were surprised at the great deal of freedom that is allowed. They would ask, "But don't the children sometimes fight together?" and then one had to say, "Yes, they do fight together sometimes," and they would go on, "And don't they beat each other?" and one had to say, "Yes, they beat each other" – and indeed they are like any other children in this way. But there is some difference too. Once an important visitor came and stayed for some time, and he was very interested in the way the children were treated, and he asked these sorts of questions. "And I told him," said Ganapatram, 'you will see they do all these things like other children, but after a week or two you will see they have something else that other children have not got.' And that very night he went to the Playground, and he found three children acting in a bad way together and abusing themselves – it was as if the whole scene was specially prepared for him so that he should see it – and he came back and said to me, 'Do you know what these children are like? They were abusing themselves…' and I had to say, 'Yes, they abuse themselves sometimes, too.' But at the end of ten days he came to me and said, 'You were right. Although these children do all these things, there is a difference from ordinary children. Today I met a girl who could read Sri Aurobindo's epic 'Savitri' and *understood* it. And I cannot do that, and I am a professor of Sanskrit, and my guru cannot read and understand 'Savitri'.' And this was a girl of fifteen years old."

And another thing about them, said Ganapatram, was their complete lack of fear. Some visitors were shocked to hear children call their own parents by their first names, an unthinkable thing outside. But that old fear of parents and grown-up people was quite gone. He remembered one incident not long ago, which illustrated this. On his building-site there was a well, an open well. And the Mother had told him to see that the children did not go near it, in case one of them should fall in. And he had explained this to the children, that the Mother wanted them to keep away from this well and they had all said, 'Yes, we understand,' – but then that would be the one place where they would try to go whenever there was an opportunity. And in the evenings he had to go over to the other side of Cottage Industries to see to some work, and then they would go and play by the well. Now one evening he knew what they were doing, and, as he was anxious about this well, he came back after he had gone off to the other place, and he saw all the children there, playing; and as he came he *shouted* at them. And they all ran away, except one. And he stood there and waited for him. And this one said to him. "Baji, I am staying because I do not think you are *really angry yet*." And Ganapatram said this tickled him so much – that the boy was waiting until he was *really* angry – that he couldn't help but burst out laughing.

*   *   *

8th February

In Purani's 'Evening Talks with Sri Aurobindo' he records a conversation about people having sudden conversions.

Sri Aurobindo does not hold that suffering or a catastrophic shock are needed to make someone completely change his life, and a disciple, agreeing with him, cites the example of Lala Babu.

213

This man was out walking one evening when he heard two fisherwomen speaking to each other. One said, 'It is late, darkness is falling, difficulties may come, let us hurry home.'

It was enough to give him the necessary push for entering the spiritual life.

*　*　*

15th February

This afternoon I went to have a talk with a senior sadhak here called Rishabhchand. I found him sitting in the Ashram Furniture Department, at his desk. He got up, and led me upstairs to his flat on the second floor. It was a large room, half bedroom and half study, with a demi-partition between. The colour scheme was grey and white, with a pale greenish-grey distemper on the walls. Everything was of Spartan simplicity and cleanliness. A typewriter stood on a small table by one wall, on a white cloth, and itself covered with a white cloth, as if it were a surgical instrument. The desk at which Rishabhchand had seated himself was covered with a number of crystal paper-weights, pens, pencils, paper-knives, blotters, and, at one end, stood a worn dictionary and a row of note-books between carved wooden book-ends.

"Would you like a glass of water?" he began. I said I would, and he disappeared into his bedroom and after a while came back with a glass for each of us.

I had said I wanted to have a talk with him, having admired his writings, but what, now, had I to ask him? We sat facing each other across the desk. He is in his fifties, or early sixties perhaps, with a lean scholar's face, and smooth black hair brushed back and round the ears down to his shoulders. He looked at me quizzically with kind eyes.

I started the conversation by saying that I was going back to England, and asked him what was the best way to help people in the West to understand Sri Aurobindo and what was happening in the Ashram.

214

He smiled and said something could be done, but that the best thing was to be, oneself, in some part a realised being. If one had found one's true self then there was no question about what to do: one's work would flower out naturally from one's soul. A certain amount could be done on the purely mental level – towards a clear understanding of the theory – but to be effective one must have some fire in oneself when one spoke of such things as God and Spirit, and one must have some experience of them, personally. One must realise one's psychic being.

I asked him if this was a thing deliberately to aim at, or if one should aim only at realising the Divine, and that the psychic being was the part of one which realised the Divine.

He replied that the psychic being was itself a part of the Divine, and one should certainly aim to find it in oneself. What else was any use? he asked. Everything else changes and is unstable. The body is never the same; now it is a child, then a boy, a man – then it grows old and dies, and what has one to take away from this life if one has not found one's true nature, and where does one go? Even if one wrote poetry like Shakespeare, or was a philosopher like Russell, what was the use if in the next life one knew nothing of it. Perhaps one would read one's own books, and not know that one had written them. There was, in the Ashram, a man who had been Victor Hugo – and now he was reading Victor Hugo!

I said how in meditation I had tried to visualise the heart-centre and concentrate on that, but that recently I had read in Sri Aurobindo that one should not do this but rather take one's stand in the heart-centre and from there aspire for the Divine. Did this mean shifting one's centre of consciousness from the head to the heart?

Yes, he replied; we start as mental beings, but the ideas and imaginary picture we have of the heart-centre can be a help towards finding it. They focus the will. One has, first of all, to make up one's mind that one must find the Divine, that nothing else matters, that that is the aim of one's life. Then one must try to go inward, deep, deep into oneself, forgetting the outer world and the body – and then "The Divine will show you what to do. Do it for a few days, and then some experience will come and help you and teach you what to do next. Perhaps it may come unexpectedly in the early morning, just after you have woken up – suddenly a glimpse, a lifting of the shutters, for just a moment, to encourage you, and then it is gone." But you must be sincere. That is the one essential condition. Once, in a children's class the Mother had asked what was the most important quality a sadhak should have. One child said, "Faithfulness." She agreed, but said there was another more important thing one should have. Other children suggested love, or aspiration, or peace, and then one said, "Sincerity," and to that she said, 'Yes, sincerity. That is all one needs – absolute sincerity, at all times, and the Divine will save you!'"

Once you made up your mind, went on Rishabhchand, that nothing else was of any value, that it was the Divine alone you wanted to find, then He Himself would help you. "He who chooses the Infinite is chosen by the Infinite." If one is sincere, then the Divine Himself comes to one's aid and works out one's problems for one. "Pray to Him, and say 'I know that I want to find my true nature but how can I do it? This and this are my difficulties…' and you will see how the Divine helps you, so that everything in one's life seems to gather together to co-operate to lead one to realisation. Books, people, events – all come and help one, just when they are needed, and one sees afterwards that nothing else could have taken their place at the time."

I asked him if one could believe that the Divine was helping even when one no longer felt the original aspiration and dedication that one had had in one's best moments of faith. Was He working on one even then, or was it only when one was open and aware of the Divine Presence that He could reach one?

Rishabhchand answered that at first it was inevitable that the aspiration should be intermittent and variable, but that one should not lose heart or worry, and that, as time went by, the alternation of light and dark would lessen until the time came when the whole of one's life was lived in the light. There were two ways in which the Mother could act on one. She could act through the subconscious, whatever one's attitude might be, so that gradually, very gradually, one changed – but this was a slow way – or she could act through one's consciousness, with one's co-operation and right attitude – and this could result in very rapid change.

Was it right, I asked him, to "work out one's desires" through experience, or did that result in a contamination and weakening of the being. I was thinking of those sadhaks who had left the Ashram to take up married life "because that experience was necessary to them." Sometimes they came back again, at a later stage, with their families.

Rishabhchand, however, said the only way to free oneself from desires was to become conscious of them and offer them to the Divine. Who ever heard of desires weakening through being given what they wanted? They grew stronger, and never became satisfied. The choice to be made was whether one could live happily without finding God, or not. If one found one could get along without feeling the need of Him, then one should find one's satisfaction through some good work, philanthropic activity, study or family life, but if *not*, if one could not be satisfied by the ignorance, then one must offer all attachments to the Divine, and He would deal with them.

He described how, in about 1917, a mystic from Bengal came to Sri Aurobindo and asked if he could stay with him. He was told he might stay. And this man had been having very high experiences – even of Satchitananda. But, when he had been in Pondy for a while, all this stopped, and he began having the most lurid attacks from all sorts of the lowest types of forces. He went to Sri Aurobindo who said yes, he knew what was happening to him, but it was all right. He should remain calm, and offer all the things that came into his mind at his, Sri Aurobindo's, feet, and they would be dealt with. The fellow went away, but came again after a few days and said he could not stand it any longer, that he would go mad if he stayed, so he was going back to Bengal. Sri Aurobindo said that was all right, that he would in time recover his former experiences of Satchitananda, but that this other side of his nature would never be transformed, but remain as it had always been, repressed, unexperienced and untransformed. The man went away.

Another question that came to me was whether one should only come to the Ashram once one had become established in a certain degree of peace, when one was ready to go on to something beyond. Rishabhchand said no; many came who had not found peace and yet had a sincere seeking for God.

Before I came away from Rishabhchand I told him of the Mother's assurance to me that I could find my psychic being within the year, and confessed that now the prospect seemed centuries away; also how I had had a foretaste of joy on the evening of my birthday – and how it had come involuntarily, like a contact with some deep-flowing current in my being…

He said it always came involuntarily. There was nothing we could do to command it, but that, once it had come, it would come again, and that one had simply to go within, telling oneself one would find what was hidden there, and then, at other times of the day, remember the Divine as often as one could.

"When I was young, I read a book by the strong-man Sandow," he went on, "and he tells one to say to oneself every time one bends one's arm that it is getting stronger and harder and thicker, *and go on bending it*, and then eventually it becomes all these things. Similarly one must tell oneself one is drawing nearer to one's true being, and that it is possible, that the Divine Guide is leading one – and then one day it will be so."

This talk has set me trying once more to go inward. Although I had known already many of the answers which Rishabhchand gave me, so that he told me little new, yet I am still ignorant of the Kingdom of Heaven that is within me, the inner light, and this, as he said, is, ultimately, the only worthwhile knowledge.

Norman speaks of 'that inner door' which, when it opens, reveals another world, so different from that of the senses, the mind and the emotions that what follows amounts to 'a reversal of consciousness.' Without experience of this one has almost no right to use the word 'spiritual', which applies to this other dimension, the possibility of the existence of which is habitually forgotten and misconceived. We are content with too limited a world and too unreal a God.

*　*　*

218

What unease holds me from going to see the Mother with full joy? Perhaps it is because I am obscurely conscious of a lack of sincerity – mine is not the child-like ecstatic devotion that I admire in others. It is spoiled by the mind and by bitterness and impurity. Yet I know that the Divine knows and pardons all, and waits with a continual sustained love and patience for me to advance out of the past to that point where I may become fully conscious of His help and presence. It is at work in me even now. It has brought me to this centre of incarnate light; it is there guiding me in the classroom and in conversation with friends. It is present when I wake in the night and there is a living stillness about me so that I have to sit up and be silent before it.

Mother, when my heart does, so rarely, rise in fullness of gratitude to you and to the Divine who shines through you, may I recognise that that is your work in me, and that when my eyes fill with tears, that that is the intensity of your joy and love momentarily born in me and returning to its source. Mother, may these moments be free from the clutch of the ego, and become spontaneous, natural and lasting, so that the psychic being in me may come more and more to the front, and so that that day may come nearer when I may realise the Divine in my heart-centre. Let me trust with all my being in your help.

*   *   *

After breakfast I go up to the roof of the little boarding house and look down over the parapet, watching the people below.

A man in a white dhoti comes out of a low house on to the street carrying a rat-trap. A boy of about twelve and a young girl come towards him. He bends over the trap and suddenly pulls out a rat tied by the hind legs with a piece of string. He dangles the rat by the string, and lets it down so it can run with its front paws on the road, then, smiling, he swings the rat high up and smashes it down on the ground. He tosses it, string and all, into the gutter, and goes inside.

It lies there for some minutes. A crow perches on a nearby tree and caws at it. Then the boy comes and looks and goes away. The little girl slowly approaches. The rat is lying still, on its side. Cautiously she picks up a piece of brick and tosses it onto the rat. She goes away to collect stones, comes back and, standing a few feet away, throws them awkwardly at the rat. Then she watches it.

The boy returns and looks at it. Then he picks up the string and pulls the rat through the dust backwards. Suddenly it is alive again, and runs with its front legs into the dirty water of the gutter. The boy pulls it back, smiling, and lets it run, then swings it back. The little girl goes to find a piece of brick. Convulsively the rat jumps and makes a hissing noise, swearing like a cat. The boy lets it run, and when it stops kicks it gently to make it go. The little girl knocks it over with a lump of brick. Several people gather and watch what is going on, and the boy plays showman, smiling.

I am turning to go down and interfere when a man aged about thirty comes and takes the string from the boy and starts to untie the rat's back legs. He has difficulty with the knot. It looks as if, finally, he bites through it with his teeth. The rat is free. But, though the man pushes it with his foot, it will only move a few feet and then stops.

There is a shadow from above. The little crowd steps back, and a kite swoops like a dive-bomber. It knocks the rat over, but misses its grip, and goes on up the street.

Again the rat moves; it is still alive. The people draw back. The kite's mate stalls overhead, with a wriggle of folded wings. It stoops, comes out of its dive almost at road-level, grips the rat in powerful claws and is gone on slow wing-beats, the rat's tail dangling below it.

Now, all is over; it is too late to intervene, and I am ashamed.

So began the Mother's birthday.

It was a dullish day. The sun was screened from the queuing crowds in the Ashram courtyard by a haze.

Prithwisingh told me there were 900 visitors and perhaps 300 local people from the town, who came for the Darshan, together with 1,200 ashramites.

Gilchrist and I went up to the main Ashram buildings soon after 9 o'clock, and sat in the court-yard on our usual seat near the garage. After about an hour and a half we joined the line of people waiting to see the Mother – old people, blind men being led, cripples, young men, girls in orange and white sarees, children in flame-coloured dresses, boys, even infants who could barely toddle – all silent and attentive in the slowly moving line. Sometimes people would greet friends and little groups of talkers would form. Others would seek out places where they could sit quietly and prepare themselves, by the Samadhi or on the stone-flagged path.

Overhead the crows cawed and flapped in the big tree, or in the betel or coconut palms. All at once, as I got nearer the staircase up to the Mother's room, I felt happy and at ease. All thoughts of anxiety and insincerity, connected with going away, left me, and I felt peaceful and at harmony with everyone, and able to love and greet them. All disturbing mental ideas and questions of attitude towards the Mother disappeared. I was to see her again, and this was sufficient cause for happiness and love to rise in me. I became conscious of being centred in my chest rather than in my head.

People went up one side of the stairs, and another file came down the other side. No-one stepped on the green stair-carpet up the middle. The atmosphere became still and intense. At the top of the stairs Nirod, and I think Nolini, were sitting on the floor of the little room between Sri Aurobindo's room and the darshan room. I tried to become aware of the rooms through which we passed, but I cannot have succeeded, for I can remember little except some fine potted dahlias, a cabinet of ivories and the portrait of Sri Aurobindo, etched on mother-of-pearl, with a light shining through it from behind.

Then, all at once, there was only one person between me and the Mother. Champaklal was standing behind a tray full of envelopes containing birthday offerings and greetings for the Mother. I dropped my envelope in, and then was face to face with the Mother. Again

I can remember nothing but the shine and love of her eyes, perhaps only of one eye, for I only looked into her right eye. She handed me the message for the day, and I was past her and already going down the stairs.

There is no doubt about the grace given at such a meeting. All is stilled. One's body is firm and compact so one can feel it as a solid vessel of the spirit. There is a pressure in the chest, a lightness and joy in the mind.

"Find somewhere where we can sit quietly," said Gilchrist. We did so, and sat for some minutes before going away to find Norman.

It seemed that Gilchrist did not find happiness in his Darshan. "I am one of those people who make their own problems," he said. "It is my own fault." Nevertheless he seemed cheerful enough, and we had a good lunch in the Dining Hall – vegetable soup, rice, brown bread, red and yellow tomatoes, bananas and a bowl of curd.

In the afternoon Ananta came to my room for a rest, not wanting to go back to his island before the next part of the day's programme. He talked and we swapped news, and then dozed until about ten to three. Then he took Gilchrist and me to the Coffee House in the town for iced coffee. He grew wild and shouted for human flesh at one stage, and Gilchrist ordered a Badam Kheerm which he said was made from crushed mice…

We then went to the Playground and saw the march-past, when the Sports Groups paraded in front of the Mother to the music of the Ashram band. This was followed by a play put on by the children for the Mother. It was a dramatisation of the Katha Upanishad, in French. Norman read out a summary in English of each scene before it began.

When this was over and the Mother had left, we came away with Norman and had a talk and drank glasses of milk with Lena in their room.

In the evening we all assembled in the Playground again, and watched about a hundred colour-slides of 'Mother in her Private Chamber'. These were excellent pictures, showing the Mother sitting and standing, and writing and reading, laughing, droll, serious, austere, humorous, weary, profound, and charged with life and light, like a very old goddess.

Then Gilchrist and I had supper at G.'s, and walked back to our rooms, through the warm deep star-packed night.

*   *   *

22nd February

"The self-born has set the doors of the body to face outwards, therefore the soul of a man gazes outward and not at the Self within: hardly a wise man here and there, desiring immortality, turns his eyes inward and sees the Self within him."

From Sri Aurobindo's translation of the
Katha Upanishad

*   *   *

23rd February

Today I met Girish Kumar. He is an Indian from East Africa who has come on a visit to see his children who are living here, attending the Ashram school.

We had lunch together, and Girish talked of the psychic being. "I think," he said, "That after one is silent, when the mind has cooled down and there is a period of quiet, then, after, one begins to go down into oneself. It is not a falling, but a going round and round," and he made a spiralling, drilling gesture, "and then suddenly one comes to a place full of light, brilliant light. And one rests there, and one says, 'This is a good place – it is all right'. And then if one has any problems, any questions, one knows the answers – you can know everything. And first it is a dazzling light, as if you were looking at the sun, but after a while it is less brilliant, but you are very happy. And you are there, and the man sitting next to you he will know nothing about what you are doing inside yourself, or where you are… And later it will go, but not for very long. Suddenly again, when you are not thinking of this thing, it will say, 'I am here, come along' and you will be there again, and not only in meditation, at any time of the day. And you know there is something in one that

223

calls out for this – not quite pain, it is not joy, either, but there is a yearning, a longing, you know, a cry…"

*   *   *

25th February

Earlier this week Norman arranged for me to have a talk with Indra Sen, who was, he said, the Ashram's best known psychologist.

He was sitting, a small thoughtful man, in a large room flooded by the evening sun. He looked as if he had been much troubled and worn by recalcitrant powers and ideas, but, like the day, had come through to a mellow late afternoon. He was at a table covered by a stained table-cloth of coloured squares, meditating or pondering, but got up with a friendly smile to meet me, and then we sat together by the table in the golden sunset light.

After I had given him some messages from friends in the West, we talked about Christianity and the Ashram.

I asked him how to reconcile an allegiance to Christ with one to Sri Aurobindo and the Mother.

He countered by asking what was the essence of Christ's teaching.

I suggested that it was to know and be able to do the will of God, how to love God and one's fellow men.

He said it was so, and that this was the Absolute, and all other matters of different religious orthodoxies and personal revelations were relative to this, and should serve it. And from this point of view there was no clash between Christ and Sri Aurobindo. Indeed there was never any exclusiveness or rivalry between forms or mediators of true spirituality.

He recounted how his mother had had a guru in Rishikesh, a family guru. When he, Indra Sen, had brought her to Pondicherry she had asked this guru how she should behave with regard to Sri Aurobindo, and he had told her to do just as the ashramites did, and to have no fears about lack of loyalty.

This reminded me of a story by Anilbaran about a Bengali Vaishnavite. This holy man had prayed all his life to Krishna to appear to him. At last Krishna came, but when he revealed himself

224

Krishna also showed the holy man a vision of the Mother, and said, "It is now no longer enough to realise Krishna, you must also find the Divine Mother." The man then sent many of his disciples to Pondicherry, where some are still living.

Among other things Indra Sen spoke of the bias of Christianity in the West towards attempting to love man without first having loved and found God, with the result that it had tended to become a rational system of ethics rather than the intuitive apprehension of the divine will, unique for each combination of circumstances. However, he spoke of Jesus himself with great reverence.

*   *   *

27th February

This month's issue of 'Mother India' has in it a long section headed 'Towards February 29, 1960'. This is composed of a series of extracts from the printed 'Messages' given out by the Mother on Darshan days, and of other announcements and comments made by her on the theme of the Supramental development. It is a résumé to help prepare people for the coming Darshan. I talked with Norman about it this morning, and he enlarged on the purpose and progress of the work that Sri Aurobindo and the Mother have been engaged on.

As long ago as 1921 Sri Aurobindo wrote, in a pamphlet called 'The Yoga and its Objects', "The yoga we practise is not for ourselves alone, but for the Divine; its aim is to work out the will of the Divine in the world, to effect a spiritual transformation and to bring down a divine nature and a divine life into the mental, vital and physical nature and life of humanity. Its object is not personal Mukti [spiritual liberation], although Mukti is a necessary condition of the yoga, but the liberation and transformation of the human being. It is not personal Ananda (spiritual delight), but the bringing down of the divine Ananda – Christ's kingdom of heaven, our Satyayuga – upon the earth."

To understand this I think one has to accept the idea of 'other worlds' –   that besides our own there are definite self-existent

225

worlds of Life and Mind, Overmind and Supermind. The worlds of Life and Mind have become native to our world of Matter; they have manifested, become incarnate on earth. This has come about because these powers are, according to Sri Aurobindo's theory and experience, already involved in the inconscient material of the universe, and when they create through a kind of yearning and dynamism, the necessary organisation and concentration of energy, the transcendent forces of the corresponding worlds can engage, get a footing, and produce a new stage in evolution. The earth aspires, as it were, and the overshadowing Presence answers to it. But it does not only answer; it may start the conversation. For the initiative of God acts from both levels – from above as well as from below. "For (the powers of life, mind and spirit) are developed here," he writes, "by two co-operating forces, an upward-tending force from below, an upward-drawing and downward-pressing force from above. For there is the necessity in the Inconscient of bringing out what is latent within it, and there is the pressure of the superior principles in the higher planes which not only aids this general necessity to realise itself, but may very largely determine the special ways in which it is eventually realised."

In our present phase of evolution individual men have been able to contact and experience the Overmental and Supramental worlds (for example Christ was conscious of Supermind), but so far these have not become native to the earth in the way that Mind has done. And much of the spiritual effort of the great religions has been directed to rising out of this earth-life into 'higher consciousness', as in Buddhism. Such effort may result in the changing of the mental and emotional lives of individuals, but the victory has always been incomplete, so that there is a perpetual struggle even in the saints, where the war in their members causes them to admit that the good that they would do they do not do, and the final victory is seen as in a heaven out of this world.

According to Sri Aurobindo it is Supermind alone that has in it the power necessary to transform the whole human being, down to the material basis of his nature. Only when this has happened will there be 'heaven on earth'.

In January 1957 the Mother gave, as her message for the New Year, "A Power greater than that of Evil can alone win the victory. It is not a crucified but a glorified body that will save the world."

To this she added the following comment. "This message, if it is understood, is just that which can lead to its goal the best human good will showing itself at present upon earth. I wrote it in answer to an immense, collective effort to awaken in men the true sense of brotherhood and to prevent all future war.

"The message has taken a somewhat special form, because the good will proceeded from a Christian country…

"It is because Evil was opposed till now by a spiritual force having no power for transformation in the material world that the mighty effort of good will made by mankind through thousands of years has ended only in a lamentable defeat, and left the world in the same state of misery and corruption and falsehood. One must – and this is the true, the only remedy – on the very plane where the adverse forces are supreme, on the material plane, secure a power greater than theirs, capable of conquering them totally in that domain itself, in other words, a spiritual force that is capable of transforming the consciousness and the material world. This force is the Supramental Force. What is needed is to be receptive to its action on the physical plane and not run away into a far-off Nirvana leaving the enemy uncontested empire over that which one abandons.

"Neither the sacrifice of the physical life nor the giving up of material power can win the victory. That only Joy can do, the Joy which the Supramental Consciousness brings, the Joy which is Force and Endurance and Supreme Courage. Certainly it requires much greater heroism to do that than to abandon all and escape, but that is the only way to conquer."

I asked Norman why, if it was possible, Christ had not brought down Supermind. Did he think that Sri Aurobindo could do what Christ had not done?

Norman replied that, at his period of history, the descent of Supermind was not the concern of Christ. It was not a question of which leaders of man's spiritual growth were the greatest – who could measure or compare them? – but rather that each had been faced by a particular situation and life-task. He got up and found a volume of Sri Aurobindo's letters, from which he read, "The traditions of the past are very great in their own place, in the past, but I do not see why we should merely repeat them and not go further. In the spiritual development of the consciousness upon earth the great past ought to be followed by a greater future." And indeed Jesus himself spoke of those who would come after him doing greater things than he had done.

Sri Aurobindo and the Mother came to the conclusion, independently, that the time was ready for some new development. In 1914 their paths crossed. The Mother has said of this occasion, "When I first met Sri Aurobindo in Pondicherry, I was in deep concentration, seeing things in the Supermind, things that were to be but that were somehow not manifesting. I told Sri Aurobindo what I had seen, and asked him if they would manifest. He simply said, "Yes." And immediately I saw that the Supermind had touched the earth and was beginning to be realised! This was the first time I had witnessed the power to make real what is true."

This was to be Sri Aurobindo's work, "a work in the consciousness, a work of connection between the Supermind and the material being." If successful, it would lead to the direct descent of the Supramental Consciousness and Power and to a radical recreation of life in terms of the spirit, so that what is true 'in heaven' would become real on earth.

"The consciousness," the Mother wrote in 1931, "is like a ladder: at each great epoch there has been one great being capable of adding one more step to the ladder and reaching a place where the ordinary consciousness had never been. It is possible to attain a high level and get completely out of the material consciousness; but then one does not retain the ladder, whereas the great achievement of the great epochs of the universe has been the capacity to add one more step to the ladder without losing contact with the material, the capacity to reach the Highest and at the same time connect the top with the bottom instead of letting a kind of emptiness cut off all connection between the different planes. To go up and down and join the top to the bottom is the whole secret of realisation, and that is the work of the Avatar. Each time he adds one more step to the ladder there is a new creation upon earth…

"The step which is being added now Sri Aurobindo has called the Supramental; as a result of it the consciousness will be able to enter the Supramental world and yet retain its personal form, its individualisation, and then come down to establish here a new creation."

The significance of the life of Sri Aurobindo lies in the claim that he was instrumental in the adding of "one more step to the ladder."

Like Teilhard de Chardin, Sri Aurobindo has linked together matter, life and mind in a theory of evolving consciousness, and predicted a further development, but his greatness rests not upon this, but rather upon his self-dedication to the realisation of the advance in his own person, and upon what he has achieved.

"There are, in the history of the earth, moments of transition when things that have been for thousands of years must give place to things that are about to manifest. A special concentration of the world consciousness, one might almost say, an intensification of its effort, happens at such times, varying according to the kind of progress to be made, the quality of the transformation to be realised. We are precisely at such a turning point of the world's history. As Nature has already created upon earth a mental being, even so there is now a concentrated activity to bring forth in this mentality a Supramental consciousness and individuality….

"Sri Aurobindo incarnated in a human body the Supramental consciousness and has not only revealed to us the nature of the path to follow and the method of following it so as to arrive at the goal, but has also by his own personal realisation given us the example; he has provided us, so to say, with the proof that the thing can be done and the time is now to do it." (The Mother, November, 1953)

• • •

A few years after the passing of Sri Aurobindo the Mother stated, "Sri Aurobindo has given up his body in an act of supreme unselfishness, renouncing the realisation in his body to hasten the hour of the collective realisation. Surely if the earth were more responsive, this would not have been necessary."

She added, "As soon as Sri Aurobindo withdrew from his body, what he had called the Mind of Light got realised here…

"The Supermind had descended long ago – very long ago – in the mind and even the vital: it was working in the physical also but indirectly through these intermediaries. The question now was about the direct action of the Supermind in the physical. Sri Aurobindo said it could be possible only if the physical mind received the Supramental light: the physical mind was the instrument for direct action upon the most material. This physical mind receiving the Supramental light Sri Aurobindo called the Mind of Light."

In 1950 the Mother had said, "People do not know what a tremendous sacrifice Sri Aurobindo has made for the world. About a year ago, while discussing things, I remarked that I felt like leaving this body of mine. He spoke out in a very firm tone, 'No, this can never be. If necessary for this transformation, I might go, you will have to fulfil our Yoga of Supramental descent and transformation.'"

The Mother, then, alone on earth, has had to continue the work.

To those who ask for evidence of the progress of this work the answer is often bound to be unsatisfactory. From the subjective nature of the material – consciousness – it follows there can be no objective or quantitative proofs. People are told to become more aware and sensitive – and they will see for themselves that in the interior worlds things are changing. Otherwise, if they do not have the capacity of inner vision necessary for verifying the statements of Sri Aurobindo and the Mother for themselves, they can take these assurances on trust – or leave them. It is true that the fact of the capacity of Sri Aurobindo's body to resist decay beyond the normal lapse of time may be instanced as pointing to the degree to which he had succeeded in supramentalising it, but there is no urge to convince or proselytize on the part of the Ashram. Its business is yoga. If the evolutionary leap is made, it will eventually be self-evident. For, if matter itself is to be affected when Supermind begins to be realised, then even the senses themselves will be able to register and the external mind take note of the change. And this material proof is envisaged as possible and indeed, since 1956, as likely quite soon. The Mother's New Year message for 1956 read: "The greatest victories are the least noisy. The manifestation of a new world is not proclaimed by beat of drum."

Then, on 29th February of that year, something occurred which led the Mother to declare, a month later:

"Lord, Thou hast willed and I execute:

A new light breaks upon the earth,

A new world is born.

The things that were promised are fulfilled."

On April 24th of that year her Darshan Day message was:

"The manifestation of the Supramental upon earth is no more a promise but a living fact, a reality. It is at work here, and one day will come when the most blind, the most unconscious, even the most unwilling shall be obliged to recognise it."

Amplifying this, she said, "The Supramental Light, Consciousness and Force have manifested. The Supramental Ananda has not come yet. When I say 'manifested' rather than 'descended', I do not mean that the Supermind involved in Matter, in the Inconscient, has emerged. That emergence is for the future, but, of course, now it is merely a question of time: the process is natural and inevitable. The manifestation is the outbreak of the Supramental world proper into the subtle physical atmosphere of our universe."

A special terminology is used, and the Mother explains it.

"What I call a descent is an individual movement, in an individual consciousness. And when it is a new world that manifests itself in an old one – as when the Mind was first diffused over the earth – I call it a manifestation....

"You may call it what you will, it is all the same to me, but we must understand each other.

"Ascending and descending are a way of speaking, they have no ultimate sense: there is really neither up nor down. We speak of ascending when we have the impression of raising ourselves towards something; and we say 'descending' when, after seizing that thing, we make it descend within ourselves.

"But when the gates are thrown open and the flood takes place, you cannot call it a descent. It is a force that spreads itself."

Norman described the Supramental manifestation as a new possibility open to mankind that has never existed before. As yet it is only the Mother who is realising in herself this possibility. But, as she says, "What Sri Aurobindo has promised and what evidently interests us who are here now is that the time has come when some chosen beings out of the present-day humanity who fulfil the conditions of the necessary spiritualisation will be capable of transforming their bodies with the help of the Supramental Force, the Supramental Consciousness and the Supramental Light and will no longer be animal men but become supermen."

I asked Norman what sort of creature Superman would be. What would differentiate him from the old Adam?

He replied that it was impossible to predict in detail how the Supermind would act. One could not predicate any definite rules for its development in and impact upon matter. Speaking in general terms, the Mother had said the Supramental body would be a better instrument for the expression of the highest consciousness. It would be characterised by its lightness, freedom from 'tamas' or inertia, by a radiance as of the 'stuff of light', and by a far greater adaptability and plasticity. It would be "supple and mobile, unlike the fixed grossly material shape. As the expression of your face changes with your feeling, impulsion, even so the body will change according to the need of the inner movement…"

Norman went on to say that it would be probable that the old organisation of the body would alter. Since energy would be converted and organised by a different process, the physical systems of digestion and excretion, of the circulation of the blood and of respiration would gradually be replaced by 'a systematic concentration of forces'. He quoted the Mother as having said that "The material organs are symbols of energy centres; they are not the essential reality, they only give a form or figure to it under certain circumstances. The transformed body will function through its real energy centres, not through their representatives as developed in an animal body. For that you must first of all be conscious of these centres and their functionings; instead of an unconscious automatic movement there has to be a movement of conscious control."

232

The sex organs too would disappear, as the creation of new Supramental bodies would take place by a process different altogether from that of previous life-forms.

Supramental beings, finally, would be characterised by knowledge, power, love and joy. In them activity would spring from insight and be carried out with mastery.

"So now," said Norman, "you see what we shall be celebrating on February 29th.

Before I left him he read me this part of a statement, an invitation, made by the Mother in July 1957: "We are attending on the birth of a new world, altogether young, altogether weak – weak not in its essence, but in its external manifestation – not yet recognised, not yet felt, denied by most; but it is there, it is there endeavouring to grow and quite sure of the result. Yet the road to reach there is a new road, that has never been traced; none went by that way, none did that. It is a beginning, a universal beginning. Therefore it is an adventure absolutely unexpected and unforeseeable.

"There are people who love adventure, and to whom then I give a call and I tell them:

"I invite you to the great adventure, and in this adventure you are not to repeat spiritually what others have done before us, because our adventure begins from beyond that stage. We are for a new creation, entirely new, carrying in it all the unforeseen, all risks, all hazards – a true adventure of which the goal is sure victory, but of which the way is unknown and has to be traced out step by step in the unexplored. It is something that has never been in the present universe and will never be again in the same manner. If that interests you, well embark. What will happen tomorrow, I do not know."

• • •

I feel, though the perspective is new and immense, that the details and future of the Supramental manifestation are, in a sense, for me irrelevant and unreal, sensational though they are. What has to be done is to take the next step towards finding the Divine within, whose existence has been verified for me by one short experience only, several years ago. How can I assess what is really happening here…?

As the Mother has said, "Those who are not conscious even in the slightest degree of their inner being and who would be embarrassed to talk of what their soul is like, such people are surely not ready to perceive the difference in the earth's atmosphere. They have a long way to go for that, because for those whose consciousness is more or less exclusively centred in the outer being – mental, vital and physical – things have to appear preposterous and unexpected in order to be recognised, and then they call them miracles."

"A new world, yes, a completely new world, is born and is here. Nothing can be more momentous. And yet, do you know, feel or perceive it? Unless things give a physical knock upon your nose, you do not believe in their reality. And yet it is there. You are blind and without sense because you are ego-bound. It is your I, My and Mine that has woven around you a web, a screen."

*　*　*

28th February

During the week between the Mother's birthday and the 29th February many sadhaks from all over India continued to arrive, and the opportunity was taken to hold a meeting in order to discuss how the activities of the various Sri Aurobindo centres might be improved.

Representatives from many centres gathered in a large room in the new school buildings, which became filled with people sitting on the floor and on seats at the back.

Puraniji took the chair, and, in a rather bustling way, said that the purpose of the meeting would best be served if as many people as possible could make simple suggestions for the better running of the centres. He did not want speeches. Everyone must be brief. He then called on one fellow to begin. He started to make a speech.

"What is the point you want to make?" urged Puraniji, and, "Yes, yes, you have said that – what is your suggestion?" and so on, until the man cut off and sat down.

Others followed, among them Indra Sen. He stood up from among those at the back of the room and gave a short statement

234

which was so measured and weighty that Puraniji did not interrupt him. He began by saying that disciples of Sri Aurobindo began their sadhana by an individual surrender to the Divine and continued by an openness to the grace of Sri Aurobindo and the Mother, and that it was therefore impossible to lay down fixed lines of development for any person or group. Each centre would develop according to its own particular circumstances and the demand of each situation as it arose. It would seem then that it was unnecessary to hold the present meeting, since it was sufficient if all the people concerned listened for the inner voice of the Divine will. However he thought the meeting could be useful as a pooling of experience of possibilities. Although no centre should feel obliged to adopt the practices of other centres, nevertheless it might serve a purpose if we were to share our knowledge of the ways an inner dedication might find expression in group activities.

Other suggestions then followed. One man proposed that the Ashram should send experienced sadhaks out as speakers and encouragers, to address meetings if necessary.

Another said that centres in regional proximity to one another should meet, or send representatives to meet, say at quarterly intervals, so each could learn what was being done by the other, and perhaps co-ordinate their activities.

The film-producer from Calcutta then proposed a national organisation to represent all the centres, which would have a central committee, with the Mother as chairwoman, and be directly under her control, and open to her suggestions and comment, with vice-chairmen, sub-committees and so on.

Another man stood up and said he thought the local centres should participate more in the social field, and suggested the starting of small child-welfare organisations, which would express the Mother's love of children and, at the same time, bring Sri Aurobindo's teaching to the coming generation and be action-points in society.

Next the suggestion was made that there should be a publication – some magazine – which would be specially for centres, reporting their activities and giving useful articles for their encouragement. A page of 'Mother India' might be given over to this.

An old man then stood up slowly from the floor and said there was a great need for clear, readable translations of Sri Aurobindo's books into local languages. He said that the Gujarati translations were especially bad. At this there was an outburst of laughter, as Puraniji himself had done these! But the man went on, saying that they were in a difficult, old-fashioned and very stiff style, and no good.

"Yes, yes," said Puraniji, laughing with the others, and making a note of the suggestion.

A small man from Bombay said that for him the point about a centre was that one could go there for quiet, and not to hear lectures or discussions. After a day's work the centre was the only place one could go to for some real peace, away from the noise of one's home and one's work and the rush of the city.

The last suggestion came from Jay Smith, an American member of the Ashram, who recommended what he had seen practised by Sri Aurobindo centres in Gujarat. And he described how they organised long weekend gatherings, in which, for three or four days, fellow disciples could live together and practise a group sadhana, with activities, addresses, kirtans and meditation.

Purani, at the end of the meeting, got up and gave the longest speech of all, but it was a good one. He said we should remember that Sri Aurobindo's yoga was not for man, but for the Divine: that we should not aim to engage in social welfare work, but to discover the divine will for our lives, and how to surrender them to it. We should certainly not get ourselves committed to big educational or philanthropic undertakings, and least of all get involved in government grants for their development, as had happened with one centre. Sooner or later it was inevitable that one would wake up to find that the original spirit had been lost. Nevertheless, he said, Sri Aurobindo's yoga was one that was to be practised by groups and communities, and not only by solitary individuals. While working in a group particular difficulties and obstacles would arise, but one should welcome them as a challenge and as opportunities for improvement and self-knowledge, which could come in no other way, and would lead to a training of the will and to skill in action.

He also said that no centre should be concerned about numbers, or go out of its way to increase membership. Numbers meant nothing. What mattered was the quality of life and the openness to the Divine Grace.

*   *   *

29th February

On the evening of the 28th February the courtyard round the Samadhi was floodlit with countless small coloured light-bulbs hung on flexes among the banks of potted flowers and arranged in the branches of the big Service tree, even as high up as the level of the Mother's window on the top floor. It looked 'like fairyland', as somebody said.

By then many hundred more people had come to the Ashram. There was a strong atmosphere of expectancy.

On the morning of the 29th the Mother's balcony was hung with golden embroidered satin, and I was told that she had the gold silk cloth to stand on, made by Cottage Industries.

There were movie men on the roof of a building on the opposite side of the street to the balcony. They had asked to be able to film inside the Ashram, later in the day, but permission had been refused.

The Mother wore gold, and was full of dignity, but her smile was full of joy and compassion.

At about 8.30 Gilchrist and I went up to the Ashram and met Norman and Lena, and together chose a place to sit in the courtyard, where we would be able to hear the Mother play on her organ.

The court was set about with many pots of flowers, brought in specially from the Ashram nurseries; there were French marigolds, nasturtiums, golden khannas, yellow and red zinnias, yellow coreopsis and double rows of sunflowers. The dominant colour was gold. Among the palms and tree-ferns beyond the Samadhi were pots of white amaryllis and magenta bougainvillaea, and the picked branches of a beautiful orange-flowered tree, the Ashram name for which, Norman said, was Transformation.

237

We had sat down on the edge of a small terrace in front of some living-rooms on the far side of the court, protected from the sun by a projecting roof. Soon people came and sat down all around us, and by half past nine the place seemed filled with people and plants, all sitting equally silent and still together – the people wearing their whitest sarees and dresses and dhotis, the plants with their finest blossoms. Many of the girls wore special cotton darshan frocks of a rich orange gold. Over all rose the Service tree, the sunlight split into moving patterns by its green leaves which played in the breeze. And among its branches the black crows.

At about half past nine a deeper stillness seemed to descend, and most people went into meditation. Then, at ten, the music began. It was strong and unfaltering, and seemed timeless, and neither of the East nor of the West. The Mother played mostly in the higher register, with the right hand only, avoiding the complications of tone and stop-combinations of which the organ was capable, and developing a line of uncounterpointed melody rather like a loud oboe solo. Later she built chords with the left hand and came into the lower registers, but initially and finally it was a single singing melody leading one over the hills and far away.

Closing my eyes, I seemed to see leaping flames, and, opening them, the tree seemed also to be full of tongues of light, everything bright, clear, firm and full of creative energy. The crows, disturbed, began cawing and flapping through the branches, but they too became part of the music. It was innocent, a pastoral idyll, a tune played perhaps by David to his flocks. Later I heard that someone, while listening, had had a vision of Krishna playing on his flute, and the Mother had said it was a true vision. Krishna was there.

It was said that the Mother would let no-one accompany her or even see her as she went from her room to Pavitra's room where the organ is, and that no-one was allowed to be in that room while she played. This might be interpreted simply as indicating that she wanted to be alone, and did not want her concentration distracted, or it might imply that she was herself embodying such spiritual force at the time that it was unsafe for others to come into contact with her.

Music, I have been told, is a unique medium for the transmission of Shakti, or spiritual force, since it acts as a transformer between the source and the recipient, and it is also free from the explicit statement of direct speech. Whatever the truth of this, it is certain that the Mother attached considerable importance to this occasion.

Later I heard that the Mother had said that what came to her was a music of Beginning; it was hard for her to stop, as it seemed unending and continually unfolding in fresh developments. Indeed at the end it did seem that she faltered in her efforts to effect a conclusion and that it was not inevitable when it came. The notes ceased but they continued inaudibly to prolong their dance. There was an outward stillness, however, and then, slowly, people began to stand up and disperse. Many waited about, hoping to see the Mother return to her own room, but I don't think they were satisfied in this, as she left very quickly after she stopped playing.

After talking for a while with Norman and Lena, Gilchrist and I went to the Dining Hall for lunch. Here, in spite of the large numbers being catered for, everything was functioning very peacefully and smoothly, and we had a good meal.

In the afternoon Ananta came and talked in my room. He has been in doubt for some time about leaving the Ashram.

"When I am here I think of Boston, but when I am in Boston I long to be in Pondicherry. Isn't it crazy?"

He admits that the Mother has given him everything he needs on his island, but, he says, he is just too restless. He asked me if I thought the Mother would live long… If he was to go away, perhaps he should get it over soon, and come back in three or four years' time, while the Mother was still here…

At half past three Gilchrist, Ananta and I went back to the Ashram. There was a long queue of people in the street, waiting to go in, but it moved quite fast.

The Mother was seated in the middle of the far side of the Meditation Hall. The aluminium of the new ceiling was dazzlingly floodlit with golden light from concealed bulbs. Otherwise the hall was undecorated. There was no splendour of flowers around the Mother's chair, but a slender ten year old girl sat beside her and kept her supplied with gilded medals and safety-pins, a pair of which the Mother handed to each of us as we came up. She smiled very radiantly and happily as she gave me mine, as if she was finding great joy in giving out love and blessings to us on this special day.

Also in the hall, some feet away, on either side of the Mother, were André, her son, who had arrived from Paris, and Champaklal, her personal attendant. These, I was told afterwards, were there to see that people did not prostrate themselves, and so hold up the queue.

The golden medallion had, on one side, a lotus flower, and, on the other, the Mother's symbol, with the dates 29.2.56 and 29.2.60.

We also received a card, describing in French and English the event that had taken place during the common meditation on the evening of Wednesday the 29th February, 1956.

After sitting a while by the Samadhi, Gilchrist and I went to Norman's room for tea. He was buoyantly happy and peaceful as he always is after a Darshan. Later the three of us went for a walk along the sea-front. We got back to the Playground in time to see a half-hour programme of coloured slides.

These were the pictures of the Mother that we had seen on the evening of her birthday, but now, of course, there were many people present who had not seen them before. I have never seen the Playground so crowded, but everyone seemed to get in comfortably, with no fuss, and sat on mats or on the sand, watching in perfect silence.

The day ended with supper at Norman's, where we were given our special issue of golden honey. A devotee in the North had sent hundreds of little pots of it for distribution in the Ashram.

Next day there was a notice chalked on a black-board, repeating Mother's message of 29th February, 1956, headed 'The Golden Day' and proclaiming 'Henceforth the 29th February will be the day of the Lord.'

The card we had received concerning the event in the Playground, four years earlier, read as follows:

"This evening the Divine Presence, concrete and material, was there present amongst you. I had a form of living gold, bigger than the universe, and I was facing a huge and massive golden door which separated the world from the Divine.

"As I looked at the door, I knew and willed, in a single movement of consciousness, that *the time has come*,' and lifting with both hands a mighty golden hammer I struck one blow, one single blow on the door and the door was shattered to pieces.

"Then the Supramental Light and Force and Consciousness rushed down upon earth in an uninterrupted flow."

THE GOLDEN DAY

Brightness fills the vibrant air,
Music penetrates my being,
The Courtyard seems all lit with fire.
Lambent flickering tongues aspire
On every face and leaf and life-thing
And the central tree that's there
Is alive with flame and light
Enfolding birds and all the crowds
Seated round in silent rite.
This is the song that built the worlds.

The sun in his splendour
Is playing his life-hymn.
We gaze on the wonder
Of a new creation.
Descending music, rarely heard,
Rhythm of the eternal word,
With fiery joy compels the earth
And air and moisture to give birth.
Surya has sent down his rays
Golden flowers send back their praise.

Symbol of life, of Eden and the Cross,
Reminder of Moses and the Burning Bush,
See how the greenness burns…
How nature is transformed in this;
The old is not destroyed, by joy made new.
All has been altered by a supreme act;
Aditi's dream now wakens into fact.
The cosmic door stands open to the light
Of the Divine distances; the herds go home.
'Euoi, euan, oh shepherd of white stars.'

*　*　*

1st March

Girish came and sat down on the empty seat next to me, near the meditation room. He was pale, and withdrawn, his eyes half-closed, and he spoke in a low voice, almost as if to himself. He was like a man emerging from deep meditation, or like a drunken man earnestly trying to steady himself and articulate what he has to communicate.

"One man may say that the basis of all the yoga is consecration, and another may say no, for him it is devotion, or again, for another, it may be sincerity, or faith, or openness – and so we cannot agree, because we are different from each other, and we mean different things by 'basis'. And for me I have to make effort, constant aspiration, all the day, and even in sleep it must be there – to find the Psychic Being. For everything is within. We do not find it by talk or discussion or argument, but by going within ourselves, to find the Psychic Being who knows everything. But it is covered over and lost. We must make effort. We must start, if you like, from the lap of the Mother – that is where we begin – but then we make own effort from there, and we work, day and night, to find this truth of our being, and year after year we aspire and seek and make this effort, and it may seem there is no result, until then, one day – 'Varoum! I am here!' says the Psychic Being, and He is there and there is no

242

doubt about it. And you know, all other effort and talk is a waste of time, except perhaps in the very beginning there is a place for it.

"And I must tell you this, too, the transformation does not begin only after we have reached Supermind. No. Here and now, it begins from where we are. And if you can see it, if you have the sight, by looking at your own hand – even now there is the beginning of the glow, a lightness and beauty on the surface of the skin…"

"How are your children?" I ask him.

"Fine, fine; they are always well and happy." He went on, "I think any child who has lived in the Ashram is going to be happy. And I will tell you this: my children, they know nothing of Sri Aurobindo's philosophy; if you talk to them of the Psychic Being or transformation they will not know what are these things, for they have no formal instruction yet in Sri Aurobindo's writings. But this they do know – this one thing – they know what the Mother would like, and they know what things she would *not* like. And they try to do only those things She would like. And I think this is very fine."

*　*　*

2nd March

About six weeks ago Ravindra fell ill. He seemed to have very severe bronchitis. He could not teach and kept to his room. Then he took to his bed and his wife allowed me to see him for a few minutes only at each visit. I was shown the Ayurvedic pills as big as birds' eggs with which he was being treated. He got no better but weaker and weaker until one day his wife would no longer let me see him. The next day when I called she said he was still alive but a special message had been sent to the Mother telling her of his critical condition.

Today I had tea with him once more; he is very nearly completely well again, and is to return to work in a day or two.

He told me that on hearing of his plight the Mother had sent him a little packet of dried flower-petals with her blessing. Ravindra had put this sacramental gift in the pocket of his pyjama-jacket and

243

drifted off to sleep. Since then his recovery seems to have been steady and extraordinarily rapid.

*   *   *

3rd March

Nirod had trained as a doctor in Edinburgh. On his way home to Bengal he had toured South India and stayed for a while at the Ashram. He had met the Mother, who had, he said, struck him as a very kind and gracious woman – nothing more. She had listened to his plans for a career, and there had been no talk or thought of his doing yoga at all. He had come away, intending to start a practice, marry and settle down in Bengal. But things worked out otherwise. He attributed it to the Mother's action on his being. He felt that she called and changed him, so that he was plucked out of ordinary life and ordinary manhood, and found himself a sadhak, and, even stranger, a sadhak near to Sri Aurobindo himself, as his medical attendant. So strangely and unforeseeably does the grace work.

Sitting in his room one morning, I asked him if leaving the Ashram, as I was about to do, was deliberately to miss a unique opportunity for surrender to the Divine.

He said no; the important thing was to retain the attitude of aspiration, and then there would be no real break with the Mother, and one's progress would continue, and one would be able to come again when the time was right.

We talked of the supramentalisation of mankind, and I asked him if he thought we would live to see Supramental beings.

He said that it depended on what I meant by such a phrase. There would be people around in our life-time – indeed were – who had realised the Supramental consciousness, certainly, but the full Supramental change, down to the physical level, was another thing and would probably take several hundred years. One might see certain physical changes, such as increased health, longevity and a radiance of the body, but the actual modification or disappearance of the digestive system, sex organs, liver and so on, would take time.

244

I also asked him if in fact it was becoming easier to make spiritual progress than it had been formerly – if the psychic conditions or atmosphere, as it were, had become more favourable.

He replied that it was definitely true to say so. People made more rapid progress now than ever before, thanks to the work of Sri Aurobindo and the Mother. Experiences came to novices now which formerly were only known to yogis after a lifetime of tapasya. Everything now depended on sincerity and aspiration. There was no limit to the possibilities of progress.

Nirod is now perhaps in his early fifties or late forties. He is small, with a large head; his features and eyes remind me of the Tibetan I met. He has at times a wistful, sad expression, which, however, can change suddenly from dead-pan to warmly smiling. He plays a good game of tennis.

JAPA

Carry, bells, across the landscape of dreams.
Carry that exultation of tongues resounding in bronze
That first chased the magical and devil's malice
From the dark woodlands and wealds of England,
When monks and missionaries first cleared the air
Ringing bells to scatter the old powers there,
As they penetrated among presences of glade and stone.
Carry, as from Oxford spires or Canterbury's
Tower of the Holy Angels – carry down-wind
Over the haunted territories of an inner homeland,
Dispelling the black, and shaking the daylight
Into sinister shadows and neglected groves
Where who knows what saturnine and primitive rites
Repeat as the habitual memory of an aboriginal past.
Oh exorcise ignorance, so nothing is left the same,
Rise bell-song and melody of a reborn age,
Rise over all as the fine song of a new courage,
Rise as the constant intonation of a well-loved name.

*   *   *

After sitting by the Samadhi, in the Ashram courtyard, I meet Girish Kumar again. He comes through the other people who are meditating there, to talk to me. As on an earlier occasion, he is no longer the middle-aged businessman. He has a certain lustre about him, his eyes at times half close, and he is smiling.

"I will tell you how it is, when we look for Psychic Being," he begins. "One concentrates, and then one goes within…"

I stop him. "There, you have passed the most difficult thing – you say, 'One goes within' – three words, but that is the problem."

He smiles, and continues, "One must be silent, of course, and know how to concentrate – then it happens. And one goes down," and he makes a diving movement with his hands in front of his throat, "and one comes to a fork in the path. And one way goes down to lower vital, but one can easily tell what sort of place it is, because of the sort of things that are happening there… yes 'turmoil' is the word. But the other way, if you go down it, leads to Psychic Being. And you know it is there because you see a brilliant light." He takes the camera that hangs from his shoulder and points to the bulb. "It is like the flash. You see it first only like this – a flash in the darkness and it is gone. But it will happen again, and each time it will be for longer time, and then, one day, you are in the light…"

Later, he says, as if describing the stupidity of some third party, "How can one talk of finding Psychic Being if one does not know how to silence the mind and concentrate? When one goes to Secondary School it is assumed one has mastered already Primary School syllabus."

* * *

The Mother, in her 'Prayers and Meditations', counsels against entertaining the distress that can come into one following the realisation of emptiness. It is easy to remember that one is still ego-bound, basically selfish, incapable of concentration, insincere, unaware of one's psychic being. One may determine to do better, goad and reproach oneself in prayer, strive and make 'a real effort'. But no, says the Mother, this is not the way. It may lead to a temporary intensification of consciousness: one may succeed in 'pulling down' some power, but there will be a reaction of darkness. It will not be sustained; it is a vital effort that has been made and its effects will be temporary because forced.

The Mother writes, "All who seek Thee with ardour should understand that Thou art there wherever there is need of Thee; and if they could have the supreme faith to give up seeking Thee, but rather to await Thee, at each moment putting themselves integrally at Thy service, Thou wouldst be there whenever there is need of Thee."

And again, "As soon as all effort disappears from a manifestation, it becomes very simple, with the simplicity of a flower opening, manifesting its beauty and spreading its fragrance without clamour or vehement gesture. And in this simplicity lies the greatest power, the power which is least mixed and least gives rise to harmful reactions…"

Her attitude is always, "I await, without haste, without inquietude…keeping watch as best I can."

To the enthusiast she replies, "In Peace and Silence the Eternal manifests: allow nothing to disturb you and the Eternal will manifest; have perfect equality in the face of all and the Eternal will be there… Yes, we should not put too much intensity, too much effort into our seeking for Thee; the effort and intensity become a veil in front of Thee; we must not desire to see Thee, for that is still a mental agitation which obscures Thy Eternal Presence… No haste, no inquietude, no tension; Thou, nothing but Thou, without any analysis or any objectivising, and Thou art there without a possible doubt, for all becomes a holy Peace and a sacred Silence."

*　*　*

6th March

Does the Mother mean that effort is unnecessary? Clearly not. She is talking, rather, of the wrong sort of effort that produces emotional disturbance, an upward anguish and stirring of dust. She is recommending an attitude that is the culmination, indeed, of a very sustained and confident will towards the Divine over many years, involving the concentration and integration of all one's being to that end – no easy optimism!

"Reject", writes Sri Aurobindo in his book 'The Mother', "the false notion that the divine Power will do and is bound to do everything for you at your demand and even though you do not satisfy the conditions laid down by the Supreme. Make your surrender true and complete, then only will all else be done for you.

"An inert passivity is constantly confused with the real surrender, but out of an inert passivity nothing true and powerful can come. It is the inert passivity of physical Nature that leaves it at the mercy of every obscure or undivine influence. A glad and strong and helpful submission is demanded to the working of the Divine Force…"

The Mother, too, in a 'Questions and Answers' dialogue with children and students, is equally severe on the dilettante.

The Mother: "You cannot do yoga if you do not take it seriously. If you are not serious, you have an aspiration for five minutes and then for ten hours do not have it; for one day you have a great urge and for a month you do not have it, and so on. You cannot do yoga under these conditions. It must be a constant, continuous thing…"

Question: "Must not one be born with a great aspiration?"

The Mother: "No, aspiration is a thing that is cultivated, like all the activities of the being. You may be born with quite a small will and you can cultivate it so that it becomes big. It is an altogether ridiculous idea to believe that things come to you like that, as a kind of grace; that if you are not given the aspiration you do not have it – it is not true… Your will is free; it is purposely left free and you have to choose. It is you who have to decide whether you will seek the Light or not, whether you will be the servitor of Truth or not – it is you – and whether you have an aspiration or not, it is you who choose."

Question: "How can one become conscious of the Divine Love, and how can one become an instrument of its expression?"

The Mother: "First of all, to become conscious of anything whatsoever, what is necessary is the will for it." And "The will is a constant, sustained, concentrated aspiration, an almost exclusive occupation of the consciousness. This is the first step…"

*   *   *

7th March

This morning a famous musician gave a performance on the Sarōd.

It took place in a large room in a palatial house once lived in by Dilip Kumar Roy. Dilip was a famous singer who became a disciple of Sri Aurobindo, and wrote several books: 'Among the Great', 'Sri Aurobindo came to me' and others. He corresponded a great deal with Sri Aurobindo on many topics, particularly poetry, and provoked many very humorous letters from him, for which I am grateful. After Sri Aurobindo's death, however, he left the Ashram 'in revolt', but the Mother, in spite of the shortage of accommodation for sadhaks, has always kept his rooms unoccupied, so that if he comes back they will be ready, perhaps because he had so genuine a love for Sri Aurobindo and was so loved by him.

THE SARŌD PLAYER

The plucked chords, the plectrum passing over the strings,
The face of the player, eyes closed, bowed, swaying,
Driven by the pressure of rhythm, slowly intensifying
Through the relaxed body to the hands,
Joined now by drum-taps – all this brings
Silence, an exclusion, an awareness of fingers,
Of fingers transforming impulse into sound,
Sound converging again on silence,
From where it came.
Out of concentration wideness is born.

*   *   *

249

This evening, an old bald-headed Indian was sitting on his bed, in the hostel, telling stories to some of the other visitors. I listened to one of them.

Now, about seven or eight hundred years ago, in Kulam, there was a man called Aker. He was a goldsmith, a very great artist, who made all kinds of jewellery and that kind of thing. He was a famous man. For some reason or other he did not marry, but lived by himself and worked hard at his craft. And when he was getting on in life, in his fifties maybe, he approached a poor widow who was living alone, and said to her, 'Sister, if you will come and live in my house, and cook for me and do my laundry, I will see to it that you do not have to work so hard in the fields, and that you always have a roof over your head and food on the table, because I have money enough to look after you. Will you join me, sister?'

And the woman agreed, and came to his house, and they lived as brother and sister, and she saw to it that he always had a loaf ready baked and a shirt washed, and he saw that she was cared for as far as money was concerned.

Now, as the years passed, the woman saved quite a bit of gold, through working for farmers at harvest time, and doing washing and so on. And she did not know what to do with those coins, for there was no Savings Bank or Deposit Account in those days. So at last she said to Aker, 'Brother, can you make me a necklace out of this gold, and then I can wear it round my neck and I shall know where it is and it will be safe.' And Aker took the gold, and melted it and made a necklace, and there was enough for what he had in mind all except for one small tola, a bead like a pea maybe. So he added that amount of gold from his own store, and finished the necklace, and the woman wore it, and it shone.

And one day a neighbour said to the woman, 'Where did you get that golden jewellery?' And the woman told her how she had taken her coins to Aker and he had made this necklace for her. But the neighbour said to her, 'How do you know he did not cheat you? No goldsmith is honest. What they do is to mix inferior metal with the gold, and keep some of it for themselves…' But the woman was indignant and said that Aker was an honest man, and would not do that. Her neighbour said, 'Well then there is no harm in having the metal tested, is there? – it will set your mind at rest, and clear Aker of any suspicion…' So at last the woman went to an assayer, and he rubbed a portion of the gold on his black stone, to test its purity. 'Madam,' he said, 'the finest gold is 22 carat, but this gold is better than that.' And then she asked him to weigh the necklace. And it was heavier than the weight of the gold she had given to Aker. So her mind was at peace.

But one day she said to Aker, 'Brother, you must have put some of your own gold into my necklace. Let me give you five rupees to make it up.'

And Aker said, 'Now, the woman I trusted most in the world, and whom I asked to live in my own house, has no faith in me, but has doubted my honesty. I will leave this miserable world.' And he left his house at once and went to Gokal, where Krishna spent his childhood. And there he found a priest in the Gokal temple, and he made him his guru, and worked for him many years, and served him. But the day came when another richer disciple arrived, and the temple priest turned away from Aker and gave all his attention to this newcomer. And Aker said, 'I have been like the ox that has its nose pierced for the ploughing.' And he left this guru and sought God alone.

Many years passed and he became wise and found enlightenment. Before he died he said, 'The mountain is very great, but it can be obscured by a blade of grass. What a pity that people cannot see the mountain.'

*　*　*

22nd March

Dear Anthony and Mary,

I am writing this in a room in a modern students' hostel in Madras. I took a train here from Pondicherry last night. It seems like a dream – the rickshaw run to the station in the dark, with my bags;

251

half a dozen friends saying goodbye on the platform, people I seem to have known for so long; the slow journey to Madras. At one time I remember the train stopping and six or seven lean Indians storming in through the windows over the passengers' not quite dead bodies. After that we pulled down the shutters when we got near a station.

Tomorrow evening I get the express to Bombay, where I am to stay for a few days with the nephew of a man I met in Pondy.

Do you remember Yehuda Hanegbi, the man from Jerusalem? Well, he wants me to call on him on the way home and tell him about the Ashram. He says I may never again be so near his part of the world. It will mean going via Egypt, the Lebanon, Syria and Jordan, since the latter is the only neighbouring country from which one can enter Israel. It will be good to see him again.

I hope all goes well with you.

Love to the family and to yourselves,

Dick.

* * *

27th March

The ship seems more tolerable now than she did a year ago. The metal trays in the self-service canteen are as greasy as if they'd never known soap-powder, and the Dormitory is crowded and the floor littered with orange-peel and nut-shells, just as on the voyage out, but somehow it seems to matter less. Perhaps having seen India's poverty and dirt one is more ready to notice the good things and play down the bad.

The Dormitory passengers, on coming aboard, were given a form to sign which outlined what was to be expected in their part of the ship. It ended, "I am fully aware of the conditions pertaining to this class, which I recognise as being of a standard lacking the amenities which are usually to be found in a more normal class of accommodation.

"I therefore undertake to make no claim against your company..."

This is, maybe, the only result of Parker's protests and petitions.

Daniel Roumanoff, who visited Pondicherry, is also a passenger, which is a happy co-incidence. He is on his way back to France, because he has received his call-up papers for national service. He will probably be sent to Algeria. I can't imagine him in the army. Today I found him sitting in the lee of a life-boat on the bow deck, wrapped in a chaddar, meditating in the lotus posture.

We both find ourselves amused by the behaviour of the white passengers, who seem living in an unreal world. This morning some people in the first class swimming pool caused some water to splash down onto the third class deck, and a man called up indignantly, "Look out what you are doing, there are French people down here!"

* * *

31st March

"One for you and two for me," said the travel agent, as we shook hands.

We were sitting on chairs on the pavement outside a café on the edge of the Suez Canal, at Port Tewfik. I had come ashore at 2 a.m. the night before. A launch, sent by the shipping agents, had come out to the boat, and I had jumped down on to its bouncing slippery deck and we had sped away to shore over a dark glittering swell, among the many ships waiting at anchor to pass through the Canal. I had slept on the floor of the agency's office, and Tony and his Armenian colleague, who had both worked there all night, had invited me to breakfast. We ate cheese rolls and pickled vegetables and drank coffee.

Soon another dignified travel agent arrived – magnificently dressed. "Two for me and one for you," he said, as he sat down.

"You fellows look prosperous," I remarked.

"Not only that," said the newcomer, "we *are* prosperous."

Anyway they were friendly. Perhaps it was obvious that I was not a business proposition to them so they could lay aside their professional acumen. Or maybe they felt more human at breakfast time.

253

They offered me a lift to the station in their car, and Tony bought me my ticket to Cairo, and actually came on to the train and began telling me where to buy three sandwiches for 1 piaster when I arrived, and drew a little map to show the place. "And don't give the porter anything. I told him we could carry your luggage ourselves, but they are always after a tip."

He told two Egyptian soldiers to look after me, and leaped off the train just in time as it moved out of the station.

One of the soldiers, a dark Sudanese with fuzzy short hair, gave me his corner seat by the window, and the other, a thin sallow man, insisted on my having one of his oranges. Neither could speak English or French, but they were full of friendliness. As it began to get hotter, the sun blazing in at the window, the Sudanese nodded and fell asleep with his head on my shoulder. Opposite me a large placid black woman in blue silk suckled her youngest child.

Was it true, as Norman had said to me, that now I had been accepted by the Mother, things, even on the material level, would never be the same again?

A free lift from four travel agents …

Epilogue

Back in Europe I kept up my connection with the Ashram, acting as U.K. distributor for the Ashram publications, and as the Honorary Secretary of the Sri Aurobindo Centre in Bell Street, London. In 1968 I sent a sample of English earth to go in the urn at the inauguration ceremony of Auroville. In 1972, I helped Nirmal Sethia organise a concert in Southwark Cathedral on the Centenary of Sri Aurobindo's birthday, with Yehudi Menuhin, Ravi Shankar and Alla Rakha; it was a magical evening of music. The profits were earmarked 'for the development of Auroville.'

To keep body and soul together I first tried teaching; then joined the excavations at Masada, but reverted to bookselling, which later led me to Watkins' bookshop in Cecil Court where I met M.E. who became my wife. After our wedding in 1978 we both came out to Pondicherry, to visit the Ashram and possibly remain to live in Auroville. But that is another story.

Behind everything there remained the search for the elusive psychic being and the memory of the flower the Mother had given me on my birthday, 28th October: 'Joy in Artistic Creation'.

Dick Batstone
February 2013

Postscript

It is now nearly fifty years since the period in the life of the Ashram described in this journal. Most of the people whose conversations I recorded are now dead. The significant year of 1967 has passed without an outward and material sign sufficient to convince a sceptical world of the advent of Supermind. The pace of change has, however, continued to accelerate.

Sri Aurobindo had written in a letter, "The Supramental consciousness will enter into a phase of realising power in 1967." There was an expectation by some that there would in that year be some dramatic material transformation inexplicable by previously accepted laws of science. The Mother refused to be drawn into making prophecies, but when she was asked, in 1967, what Sri Aurobindo had meant by "realising power", she replied, "Acting decisively on the mind of men and the course of events."

It seems natural, according to Sri Aurobindo's philosophy of evolution, that change should begin with mental orientation and awareness rather than with a new physical development. Indeed Sri Aurobindo had suggested elsewhere that it might well take a few centuries for the physical change to begin to follow the change in consciousness.

In 1967 it can be said that two remarkable developments did in fact begin to unfold – the student protests in Columbia University, to be followed by the mass unrest at the Sorbonne and elsewhere in 1968, and the advance in the planning and the actual start of the model town of Auroville, to be inaugurated by the Mother on 28th of February, 1968, a week after her 90th birthday.

The Mother also remarked, in 1967, on the birth of some children of a very special kind that had been brought to see her. She described them "as though entirely open…ready to absorb", with a thirst for light. "They have something more, already." She met a two-year old who appeared as developed as a child of six.

The period of the 1960s was, in the West, one of a psychological global warming. The ice-caps of social conventions and habits of mind began to melt and break up. Not only was it a time of repudiation by many of the young of the previously accepted materialistic aims of their parents, but also the widespread drug-experience demonstrated that there were possible alternatives to the usual way of seeing the world. It was the time of Flower Power, Woodstock, and also of the Civil Rights movement, the Prague Spring, and the protests over the Vietnam War. What connection had all these things with the lives and work of Sri Aurobindo and the Mother? Of course, though some events follow others, they are not necessarily caused by them, but an encouraging possibility remains that something deep in the psyche of western man was stirring, and that this had a connection with the prophets and pioneers of the future evolution of man.

Auroville, the City of Dawn, was founded by the Mother as an experiment in human unity. At its opening ceremony a boy and a girl representing each of 124 countries and all the 23 Indian States placed a symbolic handful of their native soil in a lotus-shaped urn in the centre of the Auroville area. "The first condition for living at Auroville", the Mother said in 1967, "is to be convinced of the essential unity of mankind and [have] the will to collaborate towards the material realisation of this unity." How was it to be achieved? "The first thing needed," she said, "is the inner discovery, to find out what one truly is behind the social, moral, cultural, racial and hereditary appearances. At the centre there is a being, free and vast and knowing, who awaits our discovery and who should become the active centre of our being and our life in Auroville." From the discovery of this inner being springs the recognition of it in others and the sense of fraternity and of unity behind variety. When asked what difference there would be between the ideal of Auroville and the ideal of the Ashram, the Mother replied, "There is no fundamental difference in the attitude towards the future and the service of the Divine. But the people in the Ashram are considered to have consecrated their lives to yoga…whereas in Auroville simply the goodwill to make a collective experiment for the progress of humanity is sufficient to gain admittance."

To make the inner discovery of which the Mother spoke, she insisted that "Work, even manual work, is indispensable." She sent a note to an Aurovilian, which emphasised this: "It is the old methods of yoga that demand silence and solitude. The yoga of tomorrow is to find the Divine in work and in contact with the world." The immediate opportunity for this was presented by the environment of Auroville itself. In 1968 the land was badly eroded. In monsoon-time the sea turned red with top-soil, carried away down deeply scoured gullies. Since then the Aurovilians have planted around two million trees and bushes and restored much of the twenty square kilometre terrain, using the methods of organic farming. Among the multifarious Aurovilian activities have been experiments in architecture, renewable energy, medicine, education and the arts. The community at present consists of around two thousand men, women and children from about forty nations – people drawn to it by the challenge of the creation of a new world based upon a new consciousness.

The Mother's life, before she died in 1973, may be said to have become the arena for an intense confrontation between the highest consciousness and all the horrendous difficulties of the universal earth-nature – not only those of the inconscient and the subconscient of mankind, but also of conscious evil. Her work continued to be the growing embodiment of the Supramental force, stabilising its presence in the world, and studying in particular its impact on the cells of her own body.

It was as if she was herself the missing link, intermediate between the old and the new species. She had what she came to call 'the superhuman consciousness' in an untransformed body. And this body became a battle ground. "I go from the most dreadful discomfort to a marvel... an unutterable bliss." She spoke of the sufferings, the unbelievable nightmare of physical life before it has been changed, alternating with "the joy and laughter of the soul".

She spoke, too, of her vital consciousness and her mental consciousness vanishing, only the psychic being and the physical consciousness remaining. She became aware of the cells of her body. And these cells were able and eager to collaborate with the evolutionary movement of transformation. "Consciousness is replacing thought," she said. And, above, a golden Force was pressing on matter to change it.

The Mother, in her last years, suffered physical crisis after crisis followed by recoveries that confounded her doctors. Her constantly repeated prayer became "What Thou willest, what Thou willest, what Thou willest…" Eventually, the forces of ageing and the attrition of the world overcame the life in the Mother's body. This may have appeared as a set-back and postponement of the goal of the yoga of Sri Aurobindo, but much had been achieved. Even by 1962 the Mother was able to record an experience of immense encouragement: "Suddenly in the night I woke with the full awareness of what we could call the Yoga of the World. The Supreme Love was manifesting through big pulsations, and each pulsation was bringing the world further in its manifestation. It was the formidable pulsations of the eternal stupendous Love, only Love: each pulsation of the Love was carrying the universe further in its manifestation.

And the certitude that what is to be done is done, and the Supramental Manifestation is realised.

Everything was Personal, nothing was individual.

This was going on, and on, and on, and on…

The certitude that what is to be done is *done*.

All the results of the falsehood had disappeared: Death was an illusion, Sickness an illusion, Ignorance was an illusion – something that had no reality, no existence… only Love, and Love, and Love, and Love – immense, formidable, stupendous, carrying everything.

And how, how, to express [This] in the world? It was like an impossibility, because of the contradiction… but then it came: 'You have accepted that this world should know the Supramental Truth… and it will be expressed totally, integrally.' Yes, yes… And the thing is *done*."

15th August 2002

259

A Biographical Note on
Sri Aurobindo

Sri Aurobindo was born in Calcutta on 15 August, 1872. When he was seven he was sent by his father to England. Here he was educated at St Paul's School, London, and King's College, Cambridge, where he was awarded a First in the Classical Tripos, Part I.

He returned to India in 1893, at the age of 20, an accomplished scholar in Greek and Latin, familiar with the literature and history of England and France, and with some knowledge of German, Italian and Spanish. He took up an appointment with the Baroda State Service, working at first in various government departments and in the Maharajah's secretariat, later lecturing in French at the State College, and finally becoming Professor of English and Vice-Principal there.

During these years, until 1906, Sri Aurobindo made up for his very western education by learning Sanskrit and several modern Indian languages, and studying the history and culture of his own country. At the same time he began to explore the possibilities of reviving a patriotism that would aim at national independence. He also worked secretly to promote opposition to British Rule through organised non-cooperation and passive resistance.

In 1906 Sri Aurobindo went to Calcutta as Principal of the Bengal National College, and for the first time came into the open as a political leader. His impact through journalism and public speaking on behalf of the Nationalist group in Congress, though it lasted only four years, was of decisive significance in rousing the spirit of the Indian people, in making independence the eventual aim of its politics, and non-cooperation and passive resistance its method of struggle.

In 1908 Sri Aurobindo was arrested on suspicion of his implication in a bomb-throwing outrage. During the year in Alipur Jail before his acquittal, he practised yoga, and had, as a result, a radical change in consciousness which was to lead to a re-orientation of his purpose in life. He described later how he was made to see the Divine everywhere – in the tree in the prison compound, in his fellow prisoners, in the Prosecuting Counsel and in the presiding Magistrate – wherever he looked he saw the Lord giving him the assurance of his love. He came out of prison dedicated to the service of the Divine, and in 1910 he left politics and moved to Pondicherry, then a French colony.

The events of the next forty years of Sri Aurobindo's career cannot be so easily recorded. As he once said to a would-be biographer, "Neither you nor anyone else knows anything at all of my life; it has not been on the surface for men to see."

It may be mentioned that from 1914 to 1921 he edited and largely wrote a philosophical review 'Arya', in which most of his major works appeared. These were later to be published as books, on philosophy, yoga, the Vedas and Upanishads, poetry, history and other topics.

In 1926 Sri Aurobindo achieved a further stage in spiritual realisation and went into almost complete seclusion, to concentrate on 'the yoga which begins where other yogas end'. The Mother, who had joined him in 1920, then took over the organisation of the Ashram which had by then grown up around him.

The years 1930 to 1938 are characterised outwardly by a very heavy correspondence carried on by Sri Aurobindo with members of the Ashram in connection with their sadhana. During the second World War he supported the Allies both in public statements and by the use of spiritual force. In 1942 he urged Congress to accept the Cripps offer. This promised Dominion Status immediately on the conclusion of peace in return for India's full co-operation in the war effort. If Congress had agreed to this, the partition of India would probably have been avoided.

On the eve of Independence Day in 1947, Sri Aurobindo was chosen to give a message to the nation on the All India Radio. He began his broadcast by pointing out that the birthday of a free

India – the 15th August – was also his own birthday, and that he felt this was not just a coincidence but 'the sanction and seal of the Divine Force' that had guided him in his life's work. He then told of his five dreams. In his early years these had looked impossible of fulfilment but they were now 'arriving at fruition or on the way to achievement', and he declared that a free India might well play a large part in their realisation.

The first dream was the creation of a free and united India. India was now free – but not united. This division had to go if the nation was not to be seriously weakened and its destiny impaired.

Another dream was for 'the resurgence and liberation of the peoples of Asia'. This, too, had largely come about, and here too, India had a role to play in its completion.

The third dream was of a world-union. This had not been realised, but there was, he said, a gathering momentum of the movement in that direction, since a voluntary unification was ultimately in the interests of all countries. There was still the need for an international spirit to grow up, as well as for the forms and institutions of a world authority. In this area, too, India had much to contribute.

A fourth dream, 'the spiritual gift of India to the world', had already begun to be expressed. India's spirituality was entering Europe and America – not only its teachings but also its practice.

The final dream which Sri Aurobindo spoke about was of 'a step in evolution which would raise man to a higher and larger consciousness and begin the solution of the problems which had perplexed and vexed him since he first began to think and to dream of individual perfection and a perfect society.'

It was this fifth dream and its fulfilment that occupied the forty years of Sri Aurobindo's life in Pondicherry, absorbing all his energies in the practice of an integral life-affirming yoga.

During his last years Sri Aurobindo continued to compose and revise his epic poem 'Savitri'. He also began a series of articles for publication in the Ashram's Bulletin of Physical Education. These were later collected as a small book under the title 'The Supramental Manifestation upon Earth' – the final expression of his views on the subject.

Sri Aurobindo left his body on 5th December 1950.

Other books published by PRISMA

Antithesis of Yoga
by Jocelyn

Finding the Psychic Being
by Loretta Shartsis

The Mother on Japan
by The Mother

The Teachings of Flowers
(The Life and Work of the Mother of the
Sri Aurobindo Ashram)
by Loretta Shartsis

Death doesn't exist
The Mother on Death, Sri Aurobindo on Rebirth
by The Mother

Passage to More than India
by Dick Batstone

The Supramental Transformation
by Loretta Shartsis

Children of Change: A Spiritual Pilgrimage
by Amrit

Memories of Auroville - told by early Aurovilians *by Janet
Fearn*

Bougainvilleas PROTECTION
by Narad (Richard Eggenberger), Nilisha Mehta

The Mother's Yoga - 1956-1973 (Vol. 1, 1956-1967) *by
Loretta Shartsis*

The Mother's Yoga - 1956-1973 (Vol. 2, 1968-1973) *by
Loretta Shartsis*

Crossroad The New Humanity
by Paulette Hadnagy

9 788195 730124